The Sacred Remains

GARY LADERMAN

The Sacred Remains

AMERICAN ATTITUDES TOWARD
DEATH, 1799–1883

Yale University Press
New Haven &
London

Set in Sabon type by Keystone Typesetting, Inc.
Printed in the United States of America.

Library of Congress Cataloging-in-Publication Data
Laderman, Gary, 1962–
    The sacred remains : American attitudes toward death, 1799–1883 / Gary Laderman.
        p. cm.
    Includes bibliographical references (p.   ) and index.
    ISBN 0-300-06432-2 (cloth : alk. paper)
    1. Protestants — Northeastern States — Attitudes.   2. Death — Religious aspects — Christianity — History of doctrines — 18th century.   3. Death — Religious aspects — Christianity — History of doctrines — 19th century.   4. Funeral rites and ceremonies — Northeastern States — History — 18th century.   5. Funeral rites and ceremonies — Northeastern States — History — 19th century.
6. Northeastern States — Church history — 18th century.
7. Northeastern States — Church history — 19th century.   I. Title.
BR525.L25   1996
306.9'0974'09034 — dc20   96-10373
                                                                    CIP

A catalogue record for this book is available from the British Library.

The paper in this book meets the guidelines for permanence and durability of the Committee on Production Guidelines for Book Longevity of the Council on Library Resources.

10 9 8 7 6 5 4 3 2 1

To my parents, Carol and Pete, my brother, David, and my wife, Elizabeth

Contents

Acknowledgments

I cannot possibly express my appreciation to all of the people who have contributed to the completion of this work. Scholars, friends, and family members have been supportive during the research and writing of this project, inspiring me with their curiosity, insights, and, perhaps most important of all, laughter. Even though I have spent the last several years reading, thinking, and writing about death and corpses, people around me made sure I kept a sense of humor. There is no doubt that the one person who has been especially supportive — intellectually, editorially, and emotionally — is my wife, Elizabeth Hardcastle. To her I offer my deepest gratitude; thank you for your wisdom, guidance, patience, and humor.

This book grew out of the dissertation I wrote in the Religious Studies Department at the University of California, Santa Barbara. In addition to its beautiful setting on the California coast, UCSB has an exceptional array of faculty, graduate students, and staff. There are many reasons why it proved to be such an advantageous place for me to study, but the most significant of these was the composition of my dissertation committee. Each member contributed to my intellectual and professional growth in her or his own way and, once again, I cannot find the words to acknowledge them adequately. It is with great appreciation and respect that I thank Robert Kelley, who died after a short illness while I was in the process of writing the dissertation, Constance

Penley, W. Richard Comstock, Catherine L. Albanese, and Richard D. Hecht for all they have done for me. Professor Penley brought her creative mind and cultural studies approach to our discussions of my work; Professor Comstock engaged in provocative conversations with me and helped in the conceptualization of the project; Professor Albanese, who deserves special mention for her careful, critical reading of every page, paragraph, and sentence of the dissertation, kept me firmly grounded in American religious history and culture; and Professor Hecht provided me with overall direction—he was my adviser during graduate school, and his counsel and friendship continue to be extremely valuable.

Fortunately, I have moved on to another exceptional academic setting. The Department of Religion at Emory University is an ideal place to begin a professional career. My colleagues here, as well as throughout the Emory community, have been encouraging and supportive while I reworked the manuscript. The enthusiasm and advice of Paul Courtright and Louis Ruprecht Jr. were greatly appreciated, and the constructive, insightful comments of E. Brooks Holifield gave me a fresh perspective on the manuscript while I was putting it into its final form. The summer research support I received from the university was also helpful as I finished putting the final manuscript together.

I would like to express my gratitude to the Graduate Division and the Interdisciplinary Humanities Center at the University of California, Santa Barbara, for research support. During the research for this project I encountered a number of generous and friendly people who made the task of searching through materials much easier. To the librarians and assistants at the following institutions, thank you for all your support: the American Antiquarian Society in Worcester, Mass.; the Baker Library and Countway Medical Library, both at Harvard University; the Davidson Library, Special Collections and Interlibrary Loan Services, at UCSB; the Huntington Library in San Marino, Calif.; the Illinois State Historical Library in Springfield; the National Foundation of Funeral Service in Chicago; the Old Sturbridge Village Research Library in Massachusetts; and the Woodruff Library at Emory. Thanks to Edward C. Johnson and Melissa Johnson Williams for access to their private collection of funerary materials. Mr. Johnson provided me with useful information about the history of embalming in the United States and burial during the Civil War. I would also like to express my gratitude to Athena Angelos, pictorial researcher in Washington, D.C., who helped me locate many of the images included in the book.

Portions of Part I appeared in a different form in the *Journal of the American Academy of Religion.* I am grateful to the journal for permission to use this material. Also, portions of the book were presented at national meetings of the American Academy of Religion, the American Studies Association, the Civil War Round Table Association, and the Organization of American Historians. A number of people who heard my presentations provided me with useful and astute comments, including Howard Kushner, Glen LaFantasie, Laurie Maffly-Kipp, Colleen McDannell, Ellen More, Michael Sappol, and Barbara Sicherman. I also presented the section on Lincoln during various "job talks," and received helpful comments from faculty and students at UCSB, Duke, and Emory. In addition, the following individuals read over all or part of this work and offered constructive suggestions about both form and content: John Gillis, Thomas Laqueur, Edward Linenthal, James McPherson, Maris Vinovskis, and Michel Vovelle.

Finally, I would like to thank Charles Grench, Dan Heaton, and the other editors at Yale University Press for their interest in my work and their assistance in producing this book.

Introduction

What should be done with the dead body? Who is best qualified to prepare the corpse for its final disposition? Does the decaying, disintegrating individual body have any symbolic value for the collective social body? These are disturbing questions indeed, yet every culture must grapple with them because of one universal, inescapable truth: death. Throughout history, however, living communities have demonstrated a remarkable range of strategies for managing and imagining their dead. While most societies have turned to religious authorities and teachings to make metaphysical sense of death, confronting the reality of the human corpse has been a particularly compelling dilemma for survivors. As sociologist Robert Hertz observed, the death of a societal member "is tantamount to a sacrilege" because society itself "is stricken in the very principle of its life, in the faith it has in itself."[1] How the dead body is cared for, and the practices employed for its disposal, can tell us as much about the animating principles within a given society as about how that society understands the meaning of death. Before turning to an investigation of these questions in Protestant culture in the northern United States of the nineteenth century, a few words about the status and meaning of the dead in contemporary American society are in order. After all, a primary goal of this study is to shed some light on how changing attitudes toward death and the dead in the previous century have led to present-day perspectives and practices.

In the United States today, corpses are handled in a fairly practical, rational, and organized way by a group of expert professionals. Family members, close relatives and friends, and other acquaintances depend on these professionals to provide confirmation that life is truly extinguished and to prepare the body for its exit from living society. Although the details of the funeral service differ according to a number of factors, including degree of religious belief and class standing, treatment of the corpse itself varies little. Throughout most of the twentieth century, the same rituals to remove the dead from the human community have prevailed, and the corpse has been kept securely within the purview of individuals who have an interest in the mortal remains at death.[2]

When death occurs, it usually takes place and is officially announced in a medical setting. The individual presiding over the transition from life to death is the doctor, who reads the body with an assortment of technological devices to make sure that there are no positive signs of animation.[3] With this pronouncement a series of actions is set in motion that ultimately lead to the disposition of the corpse out of sight from the living. Before the body of the deceased disappears from view, however, its presence as a unit of information must be recorded in a number of registers, including those managed by the hospital, the government, private agencies, religious institutions, and other social organizations that maintain demographic and biographical records.

If necessary, an autopsy is performed at the hospital, and from there the corpse is transported to a funeral home or mortuary. Here a new set of specialists begin their professional services to ensure that the body of the deceased is properly arranged for disposal. Disposal usually takes one of two forms: either the body is embalmed and then interred in the ground, or it is cremated. If the family chooses cremation, the body still may be embalmed before it is incinerated. Although an increasing number of families choose this last method of disposition, embalming and earth burial has been the most popular option for the majority of U.S. citizens throughout most of the twentieth century.[4] But common though embalming may be in the United States, many individuals do not understand — and do not want to understand — why this practice has become so ritualized.

State and federal laws require embalming only under specific circumstances. Most American funeral directors and health and safety experts, though, assert that embalming is an essential social responsibility for those who handle the dead and get them ready for their final passage.[5] A variety of federal and state agencies are interested in the practice of embalming, from local boards of health to state associations of funeral service organizations to the Occupational Safety and Health Administration. The Federal Trade Commission also has an interest in embalmed bodies because they are, in effect, commodities for use in a consumer market that generates millions and millions of dollars.[6]

When a corpse is to be buried its appearance seems to be a principal concern both to the professionals who work on it and to the survivors. The presentation of the dead, the display of an apparently serene, content figure in an expensive, comfortable, mass-produced coffin located in a "slumber" room or funeral chapel, offers the living the opportunity to gaze upon the remains of the deceased one last time before the body disappears. In order to assist in this component of the ritual, funeral technicians perform their unique duties on the dead. These duties, which usually take place out of sight of the bereaved in the privacy of well-equipped preparation rooms, include disinfecting the body, washing its surface and shaving facial hairs, draining the blood, injecting embalming fluid into the arteries, gluing the eyes and mouth shut, applying the necessary cosmetic touches, and dressing the body in formal attire.[7]

Specialists in the funeral industry claim that there are compelling hygienic reasons for the process of embalming and that, even more important to those involved in this highly lucrative business, it also offers customers who bid farewell to their loved ones a service that is therapeutic and greatly appreciated. Many survivors seem to have a strong desire to gaze upon the lifeless body before it is removed. Embalming provides a simulacrum of the living loved one, even though the secret of real death hovers over the peaceful figure "at rest" in the coffin. There is a variety of explanations as to why this practice is so pervasive in the United States, but there can be no doubt that "the embalmed body is the cornerstone of [the funeral] industry."[8] As a highly technical procedure that requires expertise, training, and some form of governmental regulation, and as a service with a sustaining consumer demand, embalming has grown from the end of the nineteenth century and throughout the twentieth century into a legitimate and fundamental element of the rite of passage leading the dead from the living community.

The routinization of the dead and their placement within a rigid, organized ritual guarantees that the survivors can turn to mediators to deal with the lifeless remains. Whether or not the corpse is viewed, the living have minimal contact with it and can choose not to bid farewell in person to their lost loved one. Although the dead become the center of a range of medical, economic, and religious activities, they can also move from hospital room to burial plot or urn without making any public appearance. Their location in society is securely regulated and controlled by numerous specialists, so the physical trace left behind at death in no way threatens the equilibrium of living society.

But the dead do not simply vanish when life is extinguished; although their final physical disposition is managed by specialists, the dead must also be accounted for in the imagination. In contrast to the relative simplicity and uniformity of the ritual activity surrounding the corpse, the life of the spirit — if it is affirmed at all — is described within a variety of symbol systems and imaginative constructs. The radical dualism that underlies this imagery about the afterlife reveals the modern indifference toward the fate of the body, a loss of interest in the semiotics of decomposition, and a sense of confidence about the spirit after death has occurred. Yet while popular, optimistic narratives of out-of-body adventure have captured much of the public's attention, darker counternarratives about the threatening return of the dead are just as powerful and popular in American culture.[9]

Surveys published in the 1980s indicate that roughly 70 percent of adult Americans believed in life after death.[10] But as Colleen McDannell and Bernhard Lang observe in their analysis of conceptualizations of heaven, "While Christians still accept heaven as an article of faith, their vigor in defining the nature of eternal life has much diminished."[11] In spite of growing interest in angels during the 1990s, specifics about the afterlife seem not to be pressing to most Christians; even with the proliferation of ideas about the spiritual world that challenge traditional religious views, many Christians remain focused on religious life in this world and spend little time or energy describing the next. On the other hand, one of the most fundamental changes in the vision of the afterlife since the Enlightenment has been the virtual erasure of images of hell from the Christian imagination.[12]

Most theologians in the twentieth century have been hesitant to offer specifics about the heavenly realm and what awaits the spirit after death. Protestant thinkers like Rienhold Niebuhr and Paul Tillich have adopted a "symbolist compromise" that avoids both literal, supernatural interpretations of the spiritual realm and scientific, rational skepticism about nonempirical realities. For these Christian philosophers "there are dimensions of reality which cannot be approached in any other way than by symbols"; they suggest that a whole range of questions relating to immortality, heaven, and the spirit are ultimately inaccessible to human understanding.[13] In contrast to the reticence of theologians, though, others within the Christian tradition have provided concrete answers about the details of death. Spokespersons for specific Protestant denominations frequently address these questions with language unhindered by philosophical ambiguity and multivalent symbolism. For many the body is inconsequential to the spirit's future prospects.

For example, in *Major Methodist Beliefs*, Bishop Mack B. Stokes asserts that people will be able to recognize each other in the next life and friendships will not only be maintained but enhanced by greater love: "Eternal life is one of peace and joy because it brings together the redeemed souls into a perfect fellowship. . . . We shall not only recognize [our friends], we shall see how truly wonderful they are and we shall more perfectly love them."[14] But the Methodist *Service of Death and Resurrection,* acknowledges that the material, decomposing or cremated body will no longer be of use at the time of the individual's resurrection. When the body is disposed of the mourners are reminded that it "has been valued and loved. When it no longer serves its purpose *in its old form*, it is returned to the elements from which it came."[15]

While American Protestant churches often frame discussions of death in terms of reunions, personal immortality, and the presence of Jesus Christ, numerous descriptions of the afterlife offer an alternative set of images, symbols, and meanings for public consumption. A popular narrative that has captured the American imagination describes the "near-death" experiences of individuals who have come back from death to provide insight into this life and the spirit's "otherworld journeys."[16] Although there are variations, the recurring themes expressed by those who claim to have died and come back include lights and tunnels, guardian angels and departed relations who serve as spirit guides, mystical insight into the meaning of life, and reentrance into the body. Most informants insist that they acquired a new, spiritual body as their physical one ceased to function.[17] Whatever the details, the primary message remains the same: at death the spirit leaves the body and begins a new, disembodied life. In the words of Betty J. Eadie, whose *Embraced by the Light* was a huge commercial success in 1994 and 1995: "When we 'die,' my guides said, we experience nothing more than a transition to another state. Our spirits slip from the body and move to a spiritual realm. If our deaths are traumatic, the spirit quickly leaves the body, sometimes even before death occurs."[18]

Death and the metamorphosis from matter to spirit constitute simply one stage in the supernatural progression outlined by those who report on near-death experiences and by scientists who attempt to provide empirical evidence of their validity. The suffering and inevitable deterioration of the physical body are overcome in these narratives, which draw on an assortment of religious systems, including Christianity, Native American mythology, and various other mystical traditions to present a syncretic, comprehensible, and highly satisfying vision of the afterlife. Considered as a cultural fashion in contemporary America, the popularity of near-death adventures reveals three specific characteristics of modern society: the increasing impotence of conventional religious traditions in making sense of death, the persistent desire to ground some form of personal immortality in medical and scientific language, and the powerful need to avoid imaginatively the symbolically potent corpse.[19]

Popular literature describing near-death journeys appeals to modern, rational, scientifically minded individuals in search of hopeful signs of postmortem existence. But on the other hand, countervailing expressions in mass media offer menacing and dangerous revenants rather than peaceful, adventurous, and ethereal spirits. From Jason in *Friday the Thirteenth* to Freddy in *Nightmare on Elm Street* to the flesh-eating zombies in *Night of the Living Dead*, horror films since the late 1960s have provided enthusiastic audiences with an orgy of fantastic violence and graphic, often sexual, brutality perpetrated by monsters who return from the grave to haunt the living. Cinematic exploits of the walking dead, through such figures as Frankenstein, Dracula, and the Mummy, have always been a successful draw at the theater. But in recent decades the horror film has attained new levels of popularity, partly as a result of the vivid and spectacular images of human destruction depicted on screen.

In these narratives all is not light and progress but instead only darkness and fear. The dead rarely assume a disembodied, spiritual form — they come back either to exact some form of vengeance or to engage in random acts of violence and destruction.[20] The insights they return with do not promote peace and promise, only chaos, injustice, and terror. The motivations and experiences of the dead in these films are inversions of what transpires in popular, out-of-body travels. Instead of visiting a realm of spiritual progress and comforting reunions, they return from beyond to *this* world to wreak havoc, sever the bonds of family, love, and friendship, and satisfy their aggressive, toxic desires. These fiends personify Death — sometimes with a degree of parody and humor — as an irrational force that can vanquish any and all individuals, regardless of faith, intelligence, or income.

The dead also return to the imagination of the living through mechanisms that exist outside the logic of conventional religious discourse and popular expressions in various media. In politics, the dead have been extremely powerful sources of national legitimation and sanctification. From Gettysburg National Cemetery to the *Challenger* disaster, the federal government has acted to preserve the memory of certain significant individuals and moments in national history.[21] Its interest in the dead goes beyond questions of propriety and respect for individuals who make up the republic; indeed, the very life of the political order has depended on trampling over the bones of indigenous peoples and glorifying the remains of figures whose significance reflects the principles and mission of the nation. Assuming a role once reserved for the church, the state confers immortality on particular national heroes and sacrality on specific locations that solemnize the sacrifices and triumphs of American citizens. In addition, the maintenance of graves, museums, and memorials contributes to the construction of sacred places on the American landscape; the celebration of such national holidays as Presidents' Day, Martin Luther King Jr. Day, and Memorial Day establishes the sacred time by which citizens orient themselves. The cosmology of American political life is saturated with death and the bones of the dead.[22]

The struggle to account for death can also be linked with a wide range of high-profile, contentious, often extremely emotional issues in American society, including abortion, euthanasia, violence, suicide, genocide, and AIDS. The public debates surrounding these issues, as well as the popularity of new-age visions of the afterlife, mourning manuals, techniques of grief therapy, and bereavement workshops, indicate that death is *not* a taboo topic, but rather a subject that is unavoidable in American culture. Although the dead—that is, the physical corpses of deceased individuals—are either disguised and made to appear in a state of peaceful repose or removed entirely from view, the broad questions associated with human mortality can be imagined in a variety of contexts and are debated vigorously in the public arena. This signals a significant change in the status and location of death in modern society.

According to the historian Philippe Ariès, by the early decades of the twentieth century death had become "hidden" and "invisible." Death was eventually understood as "dirty" and a source of pollution, which led to the medicalization of death and its banishment to the hospital. At the same time, as individuals in larger communities and major urban centers grew more and more alienated from each other, social solidarity in the face of death dissolved. The forces of life, the disappearance of hell, and the successes of medicine began to transform death into something shameful and unnatural. Under these conditions American society became "ashamed of death, more ashamed then afraid," and proceeded to eliminate it from public life.[23] Ariès concludes his 1977 study: "A heavy silence has fallen over the subject of death. . . . Neither the individual nor the community is strong enough to recognize the existence of death."[24]

Popular interest in the subject developed gradually in the United States, clearly in large part after the publication of Ariès's study.[25] Even in religious circles there was little public interest until the last decades of the twentieth century in debating and exploring the meanings, politics, psychology, and other dimensions of death that fascinate us today. The reasons for this "silence" need further exploration, but perhaps the experience of two world wars, particularly the mass destruction of the Holocaust in Europe and the dropping of the atomic bomb in Japan, contributed to this reticence to discuss the subject; perhaps, as will be argued in this work, the gradual displacement of the presence of death in daily living began sometime after the Civil War.[26]

In the following investigation I shall discuss the changing status of the corpse in the culturally dominant white, Protestant communities of the northern United States before and during the Civil War, culminating in the emergence of the funeral industry after the war. While the making of American society resulted from a mixture of religious groups and movements, immigrants and ethnic communities, and entrepreneurs and workers from various classes, the creation and acceptance of the funeral industry in the postbellum years depended on these Protestants. This was not an entirely homogenous culture, but its lineage can be traced back to the New England Puritans.[27] The imaginative and social world constituted by middle-class Protestant sensibilities will serve as the focus of this study because it was in this world that the corpse moved from a symbolically powerful though liminal object to a commodity at the heart of the nascent industry.

The time frame of this history is rather specific: it begins with the ceremonial activities associated with the death of George Washington in 1799 and closes with the assassination and funeral journey of Abraham Lincoln in 1865. A close examination of the years between the burials of the first president and the sixteenth will reveal the conditions—demographic, social, cultural, and symbolic—that led to the consolidation and professionalization of what became by the turn of the century a nationally organized confederation of market-conscious American death specialists. One of the principal services offered by technicians in the new industry—and the one that legitimated their claims to expertise in death—was embalming, a practice that offended and repulsed popular sensibilities before the onset of the Civil War.

The study concludes with the second annual meeting of the Funeral Directors' National Association in Rochester, New York, in 1883; here, at the beginning of this collective enterprise, their article of faith about embalming was articulated. At the funeral directors' first national meeting the effort to preserve the body was proclaimed to be central to American deathways and consistent with the ancient "scientific" endeavor to preserve the corpse. In the words of the first secretary of the group, S. R. Lippincott,

> From the earliest age of which we have any authentic history, it seems to have been the ardent desire of the scientific world to obtain the mystery of the art of preserving this wonderful piece of mechanism from waste and decay and dissolution, so that time should not efface or destroy it. . . . We want to know whether this lost art, if it ever really did exist, is to be again restored, and whether it has remained thus long buried in obscurity that the great American Republic may have the distinguished honor of restoring again to mankind a lost art.
>
> We have met, then, to-day, my friends, from the different parts of a great country, to lay the corner stone of a new structure to art and science.[28]

Lippincott went on to describe this task as a religious enterprise. He compared the members who were present to King David: although they might not live to see the "Temple" of the industry completed, they were involved in "preparing the materials and design" for it. But he also acknowledged that this would not be an easy task. In addition to the scientific, artistic, and religious imperatives involved in "building the Temple," Lippincott realized the economic urgency of banding together "professional" death specialists into a national organization. "Up to the present time, then, we have been but a loose aggregation of individuals, in no way united for a common purpose. Hereafter we shall be a conservative central force, that will unite and control, to a certain extent, the discordant elements among us, and save our profession from disintegration and disgrace."[29]

Before the 1880s no funeral industry existed to provide goods and services for the dead or the survivors in any uniform, dependable manner. Family members, friends, and neighbors were responsible for the actions that led to the burial of the dead. Undertakers, liverymen, and cabinetmakers offered assistance at various moments in the transferral of the dead from the living community to the grave, but they usually played a subsidiary role in the drama of death, particularly in the antebellum period, secondary in importance behind the survivors and the corpse itself. Outside of the immediate circle of relations and friends, one of the earliest expressions of managerial interest in the disposal of the dead appeared around the 1830s, in the growing urban centers of the North. In locations such as Boston, New York, and Philadelphia, the corpse began to be understood as a source of pollution and hygienic danger; the movement toward rural cemeteries, which capitalized on the public's nostalgia for pastoral settings and pious, moral instruction, became a popular middle-class answer to the horrors of bodily disintegration and putrefaction. The arguments for burial reform that proliferated during the middle of the century were informed by a combination of deep-rooted Romantic sensibilities and inspiring advancements in the natural sciences.[30]

It was only after the war that a group of professionals mobilized as a collective force, assumed a hegemonic position over the dead, and began to serve as mediators between them and the living. Their self-understanding was couched, as already demonstrated, in scientific, artistic, religious, and economic language, and their immediate impact was in the cities of modernizing America. In addition to large-scale demographic expansion, the last decades of the nineteenth century were characterized by tremendous economic and industrial growth in the North, though there were the occasional crises that convulsed the economy and led to depression.[31] The creation and growing respectability of local and national organizations or associations of professionals who legitimated, regulated, and monitored the logic of the marketplace were integral components of American — more specifically, northern — economic success in the late nineteenth century. The dead were subsumed within this logic, not only because of the nature of the capitalist urban marketplace but also because of two specific circumstances: the growing market value of corpses and other goods and services associated with death, and experiences with the dead in the Civil War.

But this study does not simply focus on the development of an institution, nor on the evolution of burial practices, as the only ingredients in the story of attitudes toward death. It is also concerned with the symbol and meaning systems used by northern Protestants to interpret and imagine the dead.[32] While the corpse was saturated with Christian symbolism in this cultural milieu, there is evidence of a gradual process of "dechristianization" that led to reconceptualizations of the meaning of the corpse and of death in general.[33] This process was twofold: on the one hand, traditional Protestant views began to lose their authority in public culture; and, on the other hand, many competing beliefs about the spirit and spiritual journeys after death became dissociated from the corpse and the church, and assumed a multiplicity of popular forms. Equally important in this process were the unconventional interpretive responses to the presence of death, which could be manifested in terms of fascination, fixation, or — for soldiers during wartime — utter disregard. The relation between the reality of death — and the material reality of the dead body — and how that reality was represented in the imagination is critical to this cultural history.

Although academic interest in death has grown in recent years, the subject has not yet attained the privileged place in American historiography that it has in the study of Europe.[34] True, historians and other scholars have identified an "American way of death" that has developed over the course of the country's history.[35] But invoking an American way of death does not do justice to the conflicts and discord surrounding the dead throughout American history in general and within Protestant American history in particular. In these northern communities before the Civil War, and even, as we will see, during the bloody conflict that united the North against the southern states, there was no one "way" to understand the proper location of the dead in society and to construct their meaning in the imagination.

In this cultural history I shall examine the formation of a new way of looking at death. In particular, I shall describe the initial yearnings for, and the transformative moment in the history of, the death industry in the post-Puritan world of the North. The two periods that are most often identified as maintaining fairly strict, rigid controls on public expressions related to death are the recent past — in which the uniformity of burial practices coexisted with a general silence on the subject — and the Puritan era in New England at the beginning of the nation's history — in which an evangelism of fear positioned the realities of death at the center of communal life.[36] The period from the beginning of the nineteenth century to the start of the Civil War, in contrast, displayed a greater degree of conflict over the place and interpretation of the dead; Protestants in the North had trouble establishing a consensus on the meaning of death in public culture. As the Puritan theocracy began to recede further and further into the past, the location of the dead in popular northern society became more and more questionable. If the dominant Protestant institutions and local communities could no longer maintain their hold on the dead, what in American culture would take their place?

PART I

Living with the Dead in the Antebellum North

George Washington's Invisible Corpse and the Beaver Hat

On January 7, 1800, the town of Providence, Rhode Island, engaged in an act of communal solidarity that temporarily transformed and united the people in a collective demonstration of sorrow. George Washington had died and the young republic had lost a revered and respected leader. Normal routines were suspended in Providence so that citizens could participate publicly in one of the most important events of the new nation. This day was to be "set apart for humiliation and mourning," and citizens were requested to close their shops, refrain from "secular affairs," and wear a mourning badge on their left arms until the end of February.[1]

A funeral procession began on the morning of the seventh, accompanied by the firing of sixteen cannons in quick succession. After this initial military display, a cannon was discharged every half-hour. Throughout the course of the procession minute guns were fired, and muffled bells tolled from morning until evening. The cortege included various military orders, a bier supported by four pallbearers, a riderless white horse, members of the local government, representatives from local trade associations and other societies, and officials from several agencies and organizations. It moved to the sounds of solemn music, which heightened the drama and impact of the spectacle for those citizens who witnessed the ceremonies in honor of the first president of the United States.

Pallbearers reverently transported the bier from the Baptist meetinghouse, which had been draped in black like most of the churches in town, to the Episcopal church in an atmosphere infused with patriotism, grief, and veneration. Religious leaders delivered orations over the bier at various stops along the procession route and provided the appropriate words for the somber occasion, conveying a combination of collective sorrow, national pride, and Christian faith. With the final discharge of three volleys, the empty bier was then deposited underneath the Episcopal church, and the procession returned to the home of a Colonel Olney to the tune of the "President's March." An individual observed that although the parade was great, "it by no means equaled the grief it was intended to express."[2]

George Washington died in his bed at Mount Vernon, Virginia, on December 14, 1799. His body was entombed on the grounds of his home.[3] One of the first heroes of the newborn republic was no longer among the living, but in death his memory and presence would be honored throughout the land. Many of the great number of obsequies, ceremonies, and observances that followed in the wake of his death, like those described in Providence, were simulations of a real burial. These activities suggested that ushering the founding father's body out of the social order had symbolic importance and served the social solidarity of the new nation. But, of course, the corpse was absent from the numerous rituals that swept both the northern and southern sections of the nation. Washington was at the center of these activities, and though his actual body was missing, the invocation of his presence in the local ceremonies and numerous speeches celebrating his death allowed the national community to collectively express their social unity. The human remains were inconsequential to the valorization of the spirit of the man.

In towns throughout the republic, however, these observances were carried out *as if* the real body were present. Philadelphia citizens not only saw a mock coffin but also a "symbolic reproduction of the Mount Vernon ceremony."[4] The funeral procession in New London, Connecticut, consisted of military and civil officers, members of the Masonic order, a riderless horse, various clergy, sixteen girls in white robes, and pallbearers carrying a bier.[5] In the city of New York the cortege was larger and even more elaborate. The vast array of symbols in these processions confirmed that in his death, the spirit of Washington was being deified in the collective imagination of the young nation. Symbols that linked Washington to the mythic themes at work in the republic included an eagle with a laurel wreath in its beak, various military trophies, and stripes from the U.S. flag.[6] Most of the towns in the North, as in other parts of the country, participated in these types of funeral activities during January.

But while funeral ceremonies were enacted throughout the country, there was only one body to be buried. Protestant public culture appropriated the spirit of Washington in these observances, but his remains were laid to rest in the private family vault at Mount Vernon. The Protestant roots of American culture discouraged any activity resembling the Catholic tradition of venerating the relics of saints in the treatment of Washington's body; in spite of its immediately recognized sacrality, the corpse would not be an accessible object to be used as a source of personal healing or other forms of miraculous activity.[7] Its integrity and its security within the bonds of his family were assured, and the material remains would not be shared with the rest of the nation. Instead, the memory of the man as a "living" symbol for national virtue and unity replaced the actual body of the dead president in the funeral ceremonies across the country.[8]

Although Washington's death caused widespread grief and mourning, Americans did not understand it as a setback to the life of the nation. It was, rather, transformed into a heroic event that regenerated and rejuvenated the body politic; the various celebrations associated with the burial of his invisible body conveyed a sense of social cohesion that many believed distinguished the American republic from other nations in the world. In addition, at the time of his death and during the services commemorating his passing, Washington continued to be imagined as an agent of Providence, remembered with a series of rituals and mythic narratives that reconfirmed the chosen, millennial destiny of the country in world history as prefigured in political and religious rhetoric from before the Revolutionary War.[9]

Efforts to memorialize Washington through mourning art became one of the many popular strategies for interpreting his death. This type of art expressed a modern manifestation of the cult of the hero, valorizing the dead iconographically through motifs borrowed from ancient Greece and Rome — the urn, the stele, and the mourner in classical maiden's dress. Also interwoven with these themes were Christian symbols of resurrection and redemption, most commonly a willow or an evergreen; Romantic motifs expressed in pastoral settings; and allegorical figures, such as America, Columbia, and Father Time. The mourning art associated with the death of Washington suggests that the act of mourning him was, "in true Roman spirit, an act of patriotism, the love of one's country and its beloved founder being equated with the love of God."[10]

In rituals as well as in public discourse, Washington's corpse was secondary to his apotheosis in the collective imagination of the early republic. In death he was not only a unifying symbol that bound disparate sections of the nation together, he was also the personification of a model citizen. His virtuous, revered life was held up as an ideal for all citizens to emulate. Many orators who delivered eulogies in communities throughout the country reminded listeners that the mortal part of Washington, which obeyed the laws of nature and God by returning to dust, was less an object of reflection than the spirit of the man. According to these speakers, his spirit must be remembered and used to nourish the soul of the country and of each citizen. But his invisible corpse, ceremoniously incorporated into the rituals around the nation, initiated the process of remembrance and civic renewal.

Another death that occurred in 1799 offers an instructive contrast to the honor, ceremony, and symbolism bestowed on Washington's absent body. In Scituate, Rhode Island, an individual with no friends or relatives hanged himself. In the early years of the republic, English Common Law was normally followed in the case of suicide: authorities confiscated the individual's personal property and, for good measure, dishonored the body by burying it either in a highway or at a crossroads with a stake driven through it. But the corpse of this suicide, though buried decently in the local graveyard, ultimately suffered a fate as disturbing as what was prescribed by the Common Law and became embroiled in a political and personal controversy that turned into one of the most famous legal cases in the early history of Rhode Island.[11]

In December 1801, charges of slander and defamation were brought against Arthur Fenner, the governor of Rhode Island, by John Dorrance, a justice on the Court of Common Pleas and onetime president of the Town Council in Providence. In his suit, Dorrance charged the governor with uttering a series of false and malicious lies through the public telling and retelling of a particular story. Fenner told the story, according to Dorrance, with the intent of depriving Dorrance of his judicial office and destroying his political character. Governor Fenner denied these charges, asserting that the story he told was indeed true.

According to Governor Fenner, Dorrance sold the corpse of the man who had hung himself in Scituate to a Dr. Pardon Bowen. The body, after being snatched from its original resting place by medical students, was allegedly left in the care of Dorrance by some of the inhabitants of Scituate. They had entrusted him with protecting the corpse and providing it with a decent reburial. Instead, the body was purportedly sold to Dr. Bowen for the same purpose for which it was first stolen: dissection. Fenner went on to say that Dorrance had received a beaver hat from Dr. Bowen in payment for the corpse and had "had the impudence to wear the aforesaid hat on his . . . head, while he . . . officiated as Moderator of a Town-Meeting of the town of Providence."[12]

Leaving aside questions of guilt or innocence and the political motivations involved, of particular interest are the sworn statements by the individuals who participated in the trial. According to some witnesses, two nights after the body of the suicide was buried it was "taken up and carried away" by medical students who were studying with Dr. Bowen and a Dr. Benjamin Dyer. A search party followed the tracks of the sleigh that carried the body from the graveyard to Dr. Dyer's house. The search party, denied entry to the house, went to Governor Fenner, who suggested that they request a search warrant from Judge Dorrance. The following day Dorrance arranged a meeting of all the interested parties and negotiated an agreement whereby the body would be reinterred under his direction. After the reburial, a group of people again disinterred the body and carried it away for dissection, this time to the home of Jabez Bowen, who lived with and was employed by a Mr. Suggin.[13]

Daniel Knight, a physician from Connecticut, participated in the two disinterments and the second burial. His deposition includes the following exchange:

> Q. Was the body put into a coffin [for the second burial] of the usual form?
> A. The body was put into a rough, pine box, not made in the usual form of a coffin.
> Q. Was the body, when put into the coffin, covered with a shirt, and otherwise laid out in a common and decent manner?
> A. It had no shirt on, and to the best of my recollection no cover at all.
> Q. How far below the surface of the earth was the coffin settled?
> A. To the best of my recollection, not to exceed eighteen inches.[14]

Knight then gave a detailed account of what transpired during the dissection.

> Q. What operations were performed on the dead body the same night after you had removed it from the grave to Mr. Suggin's?
> A. The body was opened and the entrails taken out.
> Q. What was done with the entrails?
> A. They were buried in said Suggin's shop, which had no floor.
> Q. What knowledge do you have of any operations which was [*sic*] performed on the dead body afterwards?
> A. The operation of dissection was begun the next night following, which was continued for several nights until completed.
> Q. Do you know what became of the flesh which was taken from that corpse, or the contents of the breast?
> A. I was not present when the flesh was taken off, but the heart and lights were buried in the same shop that the entrails were, but not at the same time nor in [the] same place.[15]

Later, another doctor testified that the bones of the suicide were kept by a Dr. Cleavland, who moved away from Providence sometime after the dissection.[16]

Dr. Bowen testified that during his conversations with members of the search party he attempted to persuade them of the utilitarian virtues of dissection but that his arguments fell on deaf ears. According to Dr. Bowen, cutting into the body of this suicide could be extremely useful to the living. Dissection would provide essential anatomical knowledge, a necessary pursuit "if we meant to qualify ourselves to preserve the lives and limbs of our fellow creatures." Dr. Bowen went on to explain why the suicide's corpse was the perfect specimen for medical experimentation: "He was a stranger, entirely unknown, and had no friends nor relatives whose feelings could be hurt by his dissection."[17] For Dr. Bowen and many others in the medical field, the integrity of the lifeless body could be destroyed, provided that no living relations were disturbed by its dismemberment. But the citizens of the community, though none had been close to the suicide, were scandalized by the treatment of his body and were in any case adamantly opposed to the practice of dissection.

In an odd strategic reversal, the defense lawyer for Governor Fenner attempted to demonstrate that Governor Fenner had not slandered Dorrance because no crime could be imputed from the story the defendant told. Citing Common Law, the defense stated that "when the human body is once divested of the functions of life, when once the power of death has rendered it useless and unprofitable to the surviving it becomes a cast out beyond the reach of the laws or protection of society; — it becomes a loathsome object of abhorrence, disclaimed and deserted by all the living and the human race."[18] He even asserted that the stealing of a shroud was more of a crime than the stealing of a corpse.[19]

Compared with the invisible body of Washington, which was a potent symbol of national unity in the funeral ceremonies throughout the country, the fate and meaning of the suicide's body collapsed into nothingness. Indeed, the desirability of seeing the body's interior space — of rendering what was invisible, visible — led to its ultimate annihilation. In spite of the objections of community members, individuals in the medical field argued that this corpse had no value in itself because there was no circle of close friends or family to ascribe meaning to it through an act of emotional projection. According to both the medical and legal logic of the period, the body of a suicide was an outcast from the social order. What was once a living human being was now a pure and insignificant object, thoroughly desacralized and empty of meaning. The only way for the corpse to regain value was to be reappropriated and to function in society by serving, in this case, as an instrument for the advancement of medical knowledge. For this the integrity of the body would have to be destroyed.

The funeral ceremonies for Washington and the unceremonious treatment of the suicide's body suggest the antithetical interpretations of a corpse at the turn of the nineteenth century. These interpretations, which determined meanings and prescribed actions in the two cases outlined above, reflected malleable cultural sensibilities. They also give an indication of the potential contests that could erupt over rival understandings of the place and meaning of the corpse in northern society. In order to explore these interpretations, meanings, and actions, however, we must first understand how individuals in these communities experienced death and the frequency with which they encountered the tangible, physical remains of the dead.

1

Signs of Death

Signs of death were commonplace in towns and villages in the northern states at the beginning of the nineteenth century. For most individuals death was an integrated element of everyday life. The familiarity with death and the intimacy that characterized its status in antebellum society, however, did not ease the pain and suffering endured by the survivors. Losing a child, a sibling, a parent, a friend, or any other close relation often led individuals to seek consolation and succor from a support network accustomed to the emotional rupture caused by death. Still, there was no denying its reality, for not only did death strike frequently and with cruel force, but it was also a pervasive theme in the discourses, economy of symbols, and collective imagination of the Protestant communities in this region.

The complex network of signs associated with the omnipresence of death could be expressed in a variety of forms. There were the somber tolls of the church bells, which, through a system of publicly recognized codes, provided such information as the age and gender of the recently deceased. The elaborate rules for mourning dress, followed by many women and men of the period, contributed to the public acknowledgment that a death had occurred. The funeral procession, an event often witnessed in the communities of the North, reminded citizens that death regularly intruded into the vicinity of the living. In the drama of this procession, the corpse played an unmistakably leading role. Broadsides that were posted in towns and villages often touched on the subject of death, either directly or indirectly, with words and symbols. For example, a discussion of the "funeral honours" enacted after the deaths of Thomas Jefferson and John Adams justified civic observances by describing biblical precedents occasioned by the death of certain Old Testament rulers.[1] A great number of elegies were also printed and posted, many of which incorporated an image of a coffin. They were usually written about an individual whose death could serve as a reminder of the passage of time and the inevitable fate awaiting every person:

> Our life and time, of which some boast,
> Will hasten fast away:
> 'Tis like the flow'r or shade at most,
> That quickly doth decay!![2]

The communal burying ground, both in its early rural configuration and in the later garden cemetery, offered a wide array of iconographic and textual expressions testifying to the imminence of death. The death's heads, cherubs, hourglasses, urns, and willows were only a few of the symbolic designs found on tombstones in nineteenth-century America. Besides this iconographic landscape, the textual variations found in cemetery epitaphs also conveyed a communal awareness of the omnipresent fact of death and an effort to grapple with its meaning. In addition, the location of many burial grounds, either at the center or on the periphery of the community, ensured the close proximity of the dead with the living.

Religious homilies consistently invoked death, as did much of the literature and art of the period. In the well-attended funeral sermons, mass revival meetings, and local religious services, the theme of death, on an individual as well as an eschatological level, was central to the religious language of the North. Ministers used the reality of death as a suasive tool to encourage the congregation to live morally, warn them of the dangers of sin, and prepare them for Judgment Day. In addition, numerous religious authors employed the motif of a good Christian death in the popular literature of the time because it served as a powerful evangelical device for converting community members who had strayed from, or who were never part of, the church.

According to the cultural historian Carl Bode, death was a persistent theme (along with love and success) running through much of antebellum culture.[3] The fiction, poetry, and visual arts of the period commonly incorporated the subject into narrative structures and imaginative representations. From the death of Little Eva in Harriet Beecher Stowe's novel *Uncle Tom's Cabin,* to the metaphysical musings about death in William Cullen Bryant's poem "Thanatopsis," to the human corpse serving as a footstool for Death in Rembrandt Peale's painting *The Court of Death,* writers, poets, and painters showed a fascination with human mortality. Even mourning paraphernalia — samplers, jewelry, and other mementos — were popular items in the material culture of the period.

Signs of death permeated the communities of the North, saturating every-day life in a public display of communal awareness. In order to better understand the cultural status of death in the early nineteenth century, however, we must look behind the sign systems to the more basic demographic realities of human mortality. Elizabeth Garrett, writing on the social history of the home in the United States, elaborates on the pervasive and unavoidable encounter with death experienced by nineteenth-century Americans of all ages and socioeconomic levels. Although life expectancy was on the rise throughout the century, she writes, "there were few families that did not frequently renew acquaintance with the grim reaper. . . . The pall of death was omnipresent."[4]

Accurate records of antebellum mortality rates in the northern United States are difficult to find, but demographers have been able to offer some general observations.[5] Gradual improvements in sanitation and diet helped raise health standards over the course of the nineteenth century, but up until the Civil War mortality rates in the North remained fairly stable, indicating that advancements in medical research, disease control, and scientific knowledge had not yet made a significant impact on the health of the general population. Significant fluctuations in mortality rates were often caused by severe seasonal conditions, epidemics, or other forces that were, at the time, beyond human control. In addition, changes in living and work patterns contributed to how people died. Increased urban populations and the process of industrialization aggravated the stress of living conditions in cities throughout the North, which in turn raised death rates, especially among the poor.[6] Although differences in life expectancy were minimal between urban and rural areas, mortality rates were somewhat higher in cities.[7]

According to some estimates, the crude death rate in the period before the Civil War was around fifteen per thousand in rural towns and ranged anywhere from twenty to forty per thousand in the larger cities.[8] Near the end of the eighteenth century, 80 percent of Americans died before reaching the age of seventy.[9] In general, those who were strong enough to survive the various diseases and occasional epidemics that swept through their communities could expect to live into their late thirties. For females in Massachusetts in 1849, life expectancy at birth was between 36.3 years and 38.3 years, while for males the age was slightly lower.[10]

Unfortunately many people did not even reach these ages — the chances of dying during the early years of life were exceedingly high. According to one historian, "between one fifth and one third of all children died before age ten."[11] Another historian suggests that infant mortality might have been as high as two hundred per thousand live births.[12] Between childhood, or the age of one, and adulthood, around twenty-one years, death could strike a family member without warning and without reason. Anywhere from 8 to 10 percent of the individuals in this age group could expect to die before reaching their twenty-first birthday. The death of a brother or sister, son or daughter, was a common experience in the large families that predominated in the early years of the republic.[13]

No significant decline in mortality figures emerged until after the Civil War. Compared with twentieth-century standards, the dead and the realities of death were constant and inescapable facts of consciousness for most community members in the antebellum North. They commonly witnessed, or knew about, or were exposed to, the death of a relation, friend, acquaintance, or public figure at nearly every stage of life. Signs of death circulated throughout antebellum culture, but the most significant and meaningful confrontation with human mortality arose out of the day-to-day experiences of individuals in their homes and communities.

Perhaps a better way to capture the familiarity with death evident in the everyday lives of northerners is to listen to the voices of the period rather than examine the impersonal statistics of demographers. Numbers can help contextualize the reality of death in the antebellum period, but the words of those who lived in this era reveal human efforts to make sense of this intimacy. References to death were ubiquitous in the personal writings of many individuals, who related their feelings, actions, and prayers in the face of death and often acknowledged the human inability to prevent the loss of life. And although the reflections found in the letters and diaries of the period evince a variety of philosophical temperaments and religious sentiments, the constant intrusion of death into the fabric of communal life was a frequent and commonplace event widely commented on.

The diaries of Josiah Stone, a resident of Shrewsbury, Massachusetts, contain notations on the weather, comments on town meetings, and a detailed record of deaths and funerals in his community. The following series of diary entries exemplifies the tone and frequency with which Stone recorded events related to death.

> [Monday, 1 February 1847:] Mrs Abigail Maynard, wife of Simon, died to day of Lung Fever, aged 76 [years]- 8 [months]- 23 [days].
> [Thursday, 4 February 1847:] Funeral of Mrs. Simon Maynard today at 1 P.M.
> [Sunday, 7 February 1847:] Aunt Brigham of Northboro died about 5 O'clock this P.M. aged 89 years, 11½ months.
> [Tuesday, 9 February 1847:] [Hasty] Alexander died of Consumption at the Alms House yesterday aged 32 years.
> [Wednesday, 10 February 1847:] Funeral Services at the house of Nathaniel

Brigham by the Rev. Joseph Allen of Northboro—continued cloudy [and] snowed a little in the morning.[14]

In a letter written in 1837, Sarah Walker, a farmer in Sturbridge, Massachusetts, wrote to her brother about the family's good health and the various chores they were doing on the farm. She also informed him of recent losses that had occurred in town. "Since I have wrote you, Mrs. Bullard has buried her fourth little son whome she called Charles Perez, also Mrs. Julia Rice buried her little boy, nine months old. . . . Aretus Hooker has likewise buried his wife and is left with two motherless babes. Mr. Solomon Richardson died two weeks ago he was sick only two days, within three months Mr. Barnard Bowen has consigned to the silent earth his wife and daughter and a young lady . . . who was there as a maid."[15]

The highly objective nature and the compressed factual information contained within these two examples are fairly typical of the personal accounts of daily dying in communities in the North; they also convey something of the frequency and immediacy of death in the first half of the nineteenth century. As mentioned earlier, most individuals incorporated this reality into their daily lives and consciousness largely because of the high visibility and public status of death. Diaries, letters, sermons, literature, poetry, and other texts acknowledged that human mortality was an inescapable dimension of life; cemetery iconography, works of art, mourning paraphernalia, and other visual cues reminded people of the prevalence of death in everyday life. Denying or avoiding the certainty of death, on either a personal or societal level, was an unlikely response in this time and place. Death was integrated, through a series of rituals and symbols, into the life of the community.

At the center of this network of practices and significations was the corpse, an irreducible object that evoked feelings of dread, fear, and resignation, as well as reverence, respect, and hope. The lifeless body occupied a liminal place in society, and the uncertainty that surrounded its status led to a number of competing interpretations and actions that attempted to provide it with meaning and context. From the place where death occurred, usually on a bed in the home, to the final destination of the body, in most cases a grave in the local burial ground, the treatment of the corpse generally depended on certain preestablished rituals in northern, Protestant communities at the end of the eighteenth century. And yet, during the course of the nineteenth century, the rigid structures that determined how to dispose of the physical remains began to waver, and new meanings, rituals, and technologies began to be imposed on that site where signs of death made their most impressive mark—the corpse.

2

From the Place of Death to the Space of Burial

The majority of Protestant Americans who died in the North during the antebellum period were treated to funeral services that fell somewhere between the elaborate ceremonies, national honor, and religious deification accorded Washington's absent body and the lack of ceremony, irreverence, and ultimate obliteration visited on the suicide's body. Most people considered the corpse to be worthy of respectful and dignified care. After the pronouncement of death and before disposition of the body, the corpse had a sacred quality greatly determined by its liminality: the former living being who had inhabited the body continued to be associated with the remains until they were removed from the sight of the living, and these very remains were seen as unstable, indeterminate, and ambiguous. Indeed, the feelings of horror and danger provoked by the lifeless corpse, combined with the sense of obligation and fidelity to the deceased, contributed to the religious meanings that survivors linked to the physical presence of the dead.

Not surprisingly, the journey from the place of death to the space of burial followed a remarkably similar pattern in this cultural milieu — as a liminal, sacred object that aroused ambivalence and required immediate attention, the corpse had to be ushered out of living society in a socially acceptable, religiously sanctioned manner. The pattern for disposing of the dead had three fundamental elements: preparation of the body in the home, transportation to the grave, and burial in the graveyard. Within each of these elements a variety of activities and rituals contributed to the removal of the corpse from the living community, but the basic model was rarely altered. The burgeoning urban areas of the North, however, provided a setting where modifications would take place, especially as a result of class differentiation and emerging sanitation problems. But before examining how urbanization modified burial patterns, it is first necessary to explore the traditional rural setting.

In the rural areas of the northern states, death would often take place in the home. Even when death or a life-threatening injury occurred as a result of an accident or while traveling, an effort would be made to bring the victim home. Depending on such variables as local population size and level of institutional support, it was not uncommon for death to occur in such places as almshouses or hospitals. But these alternatives to death in the home were much more prevalent in the larger cities. In the rural setting, which retained traditional values and deep-rooted sensibilities longer than the urban environment, the deathbed scene was infused with a familiar religious significance.[1]

At the moment of death, the dying person would often be surrounded by family, friends or neighbors, the local physician, and occasionally a member of the clergy. A religious figure, whether present at the time of death or not, would usually preside over the ceremonies after death either at the home, meetinghouse, or grave site. With or without a representative from the church to take the lead, interpreting the signs of religious commitment and spiritual preparedness during the critical last moments of life gave the survivors an opportunity to observe and learn from individuals who were about to enter into the holy and mysterious presence of God: How much did the dying person suffer? Did she express her faith in Jesus Christ as savior? Was he able to resign himself to divine Providence?

During the climactic period before death the religious condition of the dying individual seemed to be particularly important. Yet of equal concern in many descriptions of these last moments were the physical characteristics and pathological symptoms manifested by the fading patient. One example of this pervasive concern with the physical signs of pathology was captured in the following written account of a death that took place in Rhode Island: "I will now endeavor to give you some account of dear Harriet's sickness and final close. Except a few short intervals [*sic*] her health has been feble [*sic*] ever since She left New Garden. . . . In the course of this time watery effusion in the chest began to manifest itself accompanied with soreness of the flesh. Our family physician was called in. . . . 11 o clock I found pulsation at the Wrist had ceased but she took a little drink several times after this."[2] As historian Lewis O. Saum notes in his analysis of how antebellum Americans characterized the subject of death in their letters, "common folk recorded and conveyed, not gratuitous morbidity, but the information of pathology."[3] For the observers who were present in the house of death, the significations from the dying individual alluded to a curious mixture of spiritual circumstances and physiological processes. Both were of interest to the close relations who witnessed the body make the transition from life to death, and the nature of this transition could not be defined by either alone.

When death had finally occurred, a series of actions were set in motion to prepare the corpse for the journey from the home to the burial ground. The actors involved in these arrangements were community members, friends, relatives, and family members. Preparing the body was a duty for the close living relations of the deceased, and they rarely hesitated to participate in these activities. The intimacy that survivors maintained with the corpse preserved it, at least until the actual interment, as evidence of a valuable, and vital, social relation. Although the body had lost the spark that animated it, deeply rooted social conventions demanded that it be given proper respect and care from the living. Its uncertain status—as an empty container for the newly departed spirit, as an evocative representative of the lost loved one, as a highly charged object of reflection and remembrance, and as a decomposing, unstable cadaver—also contributed to the deliberate, careful handling by the living survivors.

The confrontation with the body thus required a number of procedures that reaffirmed its dignity and integrity and, at the same time, responded to the emotional needs among the survivors by combatting and concealing the inevitable physical traces of decomposition.[4] The first order of business in the treatment of the newly dead was to "lay out" the body. Those who assisted at the time of death ritually washed, shaved if necessary, then dressed the corpse —usually in a shroud or "winding sheet" during the first half of the nineteenth century—and finally placed it in a coffin.[5] Shrouds were made of either muslin, wool, cashmere, or a cloth material treated with melted wax or gummy matter. Occasionally individuals made their own shrouds for death while alive, but it was more often the case that this "sack" was made by friends and relatives who had come to the house to help prepare the body for burial.

Josiah Stone alluded to this activity for the burial of his wife. "[Saturday, 5 May 1847] Wind northerly & some raining in the A.M. Made some preparations of the funeral Mrs J. E. Munroe was here in the A.M. and most of the P.M. making a sack for [Emory]."[6]

The rate of infant mortality was high, and the especially tragic occurrence of a double death during the act of giving birth led to instances when a mother and infant would be laid out together. Near the end of the eighteenth century,

Martha Ballard, a midwife and nurse in Maine, wrote the following: "Shee departed this Life about 1 pm. I assisted to Lay her out. Her infant Laid in her arms. The first such instance I ever saw & the first woman that died in Child bed which I delivered."[7]

Gender seemed to be a principle factor determining who was involved in the preparation of the corpse for its exit from society. In Ballard's diary there are numerous references to the activity of laying out the dead. In her commentary on the diary, the historian Laurel Thatcher Ulrich writes that "midwives and nurses mediated the mysteries of birth, procreation, illness, and death."[8] In a Philadelphia city directory for 1810 a section labeled "Layers Out of the Dead" contains the names of fourteen individuals. Nine of these are definitely women, while the rest have only their last name or first initial and last name listed.[9] Caring for the dead had begun to be seen as a business opportunity outside of the home, but the gendered division of labor in the period suggests that responding to death, and more specifically preparing the corpse, was understood as a component of domestic life, and therefore within the purview of women's activities.

Though others support the view that midwifes, nurses, and women in general carried out the tasks associated with laying out the dead, there is also evidence that men would perform these duties under certain circumstances.[10] In the diary of Joel Clark, a teacher from Hartland, Connecticut, for example, there is an entry for January 1798 about watching Mr. Taylor "breath [*sic*] his last about twelve O clock." Later Clark assisted "about laying him out — it being the first time I was ever employed in the like occasion."[11] In a letter written from Waterville, Maine, in 1837, Samuel Francis Smith described the death of his newborn girl. When his infant died, because she could not swallow, Smith related that "our Little one was lait [*sic*] to its repose. Mr A took all care off my hands."[12]

By the end of the eighteenth and into the middle of the nineteenth century, women in the Protestant communities of the northern states indeed had the primary responsibility of getting the body ready for burial — a crucial activity performed by women in England for centuries.[13] On those occasions when the deceased was an old man or an infant, however, a male might engage in handling the corpse and preparing it for disposition. The rules for laying out the dead, probably gender-specific in most instances, were malleable and dependent on the conditions after death. In any case, the objective was to provide assistance for the surviving family members and to make the proper arrangements so that the corpse was ready for the journey from the world of the living to the silence of the grave.

In the rural communities of the nineteenth century, this journey took place in a coffin. A family member, neighbor, or, in many cases, a local cabinetmaker or carpenter assembled the coffin after death had occurred. This individual would take the measurements of the deceased and construct the encasement, usually out of pine wood. The coffin, like the shroud, might also be prepared before death. There were certain people who had a keen awareness of their own mortality and who wanted to have a hand in organizing the details of their exit from society. Most coffins, well into the nineteenth century in rural locations, "retained their characteristic and unmistakable shape — flat-sided, with a tapering hexagonal profile that fit the body."[14] Another distinctive feature of many coffins was a sliding, removable, or hinged panel that allowed the upper part of the corpse to be viewed by the family and other mourners before the entire entourage proceeded to the grave.[15]

The body of the deceased would remain in the home for a period of one to three days under constant surveillance, especially at night. It would be located in a designated room of the house, often a front room or parlor, that was marked off by such indicators as black crepe, white cloth covering mirrors, or an absence of furniture. Close relatives, friends, volunteers, or sometimes hired help participated in the vigil over the dead, often called the wake. The primary duties for those involved in the wake consisted of "watching" or "sitting up" with the corpse until the time came to remove the body from the home.[16] This type of activity allowed the survivors to be sure that death had definitely occurred, thus erasing the possibility of live burial, a prevalent concern at the time. Sometimes these watchers applied a cloth, soaked in vinegar or alum, to the face of the deceased. It was believed that this would delay bodily decomposition and assist in the preservation of the corpse while it remained in the sight of the living.[17] Another method frequently used to preserve the body while it remained in the home, especially in warmer weather, was to "put a large block of ice in a tub beneath the board [of the coffin], with smaller chunks about the body."[18]

The tone of wakes varied throughout the North. When the corpse was in the house, visitors often engaged in a variety of activities, including somber reflection, scripture reading, and socializing, which usually involved some eating and drinking. The atmosphere and degree of solemnity displayed in the house of death varied according to the cultural and denominational background of the family, but in most cases the sharing of food and drinks, which were often alcoholic, created a strong communal bond. This bond and sense of togetherness helped to counteract the fissure created by the death of a community member.

L. M. Sargent, a self-described "sexton of the old school," wrote a book in 1856 called *Dealings with the Dead*, which detailed many of his experiences with the dead in Boston and surrounding areas. This series of recollections, which also includes many of his personal reflections on such controversial issues as the Stamp Act, capital punishment, and slavery, is full of Sargent's humorous, ironic, and playful observations and commentary relating to the treatment of the dead. His remarks on funerary practices cover a range of societies throughout human civilization, from the ancient Egyptians up until his own social surroundings in New England. In one passage Sargent discusses his personal experiences as a participant in funerals in the country during his younger years and the presence of alcohol at these occasions: "In regard to the use of wine and other intoxicating drinks, at funerals . . . a table with liquors was always provided. Every one, as he entered, took off his hat, with his left hand, smoothed down his hair, with his right, walked up to the coffin, gazed upon the corpse, made a crooked face, passed on to the table, took a glass of his favorite liquor, went forth upon the plat, before the house, and talked politics, or of the new road, or compared crops, or swapped heifers or horses, until it was time to lift."[19]

Sargent also related a story, told to him by a member of the clergy in Concord, New Hampshire, of how a group of children participating in the funeral of a little boy were allowed to drink liquor. The group of youngsters, who were not more than thirteen years old, served as pallbearers in the funeral ceremony. Before these children began to transport the coffin to the grave, "a sort of master of ceremonies took them to the table, and mixed a tumbler of gin, water and sugar, for each."[20] Whether or not children frequently indulged in alcohol at funeral ceremonies is unclear, but such drinks seemed to be readily available to the adult participants at these gatherings.

When the time arrived for the body to begin its journey to the space of burial, the mourners congregated in the house of death with the surviving family members. It was a common though not universal practice for prayers or a short discourse to be given before the procession commenced. The formality and organization of the service again depended upon such factors as the economic status of the family, whether a full sermon was to be given at a church or meetinghouse along the way to the grave, or the degree of suffering in the family. Samuel Smith explained the informal nature of the services that took place after the death of his infant girl and alluded to his wife's wishes for a more subdued ceremony in a letter to his sister: "I gave no special invitation, . . . & suffering such of the neighbors as chose, to drop in, wishing on my dear Mary's account to have a quiet funeral, at a quiet hour, as being less likely to agitate her."[21]

A completely different account of how this scene might transpire is presented in an article by a folklorist in 1894. Pamela Martha Cole attempts to convey some of the more striking characteristics of traditional New England village funerals. The service in this description comes across as more of a theatrical spectacle than a somber affair, with the performative qualities emphasized over the solemnities. "The relatives and most intimate friends were generally seated in an upper room, and the officiating minister stood on the stairs, where he could be heard above and below. The service over, 'the person having charge of the funeral,' known on festive occasions as the master of ceremonies, standing on the stairs, called in a loud tone the names of the mourners in the order in which they were to come down, and family after family passed out to take their proper place in the procession."[22]

After the service, the family and other mourners were called on to transport the body to the place of burial. In some cases the designated place for the disposal of the dead was somewhere on the grounds of the family farm, perhaps in the "shade of an apple tree in front of the house."[23] This form of burial, however, became increasingly rare as the nineteenth century progressed. As towns and larger urban spaces grew in size, as higher numbers of people became more mobile, and as public health concerns about the dead led to stricter forms of regimentation in burial practices, disposal on the grounds of private homes became less and less acceptable. Instead, it was more common for the body to be carried to the local burying ground, either the local churchyard or a graveyard on the periphery of town.

There were two possible modes for transporting the corpse in the rural model of burial. In the early decades of the nineteenth century the coffin, situated on a bier with a pall thrown across the top, was carried on foot. Those who conveyed the coffin and bier were either hired assistants, friends, relatives, or young volunteers. The number of people employed in this duty varied, though often there were eight individuals, with the first four being close relations of the deceased and the next four, called "under-bearers," less closely connected to the family.[24] If a small child died it was not uncommon for other local children to carry the corpse to its grave. The task of transporting the coffin to the burial ground was relatively easy when the distance was short and the weather bearable. As towns grew over the course of the first half of the century, however, and as more people placed greater value on burial in a well-organized, delineated space, the distance to the place of interment could be imposing.

Given the potential for hardship, it became necessary to utilize other means of transporting the corpse to the grave. In cities during the colonial period, the local livery stable often made a specially designated horse-drawn carriage, a hearse, available for rent, a service employed primarily by the upper classes.[25] The hearse, which soon became available in the smaller towns and villages of the North, eliminated the inconvenience of manual transportation, so its use increased during the early years of the nineteenth century, though prejudices persisted against new technologies for conveying the dead. Community members who made efforts to prevent the use of hearses based their opposition on conservative notions of proper respect for the journey of the corpse and a guarded resistance to innovation in dealing with the dead.[26]

A "Hearse Book" from Bridgewater, Massachusetts, contained a copy of a subscription paper that outlined the benefits of using a hearse and encouraged citizens to contribute the necessary financial resources for its purchase. The document addressed some of the persistent problems associated with carrying the dead to their final resting place:

> Whereas the common practice in burying the dead hath been for men to carry the corpse to the grave this mode is frequently attended with inconvenience and difficulty specially when the distance is great or the roads bad wherefore as a remedy it is proposed that a hearse be procured for the purpose of carrying the dead from the place the funeral may be attended to the place of interment which may be done with more ease conveniency & decency than in the way & manners as now practiced & to effect so laudable a purpose we the subscribers each one for himself singly doth hereby freely contribute & promise to pay the sum of money affixed to our several & respective names.[27]

Such a clear and practical rationale for making life easier on those who were assigned to carry the weight of the dead eventually led to the purchase of a hearse in many of the smaller towns and villages of the North.[28] The shifting location of the place of disposal, along with the sheer physical labor involved in transporting the coffin, contributed to a greater willingness to modify traditional customs. In the case of Bridgewater there were enough pledges to buy a hearse for the price of $51.21.

Whether carried on men's shoulders or transported in a hearse, the coffin was often diverted to a local meetinghouse or church for a public funeral sermon and, in many cases, the viewing of the remains before being deposited in the grave. The funeral sermon placed the recent rupture in the social fabric in a meaningful religious perspective, drawing on themes related to Christian morality in general and Protestant visions of the afterlife. Stopping on the way to the burial ground also served an important social function. The members of the community, including the family, friends, or casual neighbors involved in the funeral, collectively responded to the intrusion of death in a setting without the emotional force of the deathbed and the site of disposal, one that instead provided a space in which the solidarity of the religious and local community would remind the participants of the ties that bound them together.

In addition to reinforcing social cohesion and Protestant strategies for interpreting the meaning of death, stopping at the meetinghouse offered a temporary diversion, or way station, that also served as the place where mourners had one last opportunity to view the remains of the deceased. The last look could have taken place in the home when relations planned to transport the corpse directly to the grave site or when the family was isolated from a larger rural community. But whether the body was immediately taken to the grave site or brought to a meetinghouse or church, survivors valued the chance to view it before the final disposition in the grave. Personal writings of northern community members as well as those of foreign travelers attest to this critical moment in the journey from home to grave. English visitors often complained about this practice, though it was a common feature in the treatment of the dead in English popular culture as well during the nineteenth century.[29]

In the northern Protestant communities of the United States, survivors who viewed the corpse engaged in a socially sanctioned activity that was integral to the collective rituals of death and the funerary journey.[30] Alvan Bond, a graduate from Andover Seminary, captured the habitual nature of the ritual in an account of his brother's funeral service in New England during the month of August, 1817: "The audience was then seated and the particular mourners then proceeded to look at their departed friend for the last time. After the spectators had seen him we followed our dear deceased friend in mournful procession to the grave yard."[31] Not all participants took the opportunity to view the corpse before burial, but the diversion to the local meetinghouse or church provided relations with a ceremonial space that encouraged the practice of a ritual gaze.

After the corpse had been adequately groomed, viewed, and discoursed over, it was ready for the inevitable final journey to the grave site. The end of the description quoted above refers to this next stage in the journey. The "mournful procession," often accompanied by the sound of tolling bells, usually had some kind of formal organization that depended on many of the variables mentioned before, like the degree of isolation of the family from other farms and more populated areas, class standing in the community, and number of people attending the funeral. Members of the family and community carried and accompanied the body to the burying ground regardless of how many people attended the funeral and how complex was the organization of the participants.

The procession in the rural setting was rarely an elaborate, involved, or highly intricate affair. The protagonists in the cortege were the family members, relatives, friends, neighbors, and local minister, who together made up the social network of the deceased. During the procession participants were engaged in a relatively plain and unencumbered series of actions that terminated the journey from home to grave. Although the participants often operated within a generally Protestant universe that, from the time of the Reformation, had dedramatized many of the Christian religious rituals, a tendency toward displays of symbolic behavior prevailed. In one village funeral, more elaborate than most, both the drama and simplicity of this ritual were evident: "First came twelve young girls, in white dresses, and with wreaths of evergreen in their hands. Then followed [an] old man, who proved to be the minister of the place. . . . Mourners, and a numerous train, succeeded. The procession moved on to the grave; they gathered close around it; those that bare the body stood still, and placed it on the ground. Reverently the pall was taken off, and in sad silence the coffin descended to its place."[32]

The last remaining duty of the living was to dispose of the corpse adequately. From the beginning of the nineteenth century to the start of the Civil War there were essentially two alternatives: interment and entombment, which is to say that people could be buried in the earth or in tombs above ground. Embalming and cremation were impractical if not inconceivable to the majority of the population. Indeed, any procedure that accelerated the destruction of the body and threatened its supposed integrity after death provoked outrage and horror among antebellum Protestants. Most individuals in the rural communities of the North were buried in the ground when they died. Burial above ground, in individual or family tombs, was mostly an option for the wealthier classes in these regions.

On at least one occasion a woman "borrowed" a tomb of a wealthy friend. Louisa Park of Salisbury, Massachusetts, wanted to postpone the interment of her infant because of psychological resistance to earth burial and because she wanted to wait until her husband, who was away at sea, could see their child and make a final decision about how he should be buried. She wrote in her diary after her infant died in the month of May 1801: "Captain Hoyt's politeness I shall never forget. . . . His consenting so readily to lay the corps in his tomb was a satisfaction to me. For some reason, to see him deposited there was not half so distressing to my feelings as it would have been to see him buried under the [ground]; and when his father returns he can see him, and remove him as he may think best."[33]

A local religious representative gave another discourse or prayer when a corpse finally arrived at the place of burial. Those involved in carrying the body during the funeral journey took the pall off of the coffin, which was then lowered into a grave dug in advance by family members, friends, or, if the burial was in a churchyard, the sexton.[34] This moment was perhaps the most emotional of the funeral journey, and it provided an opportunity for those in grief to be praised for their strength in the face of severe affliction, their courage for accompanying the dead on such a sorrowful occasion, or their sincerity of emotions, whether they were paroxysms of grief, restrained sentiments of suffering, or something in between.

These scenes in the space of burial had a pathetic and often poignant quality, regardless of the degree of emotional expression by the mourners. Many observers looked at this juncture, when the living relations saw their loved one committed to the grave, as a challenging and pivotal moment for those closest to the deceased. One report of a highly touching and evocative farewell scene alludes to the beauty of the moment and the emotional display anticipated by witnesses. It described the funeral ceremony at the graveyard as "a spectacle at which the Stoic might experience emotion, from which the painter might sketch his fairest subject, and on which the poet might dwell with all the glow of inspiration. . . . Here every eye was bent upon the single mourner, as if expecting a natural burst of sorrow over . . . his departed partner; but there was none. He stood calm and collected."[35]

The last act of throwing into the grave a branch, straw, or commonly dirt from the earth before leaving the place of interment was a frequent gesture recognizing the finality of the journey. Many services at the burial site concluded with this ritual drama that signified both individual and communal acknowledgment that the deceased would no longer be seen or heard from again, and that the body would be finally returning to earth. The family relations, friends, and other intimate associates standing beside the grave said any last thoughts or prayers before turning their backs on the dead and returning to the community of the living. On some occasions the mourners would stay by the grave until it had been filled up with dirt, either performing the task themselves or watching others do it.

The journey of the lifeless body from the place of expiration to the space of disposal was significant for the family and community members involved. The rite of passage from life to death, deathbed to grave, allowed the survivors an opportunity to pay their last respects and to make certain that collective action repaired the rupture in the social fabric. Throughout the journey participants in the funeral had a number of occasions to ensure that the corpse was safely and appropriately handled until reaching its final destination. It is evident that when the dead were in the land of the living an attempt was made to preserve their integrity, to treat them according to inherited conceptions of dignity, and to manage their remains in a manner that ensured familial or communal continuity.

The latter tendency helps to explain why burial on the family farm diminished over the course of the nineteenth century.[36] As the likelihood increased that future generations would move away from the homestead, the expectation diminished that family members would always be nearby to maintain and preserve the place of burial. In the first half of the nineteenth century the country graveyard came to be understood as a socially secured and consecrated space. It provided a context in which the dead could be protected by the same religious, moral, and communal values that operated in the towns and villages of the living. The transformation in the place of disposal reflected changing attitudes about the care of the dead and the relations between them and the living.

In the rural model, burial was an intimate affair in which the living were familiar, both physically and imaginatively, with the dead. During the funeral journey survivors integrated the corpse into a network of rituals that allowed the living to engage in what they considered to be approbatory behavior. This behavior was carried out by a close circle of relations, reinforcing communal solidarity, affirming the integrity of the family, and demonstrating the potent symbolic value of the corpse before it disappeared from view. In the more populated regions of the North, however, a range of interested parties and impersonal forces began to converge on the dead and alter the details of their exit from society. The simplicity of the journey would gradually be lost in the city, where new concerns — related to urban space, class status, economic opportunity, and public health — led to innovations in the treatment and disposal of the dead.

3

Simplicity Lost:
The Urban Model of Death

The corpse in the city underwent a journey to the burial ground substantially similar to that of the corpse in the country. The pattern for most Protestants who died in the antebellum urban setting contained the three fundamental elements found in the rural setting: cosmetic preparation at home, transportation to the grave site, and interment or entombment in a designated place. After an individual had died, friends and relatives transported the lifeless body from the place of death to a temporary, intermediate location, and from there they deposited it in a space marked off and reserved for the mortal remains. The handling of the dead, which included washing, wrapping, exposing, encasing, and disposal, and the methods for transporting it, were also similar.

In spite of these common features, however, the social and economic forces that were transforming the rapidly expanding cities at the beginning of the nineteenth century influenced the rituals, gestures, and practices associated with the funeral. Class divisions, more pronounced in urban areas than in rural, had a significant impact on the treatment and disposal of the dead. The growing complexity and diversification in the market and industrial economies of the North produced a new and enterprising spirit, often developed in more densely populated areas with a large concentration of potential consumers, that did not scruple to capitalize on the dead. And the increasing bureaucracy of the urbanized municipalities demanded that the dead, like the living, be governed in a systematic and organized manner.

Death has often been called the great equalizer. What better place to recognize the egalitarian and indiscriminate work of death than in a country founded on democratic notions of equality? But the history of death in nineteenth-century urban America demonstrates a litany of class divisions, racial prejudices, and gendered distinctions. Although all were aware of their common fate, this collective recognition did not lead to a common mode of disposing of dead bodies. For many urban Protestants competition for material gain and efforts to enhance social standing in life were transferred, postmortem, onto the journey of the corpse to its final resting place.

The only periods that exhibited a degree of egalitarianism in burial practices were those seasons of severe and brutal epidemics, which produced social chaos, collective misery, and a multitude of corpses. During the first half of the nineteenth century cholera was the most common epidemic disease to strike the northern United States. Intermittent outbreaks of yellow fever and smallpox, however — diseases more threatening in the two previous centuries — still inspired fear and created turmoil in the larger northern cities.[1] The impact of these diseases on the urban population was devastating; what was once a thriving, vibrant center of life could turn into a desolate landscape offensive to the senses. In a letter written on July 4, 1849, John Sherwood, a resident of Cincinnati, described the conditions on the streets during a cholera epidemic: "The cholera is very bad from 150 to 120 Persons are dying daily from it our City looks as if it was deserted we have large fires burning on every corner of the streets composed of Stone Coal Tar and Sulpher whether it will do any good or not I can not tell at any rate it is very unpleasant to the Nose."[2]

The ravages of an epidemic often affected city dwellers with equal force, though many in the middle and upper classes could afford to leave the urban boundaries of the menace. Without friends or family outside of the urban centers, nor the money to allow for a temporary refuge in the country, a great many inhabitants had no other choice but to remain in proximity of the danger. Although many people attributed the rapid spread of a disease like cholera to the moral bankruptcy, vice, and degradation of immigrants, blacks, and the poor, it inevitably made its way into the homes and businesses of individuals in the wealthier classes. Epidemics might have disproportionately affected the lower classes, but once the disease had stricken its victim and brought about the end of life, the corpse could rarely escape being seen as a source of contagion and danger to the living community.

The overwhelming number of dead victims necessitated expedient and practical forms of disposal that often did not discriminate based on class standing. Unfortunately, as the menace spread throughout populated areas and produced dead bodies from all strata of society, workers involved in the loathsome task of disposal could easily fall behind in their duties. In an insightful analysis of the cholera epidemics in the United States during the nineteenth century, the social historian Charles E. Rosenberg gives an indication of the monumental responsibility of caring for the dead: "The city seemed unable even to bury its own dead. Bodies might lie for hours, in some cases for days, in the streets before they were started on their way to Potter's Field. After being unloaded from the scows that brought them to the city cemetery . . . the dead were deposited in a wide trench some hundred yards in length, one body on top of another to within a foot or two of the surface."[3]

With the arrival of pestilence in cities, the manner in which one died and the mode in which the dead were buried had a leveling effect on the experience of death. Rich and poor alike died on the streets, in their homes, at cholera hospitals, and often alone. In these circumstances the dead bodies did not receive any special treatment, nor were they intimately cared for by the living. Instead, they were frequently piled on wagons and hearses and directly transported to potter's fields. Here they were deposited in anonymous, collective pits and covered with earth and sometimes quicklime. Some in the upper classes were able to secure disposal of their loved ones in the local churchyard, but land for burial was scarce and costly in the city. The extreme conditions brought on by an epidemic warranted pragmatic and rational action, and this often superseded privileged treatment based on class standing.

Unfortunately for the poor, the city government or church agencies consistently employed this model of burial for them whether there was an epidemic or not. That is, the journey of the corpse from the place of death to the space of burial was truncated, and the traditional symbols and ceremonies found in the rural model were frequently absent. The embellishments of the funeral — the deathbed scene with family and friends, the spectacle of the procession, and the personalized grave — were routinely denied the urban poor. In death, as in life, their fate depended on the charity of state, local, and religious organizations. Many of the poor died in the street, in almshouses or public hospitals, but even when they died in their living quarters, the corpse received attention only when there was a living network of friends or relatives who could afford to care for it. In most cases the body would simply be conveyed at the city government's expense to its anonymous resting place, entering into the community of the dead without pausing at a way station for religious sermons or a last gaze. The bodies of the poor were interred in the closest potter's field, where they would often share the ground with others on the margins of society, such as criminals, strangers, and blacks.

Many potter's fields in large northern cities before the Civil War were under the jurisdiction of the city government and often functioned as burial space for individuals who were thought to have posed a danger to the public body while alive. If a potter's field had not been established or was not convenient, these individuals would simply be buried in the public square, an expedient that local residents and public officials viewed as an intrusion in their living space. In an ordinance passed in 1812 by the Philadelphia City Council, for example, this form of disposal was recognized as infringing on the rights of "legitimate" citizens. The preamble to the ordinance stated that "for a considerable time the public square . . . had without any authority been used as a place of interment for the bodies of persons dying at the almshouse, at the State prison, and at the Pennsylvania Hospital, and of strangers not belonging to any religious society."[4] As the public square lost its legitimacy as an acceptable place for the disposal of the dead, potter's fields became even more popular repositories for the bodies of those individuals who were rejected by dominant society.

In the middle and upper classes of the dominant urban Protestant society, financial security in life led to assurances of respectable treatment in death. For all classes except the poor, the model of burial was fundamentally similar to the rural model: preparation of the body in the home, transportation to the grave, and interment or entombment. But what constituted a "respectable" funeral was informed by the emerging bourgeois sensibility of the industrializing North and depended as well on wealth, standing in the community, and other social variables. Class-dictated alterations in the ceremony surrounding the dead could turn what was a simple funeral procession in the country into an urban spectacle of dramatic proportions. In the city the journey was a public affair — a magnificent, elaborate procession through the streets aroused the interest of people with no emotional connection to the deceased. In his diary, Philip Hone, a prominent figure in New York City politics, described the public curiosity about the obsequies of the millionaire John Astor, who died in 1848: "The funeral took place this afternoon from the house of Mr. William Astor, in Lafayette Place. . . . There were six Episcopal clergymen and a long train of followers. The occasion caused great excitement, and the curiosity of the people was intense; the street was filled, the walks obstructed all the distance from the house to St. Thomas's Church, where the funeral ceremonies were performed, and in the cemetery of which the wornout remains were deposited."[5]

Along with the number of people in the ceremony, another sign sure to attract attention — and to accent the funeral's function as a rite of passage for the wealthier classes — was the clothing worn by the participants. As John M. Duncan, a visitor from England, observed in a letter from New York City, these fashion cues signified status and subscription to virtuous sentiments. He pointed out that "the dark uniformity of the dress gives to the assembly an apparent unity of purpose and feeling, which can never be attained in a motley assemblage in differently coloured coats." Additionally, he described the uses and significations of linen scarfs in the funeral, asserting that "the number of scarfs which are presented, is thought to mark in some measure the respectability of the family."[6]

When an individual from a wealthy background died, the family usually arranged funeral ceremonies meant to demonstrate both their love for the deceased and their desire to provide for the respectable treatment of the remains. Sidney George Fisher, a Philadelphia writer and diarist who attended a number of funerals in the city, referred to the ritual activity associated with the ceremonies for the dead as "the pageantry of woe."[7] The pageantry of woe seemed to be linked to the following indicators: a large number of invited guests, a long line of carriages in the procession, the prevalence of black crepe, as well as appropriate black dress and other fashion markers for the mourners and pallbearers, and the participation of the more famous members of the clergy in the pronouncements over the dead. When a military hero or other public figure died, the pageant often became more elaborate and incorporated national symbols for the sake of evoking patriotism and social solidarity.

It could be argued that, compared with the rural model, the corpse took on a secondary role in this spectacle to that of the mourners and the display of solemnity in the funeral ceremonies. But the survivors acknowledged the corpse at an integral moment in the journey to the grave. As in the rural context, this acknowledgment came in the form of a ceremonial gaze before disposing of the body. As John Duncan described the ritual, "the body is frequently placed in the hall, or an open bed-room, to give the company an opportunity of seeing it, of which many who attend avail themselves."[8]

Some evidence suggests, though, that not all mourners could participate freely in all phases of the funeral. Because of prevailing social conventions, women in many urban locales were excluded from the funeral procession and the ceremonies that took place in the graveyard. They were, however, welcome at services in the home and the meetinghouse or church. Fisher wrote in his diary that in January of 1837 he attended a funeral in Philadelphia — private, "as all funerals should be" — and that there were no women at the ceremonies.[9] In May of 1848 he wrote of another private funeral in which "no invitations were sent but the presence of Henry's most intimate friends, male friends, was expected."[10] Finally, in August of 1859, Fisher described a funeral in Laurel Hill cemetery. Although only a small crowd of people attended, "the ladies of the family were present, a thing now very unusual."[11]

But exclusivity was also a function of class, and in the cities it soon extended to the final destination of the corpse. Within the first few decades of the nineteenth century the space of the living began to impinge on the space of the dead in the urban context. As Moses King explained in his *Handbook of New York City,* "The history of New York . . . shows a constant record of pushing the dead out of place by the living."[12] The contest over space occurred in most of the larger cities of the Northeast, as population growth and urban expansion temporarily disturbed the "eternal rest" of the dead. A variety of cultural attitudes, ideological demands, and socioeconomic forces led to new perspectives on the appropriate location for depositing the corpse. But such practical problems as overcrowding, sanitation, and the unsightly character of graveyards within the city contributed more immediately to a reinterpretation of the relationship between the living and the dead.

The "rural" cemetery movement, which advocated burial grounds located just outside of the city in a natural, gardenlike setting, emerged in response to all of these considerations. Mount Auburn, the first and most famous of the new burial grounds, was created in Boston in 1831. "Rural" cemeteries gave the middle and upper classes a space for disposal more suited to their tastes and expenses than the churchyards and graveyards being swallowed up and disregarded by expanding city life. They also provided these classes with an opportunity to purchase private lots, allowing them to mark the end of their journey in a manner representative of their economic status. Many northern Protestants who could afford to prepare for their final resting place even arranged for the construction of a monument before death.[13]

Organizers and supervisors of "rural" cemeteries exhibited a strong bias in favor of interment and against aboveground entombment. A circular addressed to owners of lots in Mount Auburn discouraged the construction of tombs for a number of reasons. They could, according to the circular, become an encumbrance to the grounds during the visiting season, endanger the natural setting through the removal of trees and foliage, and, most importantly, disrupt the tranquility of the place because "the frequency with which some of the tombs are opened, and the want of sufficient tightness in the doors of others, have already given rise in the hot months, to a perceptible nuisance which, if not seasonably checked, may hereafter grow into an intolerable evil."[14] L. M. Sargent, eschewing the circumlocution of the circular, echoed its sentiments:

Tombs, not only such as are constructed under churches, but in common cemeteries, are frequently highly offensive, on the score of emanation. They are liable to be opened, for the admission of the dead, at all times; and, of course, when the worms are riotous, and the corruption is rankest, and the pungent gases are eminently dangerous, and disgusting. Even when closed, the intelligible odor, arising from the dissolving processes, which are going on within, is more than living flesh and blood can well endure. Again and again, visitors at Mount Auburn have been annoyed, by this effluvium from the tombs.[15]

After corpses from the wealthier classes were conveyed from the home to a way station and finally to the space of burial, they were deposited in individual or family tombs or, in most cases, in the earth underneath ornate markers or monuments. Their interment, in short, differed from that of the poorer classes only in style, not in substance. But major changes in the disposal of the dead were on the horizon. In the period before the Civil War an entrepreneurial spirit materialized in the North that sought to capitalize on middle-class desires for respectability, refinement, and order — and to turn a profit in a business that would never be short on customers.

The undertaker began to conduct the business of caring for the corpse in the urban milieu during the middle of the nineteenth century. In the United States the profession grew out of an amalgamation of services that had previously been performed by family and friends, such occupational groups as carpenters, liverymen, and sextons, and other members of the community who assisted in the preparation of the corpse. The undertaker might also be associated with such municipal officers as the town health official or the coroner, who investigated murders and suspicious deaths. By the middle of the nineteenth century this figure was beginning to provide all the necessary duties and make all the preliminary arrangements that would ensure the corpse had a proper funeral journey.[16]

The tasks and duties expected of these professionals and billed to the family of the deceased could include the following: providing "services" at the home, notifying families and guests about the death and funeral, tolling the bell, supplying the pall, placing the corpse in the coffin, carrying the coffin to the hearse and from the hearse to the vault or grave, furnishing a horse or a number of horses for the funeral procession, and digging the grave or opening and closing the tomb.[17] Each of these services cost the customer's family, and the total outlay did not include other necessary items for the funeral, like the coffin or the use of the hearse.

These two accoutrements — the hearse and the coffin — became viable business ventures in their own right during the first half of the nineteenth century.

They were integral components of a respectable urban funeral, and their design, symbolism, and price soon began to reflect class consciousness. The production of vehicles specifically designated for the transportation of the dead, originally the province of liverymen, became a lucrative sideline for carriage manufacturers in the urban North. Up until the outbreak of the Civil War the hearse was often a simple carriage, usually unembellished. It was long and rectangular, and the compartment that held the coffin often had windows and black curtains on each side. After the war, a fashion revolution transformed the style of this vehicle for the dead.[18]

The permanent receptacle for the corpse transformed in shape and meaning even before the war. In the course of its evolution, the coffin became a major item of commerce in an increasingly consumer-conscious market. Many of the carpenters and cabinetmakers in the larger cities who were involved in the construction of coffins began to stockpile them in the early part of the century. A linguistic change from *coffin* to *casket* reflected an interpretive strategy of the trade: the latter term was meant to connote the preciousness of the remains — and therefore announce the growing significance of an appropriate container. The coffin — commonly a plain, unadorned, hexagonal pine or mahogany box in rural settings — began to assume greater symbolic complexity and show signs of diversification in the urban arena.

The adaptations in coffin design, evident principally in the years before the Civil War, ranged from the practical to the outrageous. Because premature burial was still a concern, some coffins were designed to be "wired," so that any movement or signs of life could be detected. Coffins were made of stone, marble, glass, bronze, and metal to appeal to the aesthetic and practical concerns of the upper and middle classes. Some innovative coffins offered a new method of preservation to accommodate family members or friends who had to travel great distances to attend the funeral or corpses that had to be transported for burial. One of the most popular coffin styles was the metallic version. These receptacles came in an assortment of styles: the Mummy Case, the Cloth Covered or Ornamental case, the Bronzed Case. Most included a section of glass that allowed the face of the deceased to be seen.[19]

This development in coffin design influenced the nature of the market and the history of the craft. As Robert Habenstein and William Lamers write in their history of American funeral directing, "The small coffin shop, devoting most of its production to a craftsman's product, emerged at the end of the Colonial period and continued to flourish during the first half of the 19th century, but with the appearance of metallic burial cases a new mode of coffin construction, based on mass production methods, emerged, and became the leading method of manufacture in the second half of the century."[20]

The services of the undertaker and the attendant emerging funeral industries located the corpse in a network of commercial activity that was just beginning to operate in a heretofore untapped market. In the urban centers of the North, the dead were no longer simply prepared, transported, and buried by an intimate group of relations. Rather, they were becoming the focus of a developing economic regime that was determined by consumerism, class differentiation, and mass-produced goods. It should be stressed, however, that before the Civil War this regime was fragmented, disorganized, and irregular, and that the body itself was not yet a commodity in any sense of the word. Another innovation would have to occur before the business of death would transform the dead body into an article of consumption.

As the corpse was entering this commercial network, it had to be subsumed within a strict municipal bureaucracy in the urban centers of the North. This went beyond the registration of deaths and the demographic information that appeared on numerous bills of mortality posted in the heavily populated regions of the Northeast—data that various local officials and government representatives collected to monitor a range of items, including the age and gender of the deceased as well as the cause of death. In the early decades of the nineteenth century municipal authorities also specified certain prescriptions and codes that were enforced when managing the remains of the dead. As the social composition of urban spaces began to change as a result of increased immigration, growing class divisions, and the expansion of industry, control over the place of death required ever more vigilant attention and ritual conformity.

As "rural" cemeteries grew in prestige and popularity, the private corporations that owned these spaces gradually appropriated the power to regulate the burial of the dead. Whether the government or private companies assumed the responsibilities for disposal, the dead were subjugated to controlling forces outside the sphere of family and friends. The utilitarian nature of this control, operating according to such principles as the public good, cultural standards of decency, and social patterns of organization, contributed to the desire for uniformity and the systematization of the dead among Protestants in the North.

A broadside distributed by the Boston Board of Health in 1810 demonstrates this concern for order and social management.[21] The Board of Health set down "Rules and Regulations for establishing the Police of the Burying-Grounds and Cemetaries [*sic*], and for Regulating the Burial of the Dead, within the town of Boston, [with] the force of law." An office of superintendent was established in each of the various regions of the city, charged with maintaining the grounds, ensuring the proper order of graves, and keeping a record of burials, including such information as the name, age, sex, and family of the deceased, the disease or cause of death, the status of the deceased as a stranger or citizen, and the time and location of interment. These superintendents had to give this information to the health office each week, and from these data the board periodically published the bills of mortality for the city.[22]

Besides listing the duties of the superintendent, the statement by the Board of Health also detailed the social customs that must be followed during the funeral. All funerals in Boston were to occur in the daytime, except during severe epidemics. Only one bell should be tolled at the funeral, and a funeral car should transport the corpse of every person over ten years of age, with no more than two horses, to the grave or tomb. Additionally, after July 1, 1810, no females, except the immediate relatives of the deceased, were allowed to walk in the funeral procession. As Fisher observed later in Philadelphia, women were allowed very small roles, if any, in the public acts surrounding the burial of the dead. They may have been intimate with the deceased, but constructions of gender roles determined the level of participation for women during the journey from the house of death. The bill also noted that any and all of these provisions could be overruled by order of the board.[23]

Another section of the order recognized that certain classes of "undesirables," including African Americans, the poor, and criminals, required their own delineated space outside of the area reserved for the more "respectable" members of the urban community. Superintendents of each district were to designate a particular area for the burial of "people of color" and the order specified that the "corpse of such persons may be carried to the grave on men's shoulders as heretofore" — no hearses, that is, could be use in the disposal of blacks. This section concludes with the stipulation that funerals for this segment of society "shall be strictly conformable to these regulations in every other respect."[24]

The document from the Board of Health provides evidence that the concern with creating an ordered system in the disposal of the dead was far greater in the urban context than in the rural. All classes of society were subject to a local system of control, though the expediency and anonymity with which the poorer segments of the Protestant population were buried may have resulted in less accurate record keeping than in the middle and upper classes. Nevertheless, the municipal government was keenly interested in who was dying, why they died, and how they were buried. "Rural" cemeteries had similar interests and, for the most part, assumed control over the dead without straying from these principles of uniformity and conformity in funeral practice.

Before the Civil War, the corpse in northern Protestant society was a prisoner of the rituals and practices that structured the journey from the home to the graveyard. The rural/urban dichotomy serves to identify how the setting in which this journey took place could modify and influence these practices and rituals without effacing a fundamental pattern in the way the dead were handled. The social and economic transformations occurring in the urban centers of the North contributed to adaptations in this pattern rather than significant alterations to it.

The body could easily be placed in the grounds of a graveyard without much controversy. The interpretive placement of the corpse into a meaningful imaginative context, on the other hand, was a likelier realm of conflict and contestation. Yet even the journey to the grave and the place of burial itself were not automatically neutral fields for compatible values and symbols. As the corpse was envisioned in these fields and others outside of the funeral journey itself — in paintings, in works of literature, and even on dissection tables — its potency as a symbolic object increased. The power of the symbolism grew because the body continued to be highly charged with representational value and because, by the early part of the nineteenth century, it could be appropriated by contending interested parties who did not always subscribe to conventional Christian rhetoric about death, the dead, and the afterlife.

The responses of the Protestant communities to the physical, material trace of the lifeless body depended on a diversifying and expanding imaginative universe. The human actions in the face of death ensured that the period between the last breath and burial effectively ushered the physical body out of the living social community. Activities surrounding the corpse were instigated for three critical reasons: to reinforce communal and familial solidarity in the face of potential disorder signified by the corruptible body; to exhibit the appropriate amount of respect for the remains of the deceased as well as surviving family members; and, because of the body's persistent liminality and sacred status, to maintain the integrity of the corpse while it remained in the care of the living.

The corpse, disposed of through the proscribed procedures, also demanded collective interpretation by the living. The conditions of mortality — the demographic and semiotic impressions outlined earlier — were factors in the imaginative representations and cultural constructs produced by members of these communities to make sense of death. In spite of the rather uniform ritual structure that managed the elimination of the dead from living society, there was no fixed meaning for the remains. Indeed, the dominant rules of interpretation prescribed by New England Puritan culture were no longer viable, leaving the dead up for grabs in the public imagination of northern Protestants in antebellum America. The Puritan way of death, so compelling in the region during the seventeenth century and into the eighteenth, had lost its force by the early 1800s.[25]

A range of parties and movements reconceptualized death and the dead and submitted their visions to a rapidly growing, highly accessible populace. As the subject of death was loosed from the staid symbolic anchors of the past and opened up to democratic, free-market impulses of the antebellum period, the heretofore sacred territory of the human corpse was in danger of being profaned and violated. Conflicting discourses and contradictory representations proliferated, each attempting to render meaning from the lifeless body and locate it within an innovative, unusual, or profitable context. From the fantastic in sensational literature on the one hand to the pathetic in postmortem photography on the other, the corpse was transformed from a sacred object exclusively within the interpretive jurisdiction of religion into a symbolic commodity on the marketplace of ideas. Representations of the corpse had unprecedented exposure in the public during this period, and each representation tapped into an assortment of collective attitudes and meaningful symbols. The next three chapters will explore these attitudes and symbols, investigating how the corpse was "imagined" out of the living community.

4

The Great Escape

Throughout Western history, a prominent strategy for interpreting the meaning of death has been to encourage a division between the body and the soul, thus ensuring the possibility of some form of individual continuity and judgment after death. From this dualistic interpretive framework the physical evidence of bodily decomposition only heightened the belief that something survives outside of the corruptible flesh — in other words, some form of personal identity in the afterlife is distinctly *disembodied* and independent of the material substance of the physical world, even if the separation from the body is conceived as being temporary. In its most elementary construction, such an understanding translated into the following formula: only the body suffers death; the soul survives and is eternal. But a historically important variable is especially critical to this discussion: Will the body at some later point be raised and reunited with the disembodied soul? Does the body itself have any ultimate significance after death? The conflicts, divisions, and disagreements surrounding the status of the corpse and its relationship to postmortem existence have been especially crucial in the history of Christianity.[1]

A range of imaginative strategies for addressing these questions were available in the antebellum North. The Calvinist strain in the Protestant mentality, implanted in northern culture by the Puritans in New England during the seventeenth century, fostered the notion that Divine Providence ruled over the fate of both body and soul—thereby adding a degree of mystery and incomprehensibility to human endeavors to understand fully mortality and the life of the spirit. In spite of the profound uncertainties and intense anxieties associated with grace, judgment, and the afterlife, Puritan culture remained deeply focused on the presence and reality of death in this life.[2] While Calvinist sensibilities remained strong in some quarters of antebellum Protestant culture, constellations of innovative symbols and unconventional representations of death emerged and reconfigured earlier Puritan ideas about the body, the soul, and the afterlife. Before exploring these changes in detail, a brief overview of death in Puritan culture will be useful to the following discussion.

In the Puritan view, the corpse was a horrible sight that signified both human sin and the flight of the soul. Although many Puritans believed that bodily resurrection would occur at some future date, the details of this moment were generally avoided because, as an act of God, humans did not have the capacity to imagine or understand it. In addition, these believers stressed that judgment took place immediately at death and that the lifeless body had no connection to the subsequent fate of the soul. Although the future status of the body received little attention, Puritan leaders exploited the symbolic possibilities of the corpse and its connection to the condition of sin, using such familiar Christian motifs as the work of worms and the inevitable return to dust in their graphic descriptions. In the words of the Puritan Samuel Willard, after death had occurred the body was "to be commended to the cold and silent Grave where it must be entertained with Worms and Rottenness, and be turned into putrefaction."[3]

The tendency to downplay the cosmic significance of the corruptible body was publicly reaffirmed in the austere, plain, deritualized funerals in early New England history. As the cultural historian David Hackett Fischer writes, "The Puritans had little interest in the physical remains of the dead. They did not approve of embalming, elaborate funerals, or extravagant tombs. . . . In early New England, corpses were hurried into the ground with little ceremony."[4] Later in the seventeenth century some funerals became more elaborate, but the civic rites of separation, expensive displays of mourning, and communal demonstrations of solidarity did not signal a significant shift in attitudes toward the dead. Instead they anticipated the primary significance placed on the actions of the living, who, during the eighteenth and nineteenth centuries, were supposed to publicly demonstrate their grief and the class standing of the deceased.

The soul, on the other hand, had two possible destinations in the Puritan cosmos: eternal damnation in the fires of hell or immortality in the glories of heaven. Puritans imagined the afterlife in a rigid theological system that focused on predestination, original sin, and human inability to influence God's will. Their "intense, overt fear of death," to quote the historian David Stannard, reflected a preoccupation with what was considered the likely fate for most: the tortures of hell.[5] By the middle of the eighteenth century, however, when this vision of death began to wane and theological changes in the Protestant landscape began to alter northern religious culture, the status of the dead and the destiny of the soul could no longer be understood in such fixed, unyielding terms.

Instead of the evangelism of fear—the harsh rhetoric and emphasis on human depravity that characterized the Puritan worldview—a softer, sentimentalized imagination and religious sensibility developed near the beginning of the nineteenth century.[6] Based in part on the rise of evangelicalism and the growing Arminian outlook of Protestantism, modified religious interpretations of death began to proliferate in northern communities and replace the once-dominant Puritan system.[7] In the antebellum North the cultural force of such orthodox rhetoric had diminished—social changes wrought by urbanization, expanding markets, increased immigration, and Jacksonian democracy had turned the Puritan theological world inside out. The profound fear of death and damnation so ingrained in early New England culture no longer served as a viable source of social cohesion and personal morality. As Ralph Waldo Emerson remarked, "The terror of death will not shut one shop in the street nor stop a dance in your houses nor abate the colour in any cheek nor still the mirth of an idle song."[8] But the physical remains of the body and the realities of decomposition continued to be problems that Protestant leaders had to address if the transcendence of—and escape from—these very remains was to be affirmed.

The conservative theological wing of northern Protestantism offered a traditional perspective on the meaning of the corpse by asserting that at a particular moment in time—the return of Jesus Christ—the physical remains of the individual would be miraculously reconstituted and reunited with the previously disembodied soul. In spite of natural laws that ordained bodily disintegration, God had the power to restore life to the dead and "awaken" the body from its lifeless state. The death and resurrection of Jesus provided the faithful with primary evidence for the validity of such a belief. In this scheme the body was never inherently without value nor simply at the mercy of natural forces. While the soul rested in the bosom of Abraham or in communion with Jesus, the body—or what remained of the body—was waiting for the appropriate moment to be given a new life.

One exponent of the traditional view was John Williamson Nevin, spokesperson for the "Mercersburg theology" within the German Reformed church and one of the leaders of the High Church movement in antebellum Protestant culture.[9] His predilection for Catholic forms of thinking and worship had an impact on how believers understood death and the dead, offering them a Christocentric vision of body and soul. In one of Nevin's most famous works, *The Mystical Presence* (1846), he examined the nature of the "mystical union" of Jesus with individuals and argued that there was no theoretical separation of the body and the soul. They were, he said, "identical in their origin; bound together by mutual interpenetration subsequently at every point."[10] The body was neither a prison for the soul nor a separate entity but an essential component that, combined with the soul, formed "*one* life."[11] In a footnote Nevin addressed the question of the future significance of the body even more directly: "When the resurrection body appears, it will not be as a new frame abruptly created for the occasion, and brought to the soul in the way of outward addition and supplement. It will be found to hold in strict organic continuity with the body, as it existed before death."[12]

Other conservative religious communities, like Old School Presbyterians who resisted the diminution of Calvinist teachings, also underscored the value and ultimate necessity of the corpse for the future life. According to this perspective, the physical remains were of profound significance for the individual after death. One example of their view is found in a church constitution, published in 1822, which asserted that the bodies of members of the invisible church "even in death continue united in Christ, and rest in the graves as in their beds, till at the last day they be again united with their souls . . . the self same bodies of the dead which were laid in the grave, being then again raised up by the power of Christ."[13]

An equally commanding religious perspective on the meaning of death and the status of the dead came from the numerous evangelical communities of the period. These communities, which grew in popularity and authority in the North before the Civil War, demonstrated in various degrees inclinations toward revivalism, activism, millennialism, Arminianism, and sentimentalism. Slight variations in ideas about death and the significance of the corpse were less important than the common strategies of interpretation used by many of these Protestants. Their vision of the world was greatly determined by a combination of Reformed theological ideas — centered on notions of Divine Providence, God's revealed law, and prevalence of sin — and Methodist views on holiness, piety, and perfectionism.[14]

For evangelicals who wanted to improve and regulate American society, the symbolism of the corpse existed in creative tension with larger symbol systems found in antebellum culture. Their understanding of death required a balance between maintaining a severe evangelical emphasis on moral reform on the one hand and adopting romantic, sentimental cultural tendencies geared toward soothing the emotions of the survivors on the other. The corpse started to become a critical and powerfully evocative symbol in these evangelical communities, and new attempts to construct an effective and meaningful language depended upon satisfying both inclinations. In this context a new relation emerged between the appearance of the newly deceased, the affections and memories of the survivors, and the certainty of spiritual continuity.

Most segments of the evangelical community shifted their focus away from the corruptibility of the dead body and graphic descriptions of it in the process of disintegration—a common theme in Puritan sermons—and instead set their sights on the life of the spirit. This attitude idealized spiritual continuity after death and minimized any ultimate, enduring significance for the corporeal body. Evangelicals did not ignore the corpse—it simply began to serve a new purpose, functioning as an instrument for healing the pain of survivors who had to confront the death of a friend or relative. In a culture that was moving away from the stern, dogmatic, and oppressive sensibilities of the Puritan past and toward the Romantic, sentimental, and domestic characteristics of the nineteenth century, evangelicals reappraised how to make sense of death and the dead body.[15] The new religious culture that was emerging contributed to the establishment of four trends in northern Protestant attitudes toward death: valorization of the affections of the survivors, memorialization of the dead, augmentation of the spiritual possibilities in the next world, and domestication of the corpse.[16]

In the first part of the nineteenth century the deathbed often functioned as the location where all of these trends converged. As we saw in Chapter 2, the interior setting of the home was an integral—indeed, the most common—place for death and dying. Many novelists of the period exploited the intense emotional force of the deathbed scene with representations of this all too familiar setting. These authors articulated a sentimental attitude in their depictions of the dying, who were often children—and commonly young girls. They also used the transition from life to death as the most opportunistic moment to convey a moralistic and evangelical message, as well as their certainty of the life to come for the deceased. One of the most popular writers who captured the sentimental possibilities of home, morality, and the deathbed of a young girl was Harriet Beecher Stowe.

In *Uncle Tom's Cabin* (1852) Stowe presented the "beautiful" death of Little Eva. The beautiful death, which Philippe Ariès identifies as a dominant feature of nineteenth-century attitudes toward death, was an emotional spectacle wherein the feelings of the survivors were characterized by pathos and expressed with dramatic intensity. But the confrontation with death, and specifically the sight of the dead body, was also "both comforting and exalt-ing."[17] Writers of the period frequently couched descriptions of death in con-soling, ethereal language and encouraged hopes for some form of heavenly reunion, thus tempering the pain of separation experienced by close rela-tions. A strong sense of spiritual and moral certitude permeated the beautiful death, and the deathbed, especially of a young girl, was that sacrosanct place where religious edification could be bestowed on those who entered the death chamber.[18]

The body of Little Eva, both before and after death, is replete with evangeli-cal symbolism. After the child offers locks of her hair to those around her deathbed as a reminder to be good Christians, says farewell to her family and the household slaves by extolling the virtues of Jesus Christ, and dies in a moment of ecstasy bordering on the visionary ("O! Love, — joy, — peace!" she exclaims), Stowe describes the body in the death chamber. Draped in white and positioned on the bed, Eva's body inspires pious veneration from the living. The reverence shown to her body, and the enduring popularity of this image, suggests the existence of a cult of memory that disguises death as it domesticates and beautifies the body, making the last image more palat-able and therefore more emotionally conducive to the act of memorialization. From the "rose-colored light" that gave the "icy coldness of death a warm glow" to the "high celestial expression . . . mingling rapture and repose," on the face of the child, the corpse of Little Eva exudes Christian comfort, domes-tic continuity, and sentimental affections for the survivors.[19]

Similar representations of death were made available to the public through sentimentalized theological images presented by evangelical religious leaders, though the body did not always receive the same kind of glorification that prevailed in works of fiction. Timothy Dwight, for example — grandson of Jonathan Edwards, president of Yale College, and a key figure in the develop-ment of evangelicalism in the North at the turn of the century — downplayed the significance of the physical remains in order to highlight the meaning of their transcendence. In a funeral sermon at the death of Ebenezer Grant Marsh in 1803, Dwight incorporated such familiar Christian themes as the vanity of life and the memento mori into his discourse but refrained from any gruesome references to the decomposition of the body.[20] In Dwight's sermon, the corpse did not receive much attention, nor did it serve as a central location for impres-sive symbolic imagery — the dead body really had no bearing on Marsh's fate. Indeed, Dwight later argued that the corruptible body had no future role in the destiny of the individual, asserting in his theological reflections on the resur-rection, "It is clear from the Scriptures, that, in many important particulars, it [the resurrected body] will be greatly changed."[21] The cultivation of a proper religious attitude, the assurance of spiritual life, and the moral rigor of the survivors, on the other hand, were some of the primary topics that Dwight stressed in his attempts to make sense of the corpse.

In the sermons of Dwight and other evangelicals, allusions to heavenly reunions, evocations of personal memory of those who have passed away, and intimations of moral regeneration in the confrontation with death were rhetorical strategies employed to console, and reform, the living in their time of grief. In practice these strategies made sure that the survivors' emotional vulnerabilities did not weaken their faith and that their grief did not impede participation in daily life. The body itself — represented as a site of sin, depravity, and corruption in the Puritan past — came to have negligible importance in the symbolic economy of northern religious culture. But even as it began to recede into the background of the religious imagination, the corpse became a powerful symbol to others in the Protestant communities of the North and, for many, an object no longer suited for strictly religious interpretations.

In the process of "disembodying" death — of imaginatively relocating it outside of the body and within the destiny of the soul — a series of questions relating to morality, judgment, and spiritual regeneration came to the fore of evangelical discourse. The gradual acceptance of human responsibility and volition in the face of sin was coupled with the keen, deep-rooted awareness that death could strike at any moment. The combination of these two perspectives surely played a role in the revivals sweeping across many parts of the North before the Civil War. In the spiritual ferment of the revival setting, dwelling on bodily decay could be an emotional distraction from the pressing matter of "winning souls" and, more importantly, an anomaly in the sentimental cultural milieu of the Protestant North.[22]

Nevertheless, Charles Grandison Finney, one of the most successful and historically important evangelical revivalists of the time, conceptualized the meaning of death in a way that was in tension with Romantic culture, where feelings for others — especially family members and close relations — had priority over individual self-interests.[23] The intensity of Finney's charisma, the pressure applied to audience members to be converted and accept the saving power of Jesus, and the social, public setting of the revival itself assisted in the popularization of an orientation toward death that had been losing ground in the nineteenth century and was linked to some of the discarded Puritan values. The "death of the self," characterized in the Christian world by an acute awareness of the judgment of the individual soul at death, was important to Finney's understanding of human mortality.[24] In the religious system of his moral imperatives, confronting death was confronting the terrible justice of God — an encounter that the individual had to face alone.

But for Finney, too, the body was not implicated in the judgment of the soul—though throughout life it remained a potential site for carnality, selfishness, and pollution, and therefore of tremendous consequence for the condition of the soul in the next life. At death, however, the body simply gave way to the future destiny of the soul, and the corpse lost any of its value as an integral element of that future. Discussing the inadequacies of deathbed conversions, for example, Finney wrote: "Be it known to all men, that, as a general truth, to which there are but few exceptions, men die as they live, and no dependence can be placed upon those waverings and flickerings, and gleamings forth of a struggling mind, while the body, all weakness and pain, is breaking down to usher it [the soul] into the presence of its Maker."[25] Like the Puritans before him, Finney reminded his audience of the individual, personal judgment that took place when the soul separated from the body, though for Finney and other revivalists each person had the capacity to transform her or his destiny by making a conscious choice to be saved. From his perspective death was understood as a consequence of sin, while, on the other hand, accepting Jesus ensured "the eternal life of the soul."[26] This formula, and the distance placed in his language between "death" and the corpse, simultaneously reaffirmed the religious interest in the afterlife and contributed to a growing abandonment of the bodies of the dead by some religious groups in northern culture.

Another contemporary evangelical movement offered a new vision of the collective aspect of death. Millennialism, a religious sensibility popularized before the Civil War, fused beliefs about the imminent destruction of the world, a new age of social harmony, and the return of Jesus Christ.[27] This religious perspective, linked to the culturally popular theme of apocalypticism, centered primarily on the prophesies of William Miller, who became convinced that the world would end in 1843. His "premillennialist" scheme declared that Jesus would return at any moment, independently of human action, and inaugurate a thousand-year period of spiritual regeneration.[28] In his theological reflections, Miller presented a countervailing eschatology and focused more on collective images of death and the dead than on personal considerations of individual death. In Miller's plan the imminent moment of the second coming of Jesus was to be both an orgy of death and the end of death—as well as the end of history. He emphasized a collective encounter with Jesus over "a solitary moment of judgment at death."[29]

For Miller the miraculous return of Jesus would include midair meetings between inhabitants of heaven and earth and the onset of eternal life. The true significance of death for Miller and his followers resided in an eschatological moment that would subsume individual mortality within a larger cosmic framework. The domesticated, sentimental images of family reunions in the afterlife so popular in the evangelical imagination had no place in Miller's representation of the Last Judgment. The corpse held little significance in the larger context of Jesus' return. In Miller's vision of the Last Judgment, the distinction between the spiritual body and the physical body was absolute — no hint of the "mutual interpenetration" that Nevin imagined. The corrosive, corruptible nature of the material remains served the realism that Miller used in the description of the life of the spirit at the end of time. The destiny of the body was fixed — "a heap of ashes" — while the destination of the spirit was conditional and judged in a moment of collective activity. In a short story describing the events of the last day, Miller's sinful protagonist witnessed the spectacle unleashed by the return of Jesus and his own corporeal destruction:

> My flesh began to quiver on my bones, my hair rose on end, and all within me was suddenly turned into corruption. I felt the flame when first it struck my person; it seemed to pierce through all the joints and marrow of my frame, dividing soul and body. I shrieked with pain, and, for a moment, I was all unconscious. The next moment I found myself as a spirit, and saw the mass, of which my body lately was composed, a heap of ashes; and, although my spirit yet retained a form like that which I had dropped, yet half the pain was gone, and a moment I seemed to live again for pleasure. But the next moment, turning from the loathsome lump of ashes, I saw the flame, and in it I saw the form of the Most Holy.[30]

Beyond the Millerite perspective — and the larger evangelical culture, for that matter — were other religious meaning systems available to antebellum Protestants trying to understand the meaning of death and the status of the dead. These also encouraged the belief in transcendence over the physical remains and the continuing life of the spirit, though within a much more liberal interpretive framework. The fate of the body after death continued to be less important for religious faith in these contexts than the destiny of the spirit, and the emphasis on immortality and life beyond the grave defused anxieties about the process of bodily decay. The central task of these strategies, similar in intent to those of most evangelicals, was to provide the imagination with a vision of the afterlife attuned to the values, desires, and sensibilities of liberal antebellum northerners.

Unitarians, for example, attracted those religiously inclined citizens who distrusted or opposed the revivalistic, pietistic evangelicals making steady inroads throughout many regions of the North. Although in agreement with the evangelicals on the capacity of human volition to instigate regeneration, the liberal Unitarian creed encouraged the rationalism of eighteenth-century Enlightenment ideals instead of the wild emotionalism characteristic of nineteenth-century evangelicalism. Unitarians focused on a benevolent rather than a threatening God and, like evangelicals, believed in the perfectibility of human beings over universal human depravity. Unitarians were also theologically close to Universalists, who emphasized the doctrine of universal salvation and the denial of hell.[31]

William Ellery Channing, the "representative man" of Unitarian faith, was an articulate and thoughtful figure in antebellum religious society.[32] On the question of death, Channing expressed a familiar view that imagined the escape of the spirit and deemphasized the value of the body. Only as a container of imperishable virtue and goodness did the body truly have any usefulness, for it ultimately could not participate in the glories of the afterlife that awaited the soul. In a brief discussion of life in heaven, Channing suggested that even as our faculties, affections, and noble sentiments would remain the same, "we shall probably, too, have bodies not very different from what we now have" — but different nonetheless.[33] And in 1816 he wrote that at the time of death, "the clogs and fetters of the perishable body have fallen off, that [qualities of good in the individual] may act more freely and with more light in the grand system of creation."[34]

The dead literally shed their skin, and the body — the newly abandoned container — primarily served as a reminder for the living of the virtues, affections, and achievements of the departed who had moved on to another existence. The ugliness, fragility, and disintegration of the physical body were relegated to a secondary role in the religious imagination of both Unitarians and most evangelicals before the Civil War, if such themes were discussed at all. Instead, what held the rapt attention and answered to the hopes of many Protestants were representations that glorified the adventures of the spirit while downplaying what to many was the cruel, unacceptable order of nature — bodily disintegration. The intensity of these wishes indicates the growing importance in the nineteenth century of the feelings of survivors, who could not bear the loss of and separation from an intimate relation. Complex, thoughtful, and erudite theological explanations of human mortality and the physical remains had less and less relevancy in the antebellum Protestant world.

The popularity of "consolation" literature, written mostly by women and liberal ministers beginning in the middle decades of the nineteenth century and continuing through the postbellum period, is evidence of one form of this cultural shift. Images of the afterlife offered in this literature, often representing desired reunions between loved ones, also contributed to new sensibilities that accepted the termination of affectionate relationships, encouraged emotionally charged memories of the lost individual, and established new modes of interpreting the body. This imaginative universe transformed death into a time of hope and promise rather than gloom and despair. The deaths of children, the domestication of heaven, and detailed characteristics of the afterlife were presented as virtuous, morally uplifting scenes.[35] Most importantly, the glories of the heavenly realm and of spiritual existence after death envisioned by many in Protestant culture countered the pain and suffering associated with the material body in this world. The religious movement that best conveyed the desire to consecrate the life of the spirit, however, was spiritualism.

Spiritualism surfaced in the mid-nineteenth century as a popular and broad-based movement chiefly interested in communication with the dead and in the life of the spirit. The strong desire to contact departed spirits was facilitated by mediums — often young girls — who, through seances, collapsed the boundaries between the living and the dead.[36] But the trance physician and social reformer Andrew Jackson Davis, who connected the teachings of two critical European thinkers, Franz Mesmer and Emanuel Swedenborg, to the new movement, articulated the theoretical and metaphysical underpinnings of spiritualism most effectively. Indeed, Davis claimed to have made contact with the spirit of Swedenborg, an experience that led to his writing *The Principles of Nature* (1847). Based partly on the cosmology described by Swedenborg, Davis provided detailed accounts of six heavenly spheres and the progression of the soul through them. The metaphysics of Davis and the popular spiritual communications sweeping through many northern communities aroused the interest of many disillusioned Protestants who were intrigued by what they felt were the scientific and empirical bases of this alternate meaning system.

Davis dealt specifically with the persistent question of the relation between death, the body, and the spirit in the first volume of his *Great Harmonia* (1850). Here Davis wrote simply that "the philosophy of Death is the philosophy of change."[37] According to his view, which appealed to a collective imagination drawn toward nature imagery, death was associated with the blooming of a rosebud and the metamorphosis of a caterpillar into a butterfly. In Davis's scheme, at the end of life something was, in essence, *born* from the dying process. The mode of existence changed at death, and the material remains — the body that ultimately could not contain the eternally evolving and ascending spirit — ceased to be relevant after the change from death to new life.

The last moments of death, often full of visible signs associated with pain or discomfort, actually were deceptive and commonly misinterpreted as negative rather than positive. In an eyewitness account of an older woman's death, Davis described the spectacle of rebirth arising from material death quite literally as the birth of a new spiritual body out of the old physical one: "Now I saw, in the mellow, spiritual atmosphere, which emanated from, and encircled, her head, the indistinct outlines of the *formation* of another head! . . . In the identical manner in which the spiritual head was eliminated and unchangeably organized, I saw, unfolding in their natural, progressive order, the harmonious development of the neck, the shoulders, the breast, and the entire spiritual organization."[38]

The emergent spiritual body, a purified, perfected version of the physical body with a similar set of identifiable organs and limbs, had what Davis called an "umbilical life-cord" connecting it to the physical frame. Davis's perspective on the lifeless body ensured that no matter what fate it suffered, the eternal spirit temporarily residing in the rudimentary form would in no way be harmed or deformed. The sight of the corpse, then, according to Davis, should inspire joy and celebration for the birth and advancement of the spirit, not pain, despair, or grief. This kind of appreciation required a more profound vision, a deeper understanding of the true order of things. As Davis explained: "Could you but turn your natural gaze from the lifeless body, which can no longer answer to your look of love; and could your spiritual eyes be opened; you would behold — standing in your very midst — a form, the same, but more beautiful, and living!"[39]

As the language of Davis and other religious leaders suggests, death was unequivocally bound to conceptions of an afterlife in the collective Protestant imagination. In opposition to the natural laws of decomposition, the imaginative fancies of spiritual continuity expressed through various cultural representations were acceptable to — and desired by — many in the North. These representations offered innovative strategies for imagining the world of spirits. But whether placed in the context of a nuclear family, a spiritual journey, or an apocalyptic moment, the fate of the individual soul remained a gripping source of affection and memory for the living. It is clear that as the ideology of death began to value feelings and memory over corruption and sin, the meanings of the body in the northern collective imagination evolved.[40] Although the physical corpse was powerful because of its liminality, and therefore in need of vigilant human attention before disposal, the spiritual body began to be liberated from dogmatic theological constructs and appropriated by symbol and meaning systems circulating in the popular imagination.

5

"The Law of Nature": Revisioning Mortality and the Natural Order

A web of nature symbolism also informed representations of death and the dead in the antebellum North, though many of the interpretations used to make sense of human mortality continued to draw from deeply rooted sensibilities in the predominant Christian mentality. Although a link between nature and death had been firmly established in Western culture by the early Middle Ages, in the post-Enlightenment era, Christianity started to lose its privileged position in deciphering both; viable explanations coming from outside the realm of theology transformed their status and meaning in the collective imagination.[1] In northern communities the dissemination of new ideas about science, medicine, and the life of the spirit contributed to a breakdown of religiously authoritative positions, and exclusively Christian interpretations of the relationship between human mortality and the natural world were challenged, downplayed, or modified. Under these circumstances, a constellation of symbols drawn from nature assumed an even larger role in a variety of cultural attitudes toward death and the dead. Although a hope for postmortem survival still dominated northern public culture, the specifically Christian implications of this dream became secondary to other considerations.

"Nature" could mean many things in the antebellum North; as Americans moved across the landscape, the encounter with the environment produced a series of popular cultural themes that shaped the contours of how Protestants imagined nature and that determined how the natural world served the living. The prominent visions of Nature in these frontier communities, as well as in major cities in the Northeast, offered many citizens an alternative understanding of death. The revision in the details of death, however, did not utterly desacralize the remains. Instead, the dead could be placed in a stable, predictable, and, most important, morally instructive environment for the benefit of the social body—in other words, the corpse retained its special liminal status with Protestants. Romantic idealism, national destiny and expansion, the logic of sepulture—each of these subjects symbolically linked death and nature in new ways and preserved the imaginative viability of the dead. The natural world saved the physical body from becoming meaningless in a cultural milieu that relied less and less on traditional Christian forms of expression.

In the writings of the Transcendentalists, for example, a Romantic pantheism replaced Christian imagery with an overdetermined system of natural symbolism in the confrontation with mortality. Emerson, Henry David Thoreau, and others who subscribed to the highly individualistic and idealistic religious philosophy presented a thoroughly optimistic understanding of death: the immortality of the soul was fundamentally disconnected from the material body, which by necessity followed the organic, dynamic processes of nature.[2] In addition, the metaphysics of Transcendentalism made the problem of the lifeless remains less troublesome by valorizing the liberated soul over the transient vessel that had temporarily housed it. For Emerson the decomposition of the corpse was a sign of an inevitable natural process that did not convey the true meaning of death. In an early sermon titled "Consolation for the Mourner" (1831), Emerson announced that "the immortal soul is lodged in a dwelling place most frail and painful."[3] His interpretive propositions attempted to reduce the fear of death and the dread inspired by the dead body by emphasizing spiritual vigor over corporeal breakdown and by reading out of the natural world evidence for the eternal soul.

Thoreau expressed something similar in his short essay "Cape Cod." Here Thoreau described his encounter with a ship that had sunk near Cohasset, Massachusetts, in 1849. The St. John, a brig loaded with emigrants from Ireland, crashed on rocks near the shore. Thoreau and his companion lingered near the site of the wreck with many other curious onlookers who were in the process of retrieving fragments of the ship as well as any bodies that had washed up on the shore. Passing the location where the bodies of the dead were being collected, Thoreau wrote that he saw "the coiled-up wreck of a human hulk, gashed by the rocks or fishes, so that the bone and muscle were exposed, but quite bloodless,—merely red and white,—with wide-open mouth and staring eyes, yet lustreless, dead-lights; or like the cabin windows of a stranded vessel, filled with sand."[4] Thoreau's graphic, unyielding descriptions of what he saw on the shore suggests a cold indifference to the gruesome scene. Near the end of this essay, though, Thoreau eloquently explained his emotional predisposition as he viewed the corpses in front of him:

> Why care for these dead bodies? They really have no friends but the worms and fishes. Their owners were coming to the New World, as Columbus and the Pilgrims did, — they were within a mile of its shores; but, before they could reach it, they emigrated to a newer world than ever Columbus dreamed of, yet one of whose existence we believe that there is far more universal and convincing evidence — though it has not yet been discovered by science — than Columbus had of this. . . . It is hard to part with one's body, but, no doubt, it is easy enough to do without it once it is gone.[5]

But this form of continuity, growing out of similar impulses as those that underlay such movements as millennialism, Unitarianism, and spiritualism, was more ambiguous than belief in a simple continuation of individual spiritual life. In the Transcendentalist view, death itself was only a symbol of spiritual transition, and the material container for the mind or soul — the body — merely another expression of the immanent spiritual element that pervaded Nature. At death something of the individual survived the corruption of the body, but rather than ascending to the heavens or maintaining an individual form, the soul fused with a larger organic, spiritual unity. Emerson and the Transcendentalists preached a gospel of Nature, and in the landscape of natural symbols the corpse could easily be identified as both banal material truth and transparent sign of the divine. In the eclectic mix of influences undergirding Transcendentalist thought, including European Romanticism, Neoplatonism, Hinduism, and Swedenborgianism, death was understood as an opportunity to move beyond the confines of the material world and into a more liberated and holistic form of existence.

There were, on the other hand, less individualistic, metaphysically oriented connections between nature and death circulating in northern culture in the early nineteenth century. When linked symbolically, the natural order and human mortality could transmit particular truths about the political sphere as well, bearing especially on the long-term fate of the nation. A series of paintings from the history of art in America offers one example of this national appropriation of the meaning of human mortality. When the subject of death was addressed in American painting before the Civil War it often assumed a deeply spiritual form that found expression in the majesty of the natural order.[6] Radical variations in the Romantic imagination did not flower here as they did in Europe and England, so there were neither the frenetic nor the deeply sensual pictorial representations of death captured by such painters as Eugène Delacroix or Dante Gabriel Rossetti.[7]

Instead, an artist like Thomas Cole, founder of the Hudson River School, fused the symbolism of the natural landscape with death and national destiny through the use of majestic, mystical, and moralistic scenery. His choice of images is not surprising considering his love of landscape scenes and, according to one art historian, his "preoccupation with death and decay."[8] Cole often contrasted the transience of civilization and human life with the permanence and cyclical regeneration of nature. He developed this theme convincingly in two of his more famous series of paintings, "The Course of Empire" (1833–1836) and "The Voyage of Life" (1839–1840). Each offered a succession of allegorical scenes based on the common theme of the passage of time and the recognition that humans were destined to lose their vitality to the forces of nature.

In "Course of Empire" the signification of death and the signs alluding to human history were set against a natural landscape infused with sacrality and the power to consume life and all of society's accomplishments. Although Cole worked with an imagination deeply impressed with Christian symbolism, the nationalistic import of these landscapes overshadowed more conventionally religious sentiments. The idealized vision of nature found in Cole's paintings, similar to that in the writings of such other American Romantics as Emerson and William Cullen Bryant, exalted the American wilderness and reinforced the image of the new republic as being established in a special and providential environment—a popular view in spite of the rapid, massive, nature-destroying progress of northern industrialization. As Perry Miller observes, the painting "was exhibited over and over to fascinated throngs of the democracy. . . . [Its] moral clearly was that a culture committed to Nature, to the inspiration of Nature and of the sublime, might for a moment overcome its barbarous origins, take its place with the splendor of Rome, but it was thereby committed to an ineluctable cycle of rise and fall."[9] Signs of human and social finitude in nature, or more specifically the inevitable cycle of life and death for great societies, served to strengthen the emotional force of the patriotic content of the paintings—a bittersweet reminder to the "chosen" young republic that decay was in the natural order of all civilizations.

The spiritual and philosophical reflections offered by a popular Romantic like Cole were not the only way to imagine the relation between nature, death, and the life of the nation. Given the already potent symbolism of nature in the emergent republican religion of the national period, literally inserting the dead into the physical environment served to reinforce the sacrality of the "New Israel" and contributed to the process of westward expansion.[10] Protestants who settled the frontier believed that the ground containing the dead acquired a special significance for the young nation and therefore became the domain and responsibility of those who followed. Attachment to the dead and the location of their burial supported the rational discourse legitimating control over the land. In other words, the meaning of the dead and the marked space where they rested were related to the ideology of American expansionism and the conquest of the frontier.

The changing structure and appearance of the local burying ground was only partially driven by the acquisitive impulses of antebellum Americans. The formation of a national, as well as a more localized and communal, fund of memory depended on the simple act of burial—of some form of determined, self-conscious interment. Before the Civil War the soil of the receding frontier and the shared communal awareness of the settlers were marked by the bones of the frontiersmen, soldiers, and hunters who "tamed" the wilderness and allowed the smooth transition from wild nature to ordered culture. The moral and nationalistic imperative to remember the dead on the frontier found its most fervent expression in the practice of burying them in a delineated space, or at least in some easily recognizable place. This imperative, however, had relevance only to the European dead; Indians were seen as less than human, so their dead could be disturbed, desecrated, and pillaged.

The significance of locating the dead in secured ground is not surprising considering the deep-rooted structure of the funeral journey in early nineteenth-century northern communities: the dead body had to have a specific destination for the journey to be successful. What is distinctive about death on the frontier, however, is the manner in which the act of burial came to be symbolized in the Protestant imagination and, more importantly, what the consequences might be for disregarding this sacred obligation. Death in the wilderness assumed a number of meanings that could not, or would not, be expressed in relation to the city or town. In order for the wildness of nature to be vanquished and the success of American expansion to be ensured, the dead had to be put in their proper place under acceptable conditions and remembered by the living community.

Nathaniel Hawthorne explored the rich symbolism of death on the frontier in his short story "Roger Malvin's Burial" (1832), published in *Mosses from an Old Manse.*[11] In this pre-Revolutionary tale, Hawthorne described the fate of Reuben Bourne and Roger Malvin, two Indian fighters who had been injured in a battle and were trying to make their way back home. Too wounded to finish the journey, Malvin persuades Bourne to leave him in the forest to die—but with the proviso that he will come back and bury his colleague after recovering his health. Bourne returns to the settlement and is considered a hero by the local citizens. He marries Malvin's daughter, Dorcas, without revealing his promise to her father, a promise he fails to fulfill. As the years go by and Bourne's guilt festers, his personality and fortunes deteriorate. With Dorcas and his son, Cyrus, Bourne moves further out into the frontier to start a new life. During their search for a new home, however, Bourne tragically interprets movement behind some undergrowth as a deer, and accidentally kills his son — at the very location where Malvin's remains have decomposed and mingled with the earth.

In this story, Hawthorne linked the conquest of the frontier with the moral imperative to bury the dead.[12] On the other hand, the story also suggested that failure to perform the duties owed the dead could prove disastrous to future generations — as Bourne himself learns when he shoots his own progeny. In his characteristically subversive way, Hawthorne demonstrated the profound influence that Native Americans, who fought to preserve their lands, had on the minds of frontiersmen "settling" the wilderness for westward-moving Europeans: "An almost superstitious regard, arising perhaps from the customs of the Indians, whose war was with the dead as well as the living, was paid by the frontier inhabitants to the rites of sepulture; and there are many instances of the sacrifice of life in the attempt to bury those who had fallen by the 'sword of the wilderness.'"[13]

In spite of the ongoing battles with the perceived enemies of European civilization, those on the frontier could not escape adopting the mentality of the Other they had vowed to destroy. Hawthorne implied in this story that the absolute necessity for burying the dead related not only to a Christian responsibility but to a responsibility based on simple fear: those left unburied would, according to purported Native American beliefs, be at war with the living. For peace on the frontier, prosperity in the settlements, and success in the move West, the dead — especially those who died in the fight to control the frontier — must be buried appropriately in the very land under contention. The domestication of the wilderness surrounding the colonists, and the subsequent conquest of the frontier in the nineteenth century, required the familiar presence of a "civilized" practice — "rites of sepulture" — that could transform a harsh natural landscape into a cultured, habitable environment.

One of the ways Protestants in the northern communities negotiated the boundary between nature and culture was by making sure the dead had a decent burial with appropriate ceremony. As Hawthorne demonstrated, the rich psychological and imaginative symbolism of the dead in the frontier context could be linked to the fate of the nation. In the context of the growing urban centers in the North, on the other hand, the placement of the dead and their meanings in the collective imagination related to a completely different set of dilemmas facing the young republic. The demands of urban living and development required a reconceptualization of the relation between the living and the dead. The religious establishment, somewhat ambivalent about the spiritual usefulness of community graveyards, had heretofore accepted them as a potent symbolic force in their battle against infidelity and relaxed moral codes.

By the early part of the nineteenth century the church began to lose its close association with the space of death in and around large populated areas. In isolated regions, community members who agreed to care for burial grounds were not always reliable. The manner and logic of disposal in local churchyards and graveyards became increasingly dependent on a number of modern rationalizations having less and less to do with traditional religious and civic sensitivities. And even though the upkeep and management of these spaces fell into the hands of responsible municipal bodies and individual families, they seemed to be more of a public nuisance and distraction than deeply significant or spiritual places with any communal value to the living. As municipal bureaucracies grew more complex and families became more mobile in the first half of the nineteenth century, many graves and vaults, particularly in the larger urban centers, were being abandoned, often in a dilapidated state, and simply ignored.[14]

It was under these circumstances that the rural cemetery movement began to fascinate and appeal to antebellum sensibilities. In addition to the utilitarian and economic concerns cited earlier, the movement was rooted in the assumption that the most appropriate space for death was a "natural" setting — that is, one designed to simulate a pastoral landscape. Such a setting would be close enough for a family visit but far away from the daily business of the vibrant, dynamic urban centers where the dead no longer had a place.

At the turn of the nineteenth century a growing body of medical literature began to alert community members to the great dangers to public health ostensibly posed by overcrowded and untended places of burial. In one of the first published works of this kind, Francis D. Allen compiled a collection of "documents and facts," primarily reports from Europe, that attempted to demonstrate the potentially harmful effects of large, urban graveyards. Based on these reports, Allen contended that the close proximity of the living with the dead should be of concern because "the putrid exhalations arising from grave-yards" increased the impact of such epidemic diseases as yellow fever.[15] In his preface Allen encouraged the public to learn from the example of European urban areas and to exile the dead outside the city limits. The public good required a clean separation between the living and the dead regardless of the strong and effective memento mori inspired by the graveyards.

Another document, written by a member of the Massachusetts Medical Society in 1823, also made the case that putrid human flesh was a source of great harm to public health. The author warned against governmental approval that allowed ecclesiastical bodies to permit the interment of corpses underneath church structures in major New England cities. The natural process of putrefaction guaranteed "that the earth of cemeteries in time becomes so filled with putrid matter and effluvia, as to endanger the health and the life of all those exposed" to the unsanitary sites.[16] Other publications, similar in tone and technique, warned of the great dangers posed to urban dwellers by the remains of the dead, which they construed as a source of pollution, disease, and further death.[17]

It is clear from these documents that the dead — and disease, for that matter — were beginning to be discussed publicly according to scientific interpretations rather than theological doctrines. These assessments were based on the secularization of nature and the replacement of supernaturalism with naturalism. As the corpse began to be represented as a scientific object exhibiting natural laws dissociated from any religious significance, it started to be imagined as a source of danger to the community. And as the body became aligned with secular nature, the exile of the dead from the space of the living could be more easily rationalized.[18] The more pragmatic, utilitarian considerations associated with the scientific and medical discourses worked in concert with new antebellum sensibilities, which included the desire to beautify, institutionalize, and naturalize places of burial — outside of the daily sight of the living.

Dr. Jacob Bigelow, a physician and botanist in the Boston area, has been credited with instigating the creation of Mount Auburn, the first "rural" cemetery in the United States. He invited a number of the city's most prominent citizens to his home in 1825 to discuss burial reform, and the group soon advocated the construction of a cemetery outside of the city. To that end, they ultimately purchased more than seventy acres of wooded land close to Harvard University. Combining their interests in horticulture and their admiration for the picturesque garden with a strong desire to improve burial practices, Bigelow and his associates envisioned a cemetery securely implanted in a natural setting. This would be a place not only for the safe disposal of the dead but also a "cultural institution" that fostered a range of socially beneficial sentiments.[19] As Joseph Story suggested in his address dedicating the cemetery in 1831: "Our cemeteries rightly selected, and properly arranged, may be made subservient to some of the highest purposes of religion and human duty."[20]

In addition to moral instruction, the "rural" cemetery offered visitors a range of romantic sensibilities and liberal theological views for reflection — all concretized in the splendor of a natural context. God, nature, and the dead provided the trinity that anchored public justifications for the value of such burial grounds: "It is hallowed ground on which we tread, and the deep, dark wood is holy. The monuments of Mount Auburn mark an earthly sepulchre; but the spot itself, with its abundant and impressive beauties is, as it were, the inscribed Monument of Nature to the neverfading greatness of the supreme Judge of both quick and dead — the invincible Arbiter of our fate, both here and hereafter! Heathen must be that heart which does not worship the Almighty amidst these consecrated fanes."[21]

However, the romantic themes and Christian theology that served as the basis for the imagery and meanings identified with death in the "rural" cemetery were undergirded by the very modern, scientific perspective on the natural processes displayed by the corruptible body. In a public lecture delivered before the opening of Mount Auburn, Bigelow articulated a straightforward, scientific analysis of the inevitable process of decay operating in nature. All living organisms, he argued, tended toward corruption, including the human body. And yet, in the economy of nature the "elements which have once moved and circulated in living frames, do not become extinct nor useless after death; — they offer materials from which other living frames are to be constructed."[22]

Given the natural laws of corruption, Bigelow considered it only fitting that the dead submit to them without the slightest delay or apprehension on the part of the living. "Convenience, health, and decency," he said, "require that the dead should be early removed from our sight. The law of nature ordains that they should moulder into dust; and the sooner this change is accomplished the better." For Bigelow the finest and most appropriate place for the change to occur was quite simply a location that offered the best soil and facilitated decomposition. Also, considering the reprehensible state of graveyards in America, Bigelow, looking to European and English models, argued that what were normally "repulsive and disgusting" scenes in burial grounds could be "by the joint influence of nature and art rendered beautiful, attractive and consoling." In his concluding remarks, he expressed a naturalistic, biological construction of the dead that was somewhat at odds with religious understandings of the significance of the corpse:

> We regard the relics of our deceased friends and kindred for what they have been, and not for what they are. We cannot keep in our presence the degraded image of the original frame. . . . The history of mankind in all ages, shows that the human heart clings to the grave of its disappointed wishes, — that it seeks consolation in rearing emblems and monuments, and in collecting images of beauty over the disappearing relics of humanity. This can be fitly done, not in the tumultuous and harassing din of cities, — not in the gloomy and almost unapproachable vaults and charnel houses, — but amidst the quiet verdure of

the field, under the broad and cheerful light of heaven, where the harmonious and ever-changing face of nature reminds us, by its resuscitating influences, that to die is but to live again.[23]

Bigelow's naturalism echoed the more romantic expressions of the Transcendentalists in a scientific guise. But while in both interpretations the dead merged with a larger, overpowering natural order, there were other appealing elements to the new spaces of death. Perhaps most important, the dead could be remembered by the living community without the distracting scenes of city life surrounding the burial grounds and in a setting that conveyed the comfort of a private garden — for those who could afford it. The new, corporate-owned suburban cemeteries placed the dead in an aesthetically pleasing, emotionally tranquil, and morally enlightening location that encouraged acts of memory on the part of survivors. According to proponents of these cemeteries, the primary pedagogic value of the corpse was no longer inscribed in the body itself, but in the natural landscapes — "landscapes of memory" — surrounding the dead.[24] Such a landscape ensured that the dead would be memorialized through the physical implantation of individual and family monuments, and more importantly, visiting this kind of space would be conducive to meditation, consolation, and personal recollection of the deceased, as well as to morally uplifting thoughts related to family, love, and heaven.

Northern Protestants started to believe that the thoroughly "natural" process of decay and disintegration evidenced by the corpse was nothing to fear, nor a sign of punishment from God. It was simply a fact of nature and a reaffirmation of the natural laws that ruled the cosmos. As scientific naturalism began to gain respectability and religious supernaturalism began to lose its potency in the mainstream Protestant imagination, death became less menacing.[25] In the public culture before the Civil War, however, this view was slow to overtake traditional categories and interpretations. Indeed the innovative, modernized strategies for discussing death in relation to nature could not quiet the emotional, personal attachments to the dead. Many antebellum Protestants refused to commit to a Christian, Romantic, national, or natural interpretation of death and instead invested all of their energies into maintaining some form of connection with the deceased.

6

Morbid Obsessions

In addition to attitudes toward death that valorized spiritual continuity and natural symbolism, more diffused, less coherent attitudes existed in mainstream, Protestant culture before the Civil War. On the one hand, the immediate, individualized emotional response to the death and physical remains of a close relation did not always conform to standard, acceptable forms of behavior — the increasingly privatized expressions of grief and sadness allowed individuals an opportunity to improvise, act on spontaneous impulses, and develop unique ways of mourning. On the other hand, traces of sensationalism and imaginative innovation appeared in northern public culture; popular sensibilities that demonstrated resistance to the more authoritative positions on the dead found "authorization" through other channels. In spite of the disparate expressions, these attitudes were centered on three powerful characteristics: a refusal to allow the dead to disappear from the living community, a fixation on the body of the deceased, and a demand that the integrity of the corpse be perpetuated in the grave as well as in collective memory.

This range of attitudes was anchored in a system of symbols that grew out of the primary apprehension of, and preoccupation with, the corpse itself. Although some of these attitudes were not mediated by any cultural or religious conventions, in time they accrued their own cultural currency in America. The form and content of the emergent symbolism that captured these attitudes displayed a hybridization of currents within antebellum society: the intensification of a domestic religion that worshiped family bonds, the emergence of a strong consumer-oriented economic system that did not shrink from marketing morbidity, and the ambivalence and contestations associated with the growth of the medicoscientific field. These trends and others led to alternative interpretations of the meaning and value of the corpse in the first half of the nineteenth century.

For many Protestants the loss of a family member or close friend was simply unbearable and insupportable, and reliance on a providential understanding of life and death no longer eased their pain. In some cases, as a result, the dead became a focus of emotional projection, the grave the site of a desired reunion. This, in turn, inspired the conclusion that death itself might be a means of overcoming the suffering felt by survivors — only in death, at the side of the loved one, could the chasm be crossed by the person left behind. Few people acted directly on this wish, but a considerable number instead grew strongly attached to the body of the deceased and the location where it was housed. In letters and diaries this fidelity, bordering on the necrophilic, is a sporadically recurring theme that characterized the interaction of the living with the dead. The feeling of loss — the overbearing absence associated with the death of a close relation — often led to a fixation on the corpse as a material means to bridge the gap between the dead and the living.

One example of this sentiment can be found in the diary of Louisa Jane Trumball, a young girl who lived in Worcester, Massachusetts, during the midnineteenth century. Her little brother died of "the dropsy" when she was eleven years old. Although references to the deaths of relatives and neighbors were common in Trumball's journal, the loss of her brother remained a persistent source of anguish. The journal is also full of conflicting images of death. On the one hand, she employed standard Christian imagery conforming to established visions of spiritual continuity: "It is probable that he is now a little angel singing the praises of his Almighty God, and Father."[1] On the other hand, after questioning whether she might be better off dead and then scolding herself for having such "wicked" thoughts, she wrote five months later: "Some persons dread death, but I am *sure* I do not. When I saw my sweet brother *dead* he looked so calm, so lovely, so peaceful, that I could not *help* wishing that I also was dead and with *him*. I am going to ask Mother if I may go to the burying ground where Johnny is laid that I may see where he is put. When I die I *wish* I could be laid by his side."[2]

It is clear that Christian doctrine was a powerful force in Trumball's imagination, countering her desire for physical contact with the dead. Louisa Park, the woman who placed her infant in a temporary vault and waited until her husband returned from the sea to make a final decision about its disposal, likewise revealed that her strong impulses to remain next to her child were tempered by persuasive religious interpretations of death: "The services at the tomb were excellent, and kept me from wishing to be enclosed myself with my beloved child." The day following the child's entombment, Park walked in the burying ground and felt the urge to reestablish contact with him: "It wrung my heart [to see the tomb] — and I would have given any thing to have unlocked the door, and once more beheld my little Warren; but I was ashamed of such weakness, and forced myself away."[3]

Park's resistance proved to be the wrong choice for her mental and emotional needs; later in the day she was told by people who had visited inside the tomb "that [her] little boy remained without the least alteration." She went on to exclaim: "What would I have given to have known it! Oh what would I not have given to have kissed once more his cold cheek before it moulders to dust. What a satisfaction it would be to me — how much pleasure I should take if I could, every day, enter his gloomy mansion and there indulge in meditation and give vent to the feelings of my heart."[4]

For many in the antebellum North the lifeless body was a potential source of soothing therapy, and its appearance could provide a beneficial image to assuage grief. The preoccupation with appearance, alluded to in Park's remarks and in other statements and actions of the period, indicates that there was more than a passing interest in the visual signs of bodily decay. Josiah Stone, for example, expressed in a series of diary entries a daily concern with his wife's decomposition. On Tuesday, May 8, 1849, he wrote: "Emory & myself went up to Father Stocumb's & he went with us to the tomb about 10 A.M. — the corps had not altered much." On the next day Stone noted again that the corpse of his wife had not changed. On Thursday, May 10, Stone relayed the following information: "All went up to the tomb about 4 P.M. my wife had begun to change in appearance some." On Friday, Stone decided not to visit the tomb, "supposing she altered somewhat."[5] After this alteration the body could no longer mitigate Stone's personal distress or support the memory of the deceased in the consciousness of the living.

But the immediate fascination with the physical significations of the corpse did not depend solely on the mechanisms of memory or the search for healing; as we have seen, a consuming interest in the detailed descriptions of pathological symptoms before death appeared in many letters and diaries. In addition, the viewing of the body remained an integral ritual moment in the disposal of the dead during the antebellum period. Many people in the North had opportunities to see at least the preliminary stages of the physiological changes in the dead body. However, as the examples above suggest, in a number of instances there were departures from the conventional "last view" before interment. Salem pastor William Bentley noted in his diary that a "new kind of zeal was displayed" when a community disinterred a former minister to lay the foundation for a local monument. Bentley observed that "the Bell was tolled & the assembly were invited of all ages to come & see the corps which was exposed to public view in a high state of putrefaction. This is a new kind of curiosity, & a new way of exciting it."[6]

Even L. M. Sargent, the Boston "sexton of the old school," commented on the existence of a powerful desire to observe bodily decay, an impulse that he suggested was especially prevalent in women. After decrying the abundance of observers who gathered around the opening of a tomb "to gratify a sickly curiosity" or to steal artifacts inside, Sargent turned to the presence of what he called a "morbid desire, especially in women, which is rather difficult of analysis, to descend into the damp and dreary tomb — to lift the lid — and look upon the changing, softening, corrupting features of a parent or child — to gaze upon the mouldering bones."[7]

The morbid gaze did not emanate only from women. It was a trait, however unusual, of growing importance to Protestant antebellum culture. The desire to contemplate such mementos as locks of hair, as well as to be with the deceased, to sustain the last look, and to monitor early stages of decomposition — particularly of close relations — expressed a need for maintaining physical proximity and resisting the finality that comes with bodily disintegration. The sight of the corpse had a therapeutic effect on survivors, though an unusual preoccupation with gazing upon the remains could signal both a psychologically and culturally morbid obsession. Even Emerson, the New England Transcendentalist who discoursed on the subject of death with a fairly cool, self-possessed awareness of the true nature of human mortality, alluded to a strong attachment to the corpse of his dead wife when he admitted in a diary entry a year after her death, "I visited Ellen's tomb and opened the coffin."[8]

The corpse could not be retained among the living for very long, of course, and the natural process of bodily corruption — fascinating as it might have been to some — ensured that the survivors ultimately resigned themselves to the physical absence of a remembered friend or family member. But the desire to keep the dead among the living was gratified through other means. Mementos, such as lockets, brooches, and mourning rings, were popular with survivors as reminders of those who had passed on. These items, however, often seemed impersonal, lacking a specific connection to the one who had vanished from the family circle. Visual representation of the dead in portraiture — "posthumous mourning pictures" — was one available method for devising a more intimate, restorative image of the deceased and bringing the absent one back to the sight of the living.[9] Capturing the dead on canvas offered the survivors an opportunity to sustain the lost individual in the home — a vision of life hung on the wall.

William Sidney Mount, a New York–born painter most famous for rural genre scenes that "sum up . . . a moment of life," supplemented his income with portraits of the dead.[10] He was also a spiritualist who attended many seances and even asserted that the spirit of Rembrandt used his body as a conduit to write letters on aesthetics and painting.[11] Mount may have been interested in spiritualism because of his frequent contact with human corpses — his own writing (uninformed by Rembrandt's inspiration) indicates that he had limited enthusiasm for painting a likeness of the living from the lifeless remains of the dead. His letters are filled with remarks like, "I shall not take any more likenesses after death, while there is a living subject to draw from," and "when in health is the time for portraits," but Mount continued to take lucrative commissions for painting the dead.[12] They were, in fact, a fairly profitable source of income for him and other artists. Charging "double price" for this form of portraiture, Mount explained that he was "not paid for the anxiety of mind I have to undergo, to make my efforts satisfactory to the bereaved friends and relatives."[13] Many of his subjects were children, possibly adding to Mount's level of anxiety and discomfort at executing and reaping benefits from posthumous portraiture.

Transplanted from Europe to America in the eighteenth century, this genre of painting rose in popularity from 1830 to 1860. Through much of the antebellum period there was a fairly large market for painted likenesses of the dead, making it a lucrative sideline for individuals trying to earn their living as "legitimate" artists.[14] Raphaelle Peale, one of Charles Willson Peale's artistic sons, promoted himself as able to paint a portrait of the corpse as well as he could paint a still life. Most portraits, though taken from the physical remains before burial, depicted the deceased in a moment of life, often with symbols of death.[15] These portraits transformed the ugliness of the corpse into the beauty of a memory-image, helping to console, relieve, and revitalize the grieving relations.

Innovations in photography in the 1840s simplified and technologically purified the endeavor to sustain the image of the dead in the world of the living, allowing for more realistic simulations and lifelike representations. Over time photography replaced painting as the preferred medium for capturing likenesses of the dead. Unlike paintings, which sought to represent the deceased as active and alive, photographs represented the corpse in a state of rest or sleep, usually in the home, surrounded by family and accompanied with flowers or such religious effects as a cross or a bible.[16] In the early years of postmortem photography the brutal and inescapable signs of mortality—blood or signs of rigor mortis—might be visible, erasing any question of biological status. The photographer created a "pose" for the corpse on a couch, bed, crib, or a mother's lap. The composition was often dominated by the upper torso and the face, which on occasion was hand-colored to minimize those disconcerting tokens of death and create the illusion of life and sleep.[17]

The postmortem photograph, like the portrait of the dead, was an expensive but popular specialty item for middle- and upper-class Protestants. The widespread interest in these photographs led many photographic firms to offer accoutrements for the display of the loved one in the home, often decorated with floral designs, flying angels, and other sentimental iconography.[18] Nor was the enthusiasm for individual, memorialized representations limited to urban areas. Rural itinerants, as well as established photographic firms, would travel to isolated homes in order to capture the image of the corpse desired by the family.[19]

These portraits and photographs situated images of the dead in a safe, nonthreatening environment—the confines of a framed, domesticated picture—with the body itself playing a dual role as both prop and subject of the sentimental visual trace. The image of the deceased became a mnemonic device, which ensured immediate recognition, affectionate reminiscence, and domestic coherency. But if the photograph offered an inventive, personal way of linking the corpse to the memory of the living, numerous other cultural forms of expression directly appropriated the body to manufacture broader meanings of death linked to science and social change. Some of these expressions, in fact, rebelliously threw off the restraints of tradition and transgressed the limitations imposed by middle-class sensibilities on how the dead could, and should, be imagined.

Interestingly, these subversive representations of death and the dead did not invariably encounter collective resistance; sometimes curiosity and even captivation transformed such representations into a seductive mechanism for commercial success in northern society. On the one hand, when the cadaver was literally opened up and represented as an instrument for improving anatomical knowledge and medical care, most Protestants reacted with disgust and revulsion, refusing to accept any rationalizations for such a perspective. They considered any actions that accelerated bodily destruction to be a desecration of the worst kind—not only to the corpse itself, but also to the memories of the living. But on the other hand, when the corpse was imagined and graphically represented in a genre of writing known as "sensational literature," it became a thrilling, engrossing symbol that enhanced the entertainment value of these narratives and added to their popularity.

Sensational literature took root in American society and became prevalent in the early decades of the nineteenth century. The emergence of this form of literature began with an increase in the production and consumption of penny newspapers and trial and crime pamphlets, which described, in vivid detail, a wide assortment of atrocities and perversities. "Dark romanticism" in its sensationalistic American guise found a mainstream audience, overwhelmingly male, eager for narratives that elaborately recounted tales full of death, violence, and sexuality.[20] Those intrigued by such narratives — in contrast with the decidedly "feminine" audience for consolation literature — preferred lust over love, adventure over domesticity, and dismembered and rotting corpses over heavenly family reunions.[21]

The appetite for sensational literature aroused the interest of enterprising publishers, who did not hesitate to capitalize on these consumer tastes. Crime narratives became one of the favorite genres among readers interested in the seamy side of life in the growing, urbanizing, and diversifying nation. And as the literary historian David S. Reynolds suggests, compared with the strong religious and moral messages inscribed in earlier writings on crime, "the antebellum reports were, in the main, gloating records of unthinkable atrocities obviously designed to please a sensation-hungry public." Optimism for the individual spirit and prospects for moral reform fell flat in this literature. According to Reynolds, "In the post-Calvinist world of the crime narratives, depravity reigns while salvation is forgotten."[22]

Although the style and subject matter varied greatly, much sensational literature glorified violence, explored the more disturbing forces of human nature, and fixated on the pleasures, pain, and corruptibility of the human body. Instead of imagining peaceful death in a natural environment, many of the narratives were situated in urban settings. But the wild, untamed frontier, as much as the overcrowded, polluted city, was construed as a context that conjured the mystery, irrationalism, and dangers in human nature — even in a time of such "civilized progress" as the first half of the nineteenth century. Additionally, each of these environments provided a locus for marginal, demonic elements that inspired the most fear in white, middle-class Protestants and threatened the boundaries of what constituted the public version of the social body: wild "savages" in the dark recesses of the frontier and a class of corrupt criminals engaged in all types of vice and degradation in the city.[23]

In *The Quaker City, or the Monks of Monk-Hall* (1845), George Lippard tapped into some of the fears and fantasies percolating in the northern urban imagination and produced one of the most popular works of sensational literature in the antebellum period. (It sold more copies than any American novel before the publication of *Uncle Tom's Cabin*.) Lippard, a radical democrat and champion of the working class, offered a socialist critique of the nation's abandonment of vital founding principles, in the process depicting the urban social body as a rotting, decomposing corpse.[24] All of the moral deterioration and human depravity emanating from the centers of power had turned the city — in this case, Philadelphia — into a vile and odious place. Indeed, the opening section of Lippard's novel, explaining the "Origin and Object of this Book," used the pollution and corruption associated with the corpse as a metaphor for the reasoning behind its production — to expose the social disintegration taking place in the city of Philadelphia.[25] Although Leslie Fiedler comments that writers of sensational literature in the 1840s "exploited . . . two basic human responses: to sex and aggression," an obsession with death and a morbid curiosity about the visible, lifeless body also played a role in the popularity of the works of Lippard and other similar writers.[26]

The plot is difficult to summarize, but its main feature is Monk Hall itself, a gothic mansion located in the heart of Philadelphia where all the plots in the narrative converge. Rottenness, corruption, and death are ubiquitous in the novel and, in both a figurative and literal sense, serve as the very foundation of Monk Hall. Lippard described the mansion as a dark and mysterious place, with an assortment of trapdoors, hidden passages, subterranean vaults, and other architectural secrets. In Lippard's fictional Philadelphia of the 1840s, Monk Hall has become a den of vice used by a secret organization of "monks" — primarily upper-class professionals who work during the day as lawyers, judges, entrepreneurs, and ministers — for drunken revelries and the seduction of poor, innocent women.

The caretaker of Monk Hall, a disfigured, one-eyed black man named Devil-Bug, is literally surrounded by death and the dead. Lippard presents a modern, urbanized personification of Death, the Skeleton-Monk, whom Devil-Bug "loves . . . like a twin brother."[27] The Skeleton-Monk is the symbolic leader of the cabal, a skeleton figure who towers over the other monks in their club room, wearing a cowl, displaying a ghastly smile, and holding a goblet full of gold. This last accoutrement drew the reader's attention to a pervasive structural relationship in the story between money and death — or, rather, between the deification of wealth and the depreciation of human life. But beyond the blunt criticism of the corruption of power and the love of money rampant in the urban context, Lippard also demonstrated how entertaining the profaned corpse had become before the Civil War; the graphic, and highly titillating, scenes of body parts and decomposing cadavers added to the outrage surrounding its publication ("the most immoral book of the age," wrote one reviewer), as well as to its consumer value on the marketplace.[28]

One of the most shocking passages in the novel is described in a chapter entitled "The Dissection Room." A sorcerer named Ravoni, who has mastered the science of mesmerism and desires to institute a "New Faith," endeavors to fulfill an achievement that will initiate a new era in human history: the raising of a dead human to life. Before the demonstration, Lippard leads the reader on a tour of the "Dissecting Hall." The author not only gives his readers all the horrid details found therein, he also presents the indifferent, even irreverent attitudes of the students who study these body parts. In addition, he does not hesitate to inject sexuality into this lurid scene of mangled bodies and dismembered limbs. Discussing the upper torso of a young women, Lippard writes of the "rainbow of corruption" that "crept like a foul serpent" near her "two white globes." In his reflections on this scene, he speculates that "on this fair bosom hands of affection had been pressed or sweet young children had nestled; or maybe the white skin had crimsoned to a lover's kiss!"[29]

The attitudes of the young students in the dissection room only contribute to the scandalous nature of this section. Lippard describes an alternative response to the sight of the cadaver; instead of reverence and respect, the body inspires ridicule and aggression. Lippard had opened the theater of anatomy to the public market, and the controversial nature of his forum attests to both the fear this horrid fate aroused in Protestant mentality and the imaginative possibilities opened up by the sensational narrative. The students' brazen manhandling of the dead both disturbed and transfixed readers. One student throws the head of an old man on a table, saying, " 'I say Bob, this must have been a jolly old chap!' " Another remarks over the dead body of a young girl that many men must have desired her love, but now " 'she dont look altogether lovable. . . . And then the bosom, ha, ha! The Scalpel makes love to it now!' "[30]

The circulation of other stories—both fictional narratives and accounts based on purportedly real events—expressed a prevalent fascination with dissection rooms. Readers were hungry for shocking representations of opening, destroying, and peering inside a corpse. Dissection grew in importance as a fundamental procedure for the anatomical training of medical professionals in the late eighteenth and early nineteenth centuries. The body of physiological knowledge yielded by the practice became indispensable to the advancement of the medical sciences and the education of future doctors. A new and ultimately revolutionary "medical gaze" projected into the cadaver began to disclose previously incomprehensible signs of pathology and disease, and led to new understandings of the mysteries of death.[31] In this context cadavers became a valuable commodity for those institutions that sought to offer "legitimate" medical degrees. Students of anatomy were taught that the corpse held some hidden truth, some value that could be revealed—and therefore applied in the healing of others—only from its destruction. Unfortunately for these students, the majority of citizens in the antebellum North, many of whom were reading gruesome stories in sensational literature, still believed that anything hastening the natural processes of bodily decay or threatening the integrity of the corpse was shameful and offensive to standards of public decency.

Most American Protestants refused to see the dead in a medical light until after the Civil War. Christians had already begun to abandon the body, and in America the prevailing religious sentiment envisioned a spiritual birth after death and exhibited a decreasing interest in the "mortal coil" left behind. But over the first half of the nineteenth century, dead bodies had no firm, agreed upon location in the social landscape. Even though their place in the growing consumer market of the national period had not yet been settled, certain acts remained unequivocally outside the moral boundaries of public Protestantism, and dissection continued to incite disgust and moral indignation in northern communities.

There were many reasons for community members to be outraged when a corpse disappeared from a local graveyard, presumably bound for a dissecting table. One reason for outrage related to a lingering sense of something sacred about the remains, a sense that the identity of the deceased could still be associated with the body. Further, it robbed the community of its control of the dead. But the outrage was particularly aroused by the manner in which corpses were acquired for dissection. Body snatching, performed by a class of men often called resurrectionists and hired by individuals within the medical community, was a recurring problem in both England and the United States in the nineteenth century.[32] The idea of robbing a grave for money, coupled with the imagined, horrid scene of the dead body on a table surrounded by strangers who cut into it and destroyed its integrity, was repulsive to many.

And yet in the name of progress, science, and the advancement of medical knowledge, medical professionals required cadavers for dissection. Although most of the bodies came from executed criminals, the poor, and those who died without family or friends to tend them, an occasional corpse came from the middle or upper classes.[33] Children, fathers, mothers, young men, and young women—any and all bodies that could be easily snatched from their resting places—were removed by the resurrectionists. Resolve to protect the corpse from being stolen also contributed to the emergence of "rural" cemeteries. Those who could afford a burial plot in a "rural" cemetery knew that their remains, and the remains of their loved ones, were less likely to end up on a dissection table.

Episodes of body snatching sometimes inspired enough disgust and indignation to create an angry mob, its rage focused against local medical institutions approving of or participating in the dissection of corpses. In one of the most famous cases of mob action, a group of furious citizens rallied against Castleton Medical College in Vermont in 1830. When the body of a young woman was found to be missing from its grave, a group of about three hundred people marched to nearby Castleton and surrounded it. After some negotiations, officials at the College allowed a group from the mob to search the building. One of the individuals in the search party noticed some loose floorboards and tore them up. The body of a woman was found beneath, but she had been decapitated and could not be identified. During the ensuing commotion a student wandered out of the building with a bundle hidden in his clothes and deposited it in a nearby barn. The sheriff demanded the head, and the dean agreed after securing a promise that there would be no arrests. The same student returned to the barn and retrieved the head of the young girl. The body was reinterred, and no charges were brought.[34]

Medical schools demanded bodies — they were, in their own way, obsessed with the dead. But their interest in the cadaver had particular, and practical, consequences for the social body. The conflict between the medical fixation on cadavers for study and the Protestant demand for postmortem tranquility was ultimately mediated by legislation, at first drafted to prevent civic disturbances and prohibit the creation of a market in cadavers — the commodification of corpses. But while the laws tried to take into account the concerns of citizens, they did not discourage the study of anatomy. Most Protestants did not recognize or appreciate the reconceptualization of the corpse by medical professionals, yet lawmakers based their explanations for legislative action on the reasoning of those involved in the practice of medicine. An enlightened, pragmatic approach to the physical remains began to find support in numerous statehouses and political discussions on death.[35]

In a rather biased report to a select committee of the House of Representatives in 1830, the two sides of the argument over the appropriate interpretation of the corpse were outlined in broad strokes.[36] On the one hand, uneducated, superstitious individuals held to prejudices and simplistic reflections that prevented them from understanding fully the benefits of opening a corpse. According to the authors of the report, the reverence and sacrality projected onto the body were misplaced: "It is ever the common result with the uninformed mind, to bestow that reverence on the external form, which if properly directed, should be given only to the *acting cause and controlling spirit*."[37] Anatomy, the report went on to say, was shrouded in secrecy as a consequence of deep-rooted prejudices and sensibilities. This led the medical field to resort to surreptitious means of acquiring bodies for dissection, means that scandalized community members.

On the other hand, rational minds of liberal individuals interpreted the human frame in an appropriately philosophical and Christian manner, the report argued. Instead of the corruption and decay fated for the human body, why not allow it to be used for the betterment of the living? The socially beneficial knowledge obtained through the study of anatomy would help the medical profession better serve the very community so opposed to dissection. Legislators, the report continued, must adopt a similarly enlightened attitude toward the dead and move beyond popular superstitions and reverence. They must confront death according to a different set of values: "Who would not prefer, were his own feelings only concerned, to be useful even after death, to his survivors, rather than fester and decay—to feed the numerous worms and undergo the slow and disgusting process of chemical decomposition?"[38] Dr. Bigelow and the Romantics, as well as many other Protestants, obviously would have disapproved of such a negative representation of the fate of the body.

The report concluded that the insufficient supply of bodies for dissection must be addressed by lawmakers in an equitable and judicious manner. The increasing number of shady characters trafficking in corpses represented a danger to the welfare of society, and the problem threatened the legitimacy of medical schools. Further, the substance of older laws, which included dissection as part of the punishment in capital crimes, encouraged popular biases against dissection. The authors looked to France as a model for proper anatomy legislation. There the body of any patient who died in a hospital was sent to the medical schools for dissection if no one claimed it within twenty-four hours. In praising such an approach the report presented the medical profession's understanding of the meaning and value of the corpse: "This system is a philosophical, liberal and truly Christian one;—it makes the mortal and earthly frame what it ought to be—subservient to the intellectual development, improvement and power of man."[39]

The arguments appealing to reason, liberalism, Christian morality, and scientific progress notwithstanding, the study of anatomical medicine owed as much to a specific attachment to the dead as did any straightforwardly personal stance toward revered remains. In contrast to attachments rooted in the refusal to accept the death of a loved one or the links established between death, violence, and sexuality, the clinical devotion to the cadaver was ostensibly dispassionate, utilitarian, and scientifically advantageous. The medical community challenged the irrational romanticization of the corpse—a challenge that received full support from key government institutions—so that they could have access to dead bodies. But legitimating a clinical obsession with dead bodies proved to be more difficult for the medical field than marshaling support from the government. Doctors, in order to convince the Protestant community that their fascination with the dead was legitimate and valuable to the health of society, needed an opportunity to make the public recognize that medical knowledge and death share common ground. Until they did that, their search for more bodies would have to continue in secrecy.

The opportunity came with the carnage produced by the Civil War. During the conflict, where so many young men from the North perished for the Union and the abolition of slavery, older models for interpreting the meaning of death, as well as for disposing of corpses, were no longer viable. Scientific and medical perspectives on the dead body gained legitimacy during the war and contributed to a shift in understanding the meaning of death. But other practices, attitudes, and meaning systems emerged as well. Some represented predictable evolutions of past systems, but other imaginative responses to the realities of death had profound consequences for the location of the dead in the northern Protestant consciousness. In addition to the economic, social, and political changes that the crisis produced, the fighting transformed attitudes toward death and rituals surrounding the dead.

PART **II**

Death in the Civil War

John Brown's Body and a Soldier's Experiences of Death on the Battlefield

The beginning of the Civil War is commonly associated with the Confederate attack on Fort Sumter on April 12, 1861. In one of the many ironies of this war, no deaths occurred during the bombardment. The bloodiest war in the nation's history began with a battle that yielded no loss of life. But blood had been spilled and individuals had died on account of the polarizing divisions over the slavery question in the years preceding the attack. In November 1837, a mob in Alton, Illinois, dumped the murdered body of Elijah Lovejoy, an abolitionist editor, into the Mississippi River, along with his printing press. Throughout the 1850s, much of Kansas was embroiled in the conflict over the future of slavery, and murders, massacres, and mayhem prevailed in the "bleeding" state. One of the most terrifying acts of violence took place near Pottawatomie Creek in 1856, when five proslavery men were hacked to death with broadswords.

John Brown, an unsuccessful businessman turned antislavery zealot, instigated and directed the Pottawatomie Massacre. Though never captured and convicted for these crimes, he eventually attempted to invade the South in order to ignite a slave insurrection and overthrow the slavocracy that he saw destroying the country. Brown's campaign began and ended in October of 1859 at the federal arsenal at Harpers Ferry, Virginia, when his raid failed to produce an immediate uprising of slaves. The plan seemed doomed from the start, and after thirty-six hours, Virginia military authorities, including two of the South's best-known officers, J. E. B. Stuart and Robert E. Lee, apprehended Brown and his cohorts. He was subsequently found guilty of treason against the state of Virginia and sentenced to hang. His death served as a portent, if not the defining moment, of the conflict that was to follow.[1]

John Brown believed that his defeat and death would be the beginning of the ultimate destruction of slavery. Like the Old Testament prophets he so admired, Brown traced the hand of God in future events and was convinced that his martyrdom would transform the fiasco at Harpers Ferry into a prelude to victory. Brown wrote in his last letter to his family, "I am waiting the hour of my public murder with great composure of mind and cheerfulness; feeling the strong assurance that in no other way could I be used to so much advantage to the cause of God and humanity. . . . I have no doubt but that our seeming disaster will ultimately result in the most glorious success."[2] Brown proved a better prophet than insurrectionist. From the moment of his execution on December 2, 1859, John Brown's body did more for the abolitionist cause he so fervently embraced than all of his violent schemes and actions combined.

Although many northern abolitionists disapproved of Brown's violent methods, many thought that in death he could serve as an irresistible symbol in the fight against slavery. Emerson, for example, predicted that this "new saint" would "make the gallows glorious like the cross." The popular and influential liberal Protestant minister Henry Ward Beecher concluded that the failure at Harpers Ferry could be redeemed only through Brown's execution. Henry David Thoreau, Lydia Maria Child, Theodore Parker, and a chorus of other voices in northern public culture were sure that the battle over slavery had acquired its first true martyr, and that the work of the hangman in Virginia had done more for the antislavery cause than all the editorials, regional violence, and political grandstanding ever could.[3]

Compared with the unity demonstrated at George Washington's funeral ceremonies, John Brown's public execution and subsequent burial signaled a moment of national dissension that was nearly unprecedented in the young United States. Southern citizens, and many in the North, demonized Brown and desired the worst possible indignities to be suffered upon his body. A northern physician even suggested that it be given over to a medical school for the most complete destruction possible: dissection.[4] But Governor Henry A. Wise of Virginia, spurning the bloodthirsty crowds, allowed Brown's body to be cared for by his wife, Mary, and transferred from the gallows to the location where he desired to be buried, the family farm in North Elba, New York. The conveyance of the body stirred intense feelings among both pro- and antislavery forces, and there was a reasonable fear that even as a corpse John Brown could pose a danger to the divided nation.

No incidents had occurred when state authorities handed the body over to Mary Brown at Harpers Ferry, but, according to witnesses, she opened the coffin to ensure that all was in order before transporting it to the Brown farm. When the funeral train arrived the next day in Philadelphia, a sizable crowd that included blacks, abolitionists, and proslavery sympathizers had gathered at the station. In consultation with Mary Brown and her escorts, the mayor and his associates devised a plan to avert mob violence. They used a decoy to fool the crowd into believing that Brown's coffin was being taken to the local undertaker's office. While the crowd followed the decoy, Mary Brown and the others sent the coffin actually containing the body to the wharf, where it was shipped by boat up the coast to New York. The widow then took the train on the following day and rejoined the remains of her husband in New York City.[5]

From New York City to its final destination in North Elba, the corpse of John Brown caused great commotion in communities small and large along the way. Bells tolled, crowds gathered, processions formed, and, in at least one instance, local officials summoned a guard to protect the body for the night.[6] People clamored to see and be near the box that contained the individual many leading northern religious and political figures identified as a national martyr; the symbolism of Brown's remains had attained a cultural potency rarely achieved in northern society — perhaps second only to the remains of Washington. When the coffin finally arrived at Brown's farm on December 7, a small group of family members, friends, and neighbors viewed the corpse, which had been placed in the front room of the house. The next day, after funeral services, John Brown's body was buried quietly in the family graveyard.

The memory of Brown's passionate crusade against slavery and the resonant symbolism of his execution remained fixed in both the northern and southern imagination after his real corpse was long gone. Throughout the war Union soldiers remembered his body "a-mouldering in the grave," in the words of one of the most popular songs in the federal armies — a song that would eventually be given new lyrics by Julia Ward Howe and become a national treasure known as "The Battle Hymn of the Republic."[7] Brown's actions had a dramatic impact on both sides of the slavery debate and led to concrete steps in the preparation for the oncoming war. Thanks to Brown's raid at Harpers Ferry, southern fears of a violent confrontation over slavery translated into greater military preparedness in the years leading up to the war.[8] On the other hand, Brown's death forced the North to recognize the stakes involved in the fight against slavery.

The meanings attributed to John Brown's body were related to the political strife, cultural dissension, and emotional turmoil erupting over the future of slavery in the years before the war — his corpse became a virtual arena where larger social conflicts were represented for all sides in the debate. While

Brown's body was ultimately given a respectful burial and interred in land owned by his family, many Union soldiers received less humane treatment when they died fighting the southern enemy; the meaning and disposal of their bodies were shaped by northern attitudes that did not always depend on the political symbolism used to make sense of Brown's corpse. They were treated by their own comrades as nothing more than "sticks of wood" and buried en masse in what many northern Protestants considered to be "profane" southern soil. The written observations and ultimate death of one Union soldier — coincidentally, less than twenty miles from Harpers Ferry — suggests that, despite the political nature of the conflict, in the midst of war the dead could be imagined according to a range of meaning systems — or as having absolutely no meaning whatsoever.

During the late summer of 1864 Martha Gable received a letter from Thomas Patterson, chaplain of the Twenty-Second Pennsylvania Cavalry. Patterson imparted to Mrs. Gable the news that her son, William Marton Gable, had been killed during a battle near Berryville, Virginia, in the Shenandoah Valley. As the young Union soldier had performed his duty on the skirmish line, Confederates shot him in the leg, which was amputated later that evening. William survived only about twenty minutes after the surgery. Patterson went on to inform Martha Gable that, although he was not present when her son died or at the burial, William "was buried the next morning on an elevation near a farm house about a quarter of a mile from Charleston." The last words of the letter were intended to convey support and concern to the grieving mother and sister: "May it be one consolation in your trouble that he fell in battle defending his country. I had not yet formed his acquaintance and did not get to speak with him in regard to his future prospects. I hope all is well with him."9

When Gable first joined the Union army as a private in the Forty-Fifth Pennsylvania Infantry, he was sent from Camp Curtin in Harrisburg, Pennsylvania, to Washington, and from there he eventually moved to Braddock's Point on Hilton Head Island in South Carolina. Although Gable expressed little interest in the war effort in his numerous letters home and occasionally exhibited disdain for the blacks he met in the South, he realized that his participation in the war could cost him his life. In a letter dated January 20, 1862, Gable wrote home that he was about to engage in a battle near Savannah and that he was aware of what might come. "May god bless you all if I should fall in battle if this battle is over we will soon be home a gain."10

He survived what turned out to be a relatively minor battle and began to serve as the cook in his company. It soon became clear to Gable that the war would last longer than he and most soldiers expected, and like many other men in the Union army, he began to question why they were fighting. "I dont [k]now when I will get home not for a year yet I ges they dont [appear] as if they want to close the war the big men are making the money."[11] In the summer of 1862 Gable suffered a severe attack of dysentery and thought he was going to die. But he survived this sickness and, by the end of summer, moved on to Camp Wright in Virginia. He wrote home often, stating in one letter his desire to see his family, wondering in another when the war would finally end, and in yet another claiming that the war did not mean much to him.

In September of 1862, Gable sent his family a letter from Middletown, Maryland. He had just participated in his first major battle at South Mountain and wrote that he could not adequately report to them what he had witnessed. "There was a grate maney of our men kild and wounded it was afull I was in it all I was not hert but I had four barils thrue my close."[12] After this battle Gable's commanders assigned him the duty of tending the wounded in the hospital at Middletown. Another of his responsibilities was to go back to the battlefield in search of injured soldiers. He wrote that the field, with bodies piled two and three deep, was a "site to see." Back at the hospital the sights and sounds were even more shocking. In a letter dated October 9, Gable informed his family that he had another bout of dysentery but that he recovered fairly quickly. He then described life — and death — in the hospital: "There are a grate maney duying there is a bout theree a day it dont pere odd to see a ded man or to see a man's leg or arm cut off I have seen a grate many takin off since I have been in this hospittle. . . . There was twenty five legs and a bout the same number of armes takin off at this place it is an afull site to see and to here the moaning and lamenting there is a very bad smell. . . . I dont know when I will go home per haps never." Although Gable remarked that it took a strong stomach to deal with all of this carnage, he thought that it was possible to get used to it: "I could dres the worst wound in the house and then go and eat with out washing my hands."[13]

As winter began to settle in, Gable wrote home expressing his desire to rejoin his regiment, which had moved on across the Potomac without him. His letters also attempted to convey the scenes of hospital life, and, in a letter dated November 28, Gable conveyed his realization that his attitudes about death and the dead had changed dramatically: "We dont mind the deth of a man we have seen so many you [k]now that I never would tuch a ded person I dont mind it now I can pick them up and handle them as if they ware a stick of wood."[14] By the beginning of the new year Gable moved with the hospital to Frederick City, Maryland, and though allowed to rejoin his regiment after the move, he injured his ankle and had to be sent back to the hospital. In April, Gable decided to take a discharge from the army and returned to his family.

Then in the spring of 1864 Gable reenlisted, perhaps as a means to earn some extra income for his struggling family. He was given the rank of corporal in the Twenty-Second Pennsylvania Cavalry. The letters he sent home through the summer included some, if not all, of his pay, and they frequently addressed financial considerations at home. As a member of Phil Sheridan's Army of the Shenandoah, he moved from camp to camp in Maryland and West Virginia. On August 9, 1864, Gable wrote what was to be his last letter home from Pleasant Valley, Maryland. In it he explained that the rebels were closing in and that his company had been run out of Martinsburg, West Virginia.[15]

The Twenty-Second began to move in the direction of Winchester, Virginia, on the morning of August 18. After Gable's unit crossed the Opequon Creek, the enemy soon appeared and engaged them in an exchange of gunfire. The Confederates opened fire with heavy artillery early in the day on August 21 and inflicted serious damage. When a request was made for volunteers to form a skirmish line, Corporal Gable offered his services, along with a sergeant and a private. During the course of the battle of Berryville, the sergeant received serious wounds, the private was taken prisoner, and Gable lost his life. In the words of the sergeant of Company K, "Corporal Gable was brought off the line and laid on the porch of a farmhouse in the rear of our line of battle. He was the only support of his mother and sister and spoke very touchingly of them, and his fears for their support in the event of his death. He died during the night, and was buried near Charleston."[16]

After the family received the letter from Patterson informing them of William's death, his sister requested more information about the circumstances of his burial, whether it would be possible to find his remains, and other pertinent information. In a reply dated October 27, 1864, Patterson wrote that Gable was buried in a hurry, "as well as circumstances would admit" considering the advance of the enemy toward their position. He continued: "I think an unnailed box placed in the grave was used for a coffin. He was not buried in a grave yard. I don't know whether his grave was marked or not. I think it would be possible for you to find his grave and remove his remains if you wish. I am not able to say whether his mother is entitled to a pension or not. Ask some man of the legal profession. His mother is entitled to all the money due him from the government at the time of his death."[17]

Whether Mrs. Gable retrieved the remains of her son is not known, but his body, like John Brown's, had to be accounted for and made meaningful — not only to his own family but to the entire Union. Although Gable himself articulated an indifference that many others participating in the battle felt toward the war dead, in death he was, like Brown, of particular value to Union ideology as well as to a family that wanted to secure his physical remains. The cases of both Brown and Gable indicate that over the course of the war years, the federal government grew increasingly concerned about the dead and the meanings of death. But in the midst of war, where scenes of destruction and bodily mutilation were commonplace, soldiers began to see death in a new light; the sight of death and the site of the remains held radically different meanings for them than those formulated by leaders in northern culture and those held by family members back home.

By the time John Brown was put in his grave the conflict over slavery had been transformed into a violent and deadly crisis; when William Gable was laid to rest, the war had already yielded enormous casualties. Such excess of violence and human destruction during the contest was heretofore unknown in the history of the republic, and under these circumstances the symbolism constructed around the dead began to demonstrate significant changes. In addition, the physical vestiges of this excess demanded immediate attention. The corpses produced as a result of the fighting could not be left unattended on or near the zones of combat, and their disposal required unconventional practices that were unfamiliar to many northern citizens.

7

Death During Wartime

The Civil War was the most deadly conflict in the nation's history, with the North and South losing a total of more than 600,000 individuals. Fatalities during the war astounded contemporaries who lived through the conflict as well as subsequent generations who study and read about it. The number of American soldiers who died during the Civil War greatly exceeds the number of military deaths in any other war—roughly twenty-five times as many as the American Revolution (25,324 deaths), forty-five times as many as the Mexican War (13,271), five times as many as World War I (116,516), and ten times as many as the Vietnam War (57,777). Only World War II, with 405,399 U.S. military deaths, is on a similar scale. Even so, as the social historian Maris Vinovskis remarks, "before the Vietnam conflict, the number of deaths in the Civil War almost equaled the total number killed in all our other wars combined."[1]

The carnage that resulted from the Civil War and the fratricidal nature of the conflict had a tremendous impact on attitudes toward death in northern Protestant communities. In spite of the familiarity with death and the intimacy with the dead evident in the antebellum period, the destruction of life during the Civil War made the awareness of death even more compelling and challenged established patterns of thought and action for both soldiers and civilians. On the one hand, the war had an impact on attitudes toward the body, leading to alternative and unorthodox practices for disposing of the dead. On the other hand, the symbolism of death, its connotations and meanings, were reconceptualized according to a series of ideological and social imperatives because of the political stakes in the war and the amount of human sacrifice necessary to achieve victory. But underneath all of the rhetoric and political rationalizations legitimating the war effort, behind all of the efforts to make sense of the violence and put the dead in their place, the brutal demographic facts of the Civil War tell a tale of blood and dismemberment, grief and suffering.

Vinovskis asserts that one out of sixteen white males in the North in 1860, aged 13–43, died during the conflict.[2] The numbers become even more shocking when Union casualties are counted for particular battles. As a result of the fighting that took place during the battles of the Wilderness and Spotsylvania from May 5 through May 12, 1864, 26,815 soldiers were killed or wounded, while 4,183 were documented as missing. At Gettysburg, 3,155 soldiers were killed, 14,529 were wounded, and 5,365 classified as missing in three days of fighting. In one day of fighting during the battle at Antietam, the Federal Army lost more than 12,000 soldiers, with 2,108 killed, 9,549 wounded, and 753 missing.[3]

And misery, suffering, and death were consequences not only of the activity on the fields of battle. Disease was an even greater threat to human life during the conflict, particularly during the early years, than the firepower emanating from enemy lines, a threat that could cripple a regiment by half of its fighting force even before they went into battle. According to the best estimates, twice as many men died from disease than on the battlefield. A soldier was five times as likely to lose his life from disease than a male civilian of military age.[4] Some of the most fatal diseases were diarrhea, typhoid fever, and pneumonia; others equally feared were smallpox, malaria, and measles. The living conditions of the soldiers included contaminated water, poor diet, inadequate clothing and shelter, and a general inability to ensure effective sanitation. These and other circumstances contributed to the deadly impact of disease in the camps. An underdeveloped body of medical knowledge — especially the lack of practical understanding of germ theory — also contributed to the lethal presence of disease in Union camps.[5]

Soldiers could not avoid contact with corpses, and this intimacy, a common feature of their lives throughout the course of the war, was quite different from their experience of death back home. In the context of the Civil War, the dead body began to reflect a range of wartime significations and to assume a series of novel meanings far removed from the northern Protestant traditions. Although the corpse itself lost much of its power and multivalence as a religious symbol — there were simply too many of them to accommodate time-consuming reflection and proper, respectful treatment — under certain circumstances it could be understood by Union soldiers as a startling reminder of military discipline as well as Confederate barbarity. And messages relating to death were transmitted from the battlefield to Protestant communities in the North through letters, newspapers, and photographs, destabilizing familiar associations and sometimes replacing them with those more suited to the wartime context.

At the same time, reports of mass death on a particular battlefield influenced both national and international interpretations of who had the upper hand in the conflict. For example, the consequences of the battle of Antietam — where the Confederates lost 50 percent or more of their soldiers in several regiments — led France and Britain to drop plans to mediate the conflict and perhaps to assist the southern cause.[6] The Union victory there also led to an even more historic moment: Lincoln gained the political capital he needed to issue the Emancipation Proclamation.[7] Although the number of soldiers killed on a battlefield did not necessarily translate into victory or defeat, a casualty report did become a simplistic device for measuring which army got the better of the other, and it could sway perceptions about the direction of the war. As the chaplain of the Second Massachusetts, Cavalry Volunteers, wrote in his memoirs, "We could mark the fluctuating fortunes of the battle by the numbers and positions of the dead."[8]

For the North, a landscape covered with mangled and broken bodies also symbolized the righteousness of the Union cause — the large numbers of young northern soldiers slaughtered on the fields of battle became evidence of Union patriotism and virtue. Leading political and religious figures pontificated on the meaning of the bloodshed, and the meanings drawn from the reality of the overwhelming, if abstracted, war dead led in two directions. On the one hand, Protestants in the North understood the blood being spilled as a sign of past national sin, corruption, and punishment. Certainly, they believed, slavery was the most important reason for the disgrace of the nation and the suffering in it. But some Northerners saw other reasons for the war: greed, materialism, and lack of appropriate humility in the antebellum North itself.

A more common assessment of the true and ultimate meaning of the carnage, employed by Protestant religious and political leaders, as well as some military officers, took this theory a step further: Union blood had an extraordinary status as a curative, a source of regeneration for these sins. This interpretation, expressed in political speeches and religious sermons throughout the war, looked more to the future than the past to grasp the fundamental truth behind the tremendous numbers of war dead; from this point of view the numerous martyrs on the battlefields meant that the nation's prospects in the unfolding trajectory of world history were favorable and promising, particularly as seen from the rubric of Christian eschatology. Many poems and songs of the period expressed a similar point of view—the glory of the Union cause and the nation's salvation through the sacrifices of fighting soldiers had a social, political, and cosmic significance.

But while those far from the fighting attached collective, abstract meanings to mass death, the reality was more immediate to the individual soldier, his visual and visceral experience supplemented by the persistent strains of the "Dead March" and the stench of decomposing corpses. And certain deaths had a specific, and unmistakable, impact on the soldiers. One of the most indelible sights in the Union camps—and an event that occurred more frequently in the Civil War than during any other American war before or since—was the execution of fellow soldiers. Offenses that could lead to the death penalty included treason, murder, rape, and—one of the most common infractions—desertion. Soldier's diaries and letters commonly referred to executions, indicating that this form of military punishment was an important tool in the attempt to instill fear and maintain discipline in the federal armies. In the midst of chaotic battles, uncontrolled violence, and thoughtless killing, the formal spectacle of the military execution signified the primacy of law, order, and the Union cause.

Executions followed a basic pattern in northern camps throughout the war, although the method of punishment—death by hanging or by firing squad—determined the particulars. Napolean Radcliffe, a first sergeant in the Army of the Potomac, gave an account of a soldier who was executed for raping a woman in her sixties. After officers ordered the entire division to assemble around the gallows, which had a grave dug at the base, the escorts brought the prisoner from division headquarters. The band, playing the "Dead March," the provost marshal, and the provost guard all preceded the prisoner, who was seated in a wagon and accompanied by the chaplain. When the condemned man had ascended the steps of the gallows, the adjutant general read the terms of the court martial to the prisoner. Finally, at the conclusion of a short religious service, attendants placed the rope around his neck and at the appointed time released the floorboard.[9]

Although most executions went flawlessly, inevitably some were bungled, and Radcliffe described the slight miscalculation at this one: "I heard the sound [of the body dropping] very plain where I was, I had a small glass and was looking at him the instant the drop fell. Presently I saw two men on the platform doing something with the rope. When the men came in I learned the rope had been tied too long, his feet touched the ground, they hauled him up and shortened the rope, he swung around several times by the wind, but I could not see he made any struggles, I believe he moved his hands a few times." The death of the prisoner did not end the lesson for his comrades. The body remained on the gallows so that the various regiments in the division could march past the hanging corpse before heading back to their quarters. Radcliffe noted that the corpse hung for thirty-three minutes before assistants took it down. Within an hour the platform itself was disassembled and, according to Radcliffe, "all we could see was a little mound of dirt which is the last resting place of [the soldier]."[10]

The federal army had an obvious interest in controlling the meanings of death for its own troops, but in some instances Confederate soldiers determined how the Union dead were symbolized. In particular, there were rumors—and apparently some artifacts to back them up—that southern soldiers had desecrated the dead and used their remains as battlefield trophies. A few soldiers' diaries and letters referred to skulls of the Union dead that had been shaped into cups or soup bowls and to bones that were used as rings. When Samuel Derrick Webster, a soldier in the Thirteenth Massachusetts regiment, passed a deserted rebel camp near the first battle of Bull Run, for example, he remarked that the Confederates seemed to have lived well. He also noted that at the nearby burial ground "a number of graves, supposed to be of those who fell at the battle of '61, appear all more or less disturbed, and tending to prove the horrible stories related of cups made of skulls, and rings of bones, etc. In fact, I understand that some *unfinished* cups have been found —I have seen none, however."[11] Charles Page, a war correspondent for the *New York Tribune,* wrote that after the battle of Gaines Mill in June of 1862, Union soldiers confiscated a rebel knapsack, "hung to which was half a skull, used evidently as a drinking vessel. An inscription upon it stated that it came from Bull Run."[12]

In another, more fanciful example of northern perceptions of atrocities visited upon Union dead by Confederates, one issue of *Frank Leslie's Illustrated* contained a woodcut entitled "The Rebel Lady's Boudoir." In it a woman sat comfortably reading a letter, with her small child playing on the floor beside her. The walls of the room were covered with skulls and crossbones, rib cages, and other skeletal remains. A skull could be seen in a glass case on the table behind her, and another skull, which had been turned into a teapot, rested on the table next to her. The little child beside her amused himself with a skull as well. Immediately under the image was an excerpt from the Report of the Congressional Committee on the Conduct of the War that read, in part, "The outrages upon the dead will revive the recollections of the cruelties to which savage tribes subject their prisoners." Underneath this caption was another, relating specifically to the illustration itself. It informed the reader of the content of the letter in the lady's hand: "My dearest wife, I hope you have received all the little relics I have sent you from time to time. I am about to add something to your collection which I feel sure will please you — a baby-rattle for our little pet, made out of the ribs of a Yankee drummer-boy."[13]

The abundance of dead bodies, their immediacy in the lives of northern soldiers, and the circumstances of the war itself tended to politicize the significations of death. This was especially evident when bodies arrived back home for burial. In many cases, perhaps more in the cities than in the rural areas and more often with high-ranking soldiers than with others, funeral processions for fallen soldiers were elaborate affairs replete with patriotic symbols and rites. American flags, national guards, funeral dirges, reverential crowds, and speeches and sermons all contributed to the solemn proceedings and ensured that these bodies evoked ideas of national unity and the righteousness of the Union cause. Most citizens in the North never witnessed the terrible destruction of human life on or near fields of battle and did not feel the numbing affects of such scenery, so when a body arrived it could be easily reincorporated into the community by virtue of its sacrificial nature. Even the lists of names of those who died in battle, found in newspapers and soldiers' letters, could not be read without recognizing the political meaning of their sacrifice.

The horrors of the battlefield, the gruesome sights of bloodied and battered soldiers strewn across the landscape, could not avoid being associated with a system of meanings determined by the nature of the conflict. The soldiers became increasingly desensitized to these scenes, sometimes utilizing humor in their confrontation with the dead, other times assuming an attitude of complete indifference. But beneath the jokes and the silences was a simple question of survival — for both the individual soldier and the nation itself. The stillness of a soldier on a battlefield, a half-buried body slowly disintegrating in the warm summer sun, or a unit mowed down during a frontal assault may not have uniformly provoked feelings of grief. But such scenes inevitably led contemporaries to reflect on the larger issues facing the nation. Perhaps that is one reason why photographs of the war dead became so popular. They were not only black-and-white representations of the realities of war; they also challenged the audience to question whether the costs of the battle were worth the price.

For although slavery was restricted to the South, that region had no monopoly on racism. In a particularly perverse strain of that impulse, African Americans were linked symbolically to death and corruption. Physiological processes of decomposition reminded some observers of markers that differentiated the races, particularly skin color. On October 11, 1862, *Harper's Weekly* included a description of the carnage on the Antietam battlefield. After providing the reader with a fairly graphic account of the dead on the field, the correspondent wrote that "the faces of those who had fallen in the battle were, after more than a day's exposure, so black that no one would ever suspect that they had been white. All looked like negroes, and as they lay in piles where they had fallen, one upon another, they filled the by-standers with a sense of horror."[14]

As the political rhetoric in the North began to shift away from the goal of preserving the Union and toward one of eradicating slavery, blacks themselves became more involved in the war effort. In turn, as their involvement increased, so did their proximity to the dead, not only in the morbidly representational terms of the *Harper's Weekly* account, but literally as well. At first African American contact with the Union dead was limited to their assignment to burial duty, but they soon won the right to bear arms and thus entered the dominant Protestant imaginative universe — especially after the failed assault by Colonel Robert Shaw and the all-black Fifty-Fourth Massachusetts Infantry on Fort Wagner in South Carolina in July of 1863.[15] After this defeat, many in northern society recognized for the first time that slaughtered black soldiers stood for the same virtues of courage, sacrifice, and patriotism as did fallen white soldiers.

During the Civil War the bodies of dead soldiers became increasingly politicized; northern Protestant leaders, citizens, and soldiers themselves began to apply a set of new discursive and symbolic rules in their interpretations of the meaning of the carnage around them. The problem of the corpse, its social and imaginative status, required unconventional responses because of the nature and context of the bloodshed. Death during wartime transformed some attitudes, enhanced others that already existed in Protestant culture, and produced original, and ultimately long-lasting, attitudes as well. In order to understand the contours of these changes in attitudes better, we must move from a general discussion of how death and the dead appeared in northern culture to a more detailed analysis of the treatment and management of the dead.

8

"Let the Dead Bury the Dead":
The Search for Closure

The destruction on Civil War battlefields and the ravages of disease in camps and hospitals forced northern Protestants to reevaluate their priorities and responsibilities when confronted with the dead. Back home corpses were generally handled with reverence and honor, reflecting their liminal status in society, their uncertain placement within the Protestant universe, and the ambivalence many felt toward them. The conditions brought on by the war not only changed the scenery of death, they also challenged the conventional and deeply rooted attitude about communal responsibilities, religious solemnities, and individual respect demanded in the disposal of a corpse. The exigencies of combat ensured that what had been considered proper and respectful treatment of the dead in peacetime no longer applied during war. For young men in blue, encountering death now meant responding to bodily chaos that was often more violent than they experienced back home; dismemberment, diarrhea, and bleeding to death were only a few of the common and horrific ways the transition from life to death played out.

The dead were rarely abandoned, however, especially early in the war, when many units consisted of individuals with either familial or communal ties. Soldiers made efforts to perform at least minimal acts of closure, such as covering them with dirt from the earth, no matter what condition the bodies were in, and some burials incorporated a high degree of ceremony, either in camp or in a hospital. The specifics of disposal depended on a range of circumstances and interests. When a body was sent home, the distance between the family in the North and a southern battlefield required logistical accommodations by family members or friends. The Union itself also had an interest in these war dead, and if the government was going to maintain the confidence and support of the citizens of the North, it had to find an emotionally satisfying way to account for and handle the fallen soldiers.

In general, Union dead were buried unceremoniously near where they fell during an engagement, either in individual graves or mass trenches. They would usually be buried in their uniforms or wrapped in a blanket before interment. Soldiers were buried in containers or pine boxes only if provisions were available and there was time for such care. If the northerners controlled the field when the fighting had stopped, a regiment might be assigned the unappealing task of burial duty. For example, the 130th Pennsylvania was called upon to bury northern men after the battle of Antietam had ended. When possible, individual graves of Union soldiers were designated with a wooden or cardboard marker that identified the name and regiment of the deceased. After the Federal troops were buried, the Confederate dead were interred in long trenches, with as many as thirty corpses together.[1] Northern soldiers were for their part haunted by the fear that if they died in a losing battle, the Confederates might execute the formalities of burial—if at all—with recklessness, disrespect, and malice.

The practicalities of war limited the priority given to the burial of the dead. Men were prevented from going back onto the field to bury their comrades for a number of reasons, including the rapidity of troop movement, the urgency of other war-related activities, and sheer exhaustion. When northerners had only limited time for burial, covering the dead with dirt where they lay was an expedient option. Soldiers commonly encountered the half-covered remains of individuals killed in battle, and what may have appeared as a macabre, grotesque scene early in the war in time became simply another banal observation in their letters and diaries.

Elisha Hunt Rhodes, a member of the Army of the Potomac throughout the war, remarked in his diary in June, 1862: "We crossed the old battlefield of Seven Pines which is a graveyard, and many of the bodies are only half buried. Some only have a little earth thrown over them and are partly exposed."[2] Correspondents exploited the literary potential of such scenes and graphically described the morbid details. A journalist in *Frank Leslie's Illustrated* wrote about what he saw on the battlefield of Bull Run: "Through the thin layer of soil that hides the nameless hero who gave his life for his country, one sees the protruding ribs whence the rain has washed their covering, a foot or an arm reaching out beyond its earthen bed; and once I saw one of these long sleepers covered snugly up to the chin, but with the entire face exposed and turned up to the passer-by."[3]

Soon after an engagement had ended and the warring sides moved on to other positions, the cries of the wounded, the mangled remains of soldiers, and the stench of rotting corpses presented a variety of sounds, sights, and smells to those who ventured onto the field, especially those assigned to burial duty. Their task was always distressing and repugnant—and the summer season could make it particularly unbearable. Three days after the battle of the Crater in July of 1864, the Thirty-Fifth Massachusetts, along with a black regiment from the Fourth Division, received the order to bury the war dead. The burial brigade made an effort to identify the dead, but the swarming flies and maggots, offensive smells, and rapidly decomposing corpses necessitated hasty interments.[4]

Sometimes a battle would rage intermittently over a long period, and flags of truce would be exchanged so that the dead of both sides could be buried. A lull in the fighting might prompt such a truce, or perhaps a maze of wounded on the battlefield, or even an intolerable odor emanating from decomposing bodies located between the combatants. Charles Johnson, a doctor in the Union army, wrote that during the battle of Vicksburg the two sides called for a brief armistice because of the stench of corpses disintegrating in the hot sun. Again, under these unfortunate circumstances, the burial of the dead was rushed and haphazard: "The time allowed was too short for a regular interment, hence dirt was thrown over the dead bodies where they lay, and in cases where they could be identified, a piece of board put at the head, upon which, in rude letters, were the names and commands of the fallen ones."[5]

The federal government and the soldiers themselves made efforts to ensure that some form of identification marked the bodies of the dead. This concern preoccupied some of the living soldiers, who began to take matters into their own hands; some pinned their names and positions on their clothes before going into battle—a precursor to the use of dog tags in World War I. When a dead soldier could be identified, he might be interred with a vessel containing all of the necessary information, particularly if a close friend was involved in the burial. Armstrong B. Hallock, a chaplain who attended Princeton Theological Seminary before joining the Pennsylvania Volunteers, wrote during the Siege of Petersburg in 1865 that before burial "care is taken to keep the body identified. In each grave a sealed bottle is placed containing discriptive list etc. Besides most of the boys have plain rings, with their name and regiment engraved." He went on to explain that while the army was on the heels of General Lee, the dead did not always receive the attention they deserved: " 'Let the dead bury the dead' is the motto for the present. . . . The dead are all buried too, but they are only just covered with earth. I saw them buried where the box was even with the top of the ground. And many were buried without even a rough box. The blankets were their winding sheets. Of course we could have no religious ceremony."[6]

An article in *Frank Leslie's Illustrated* in February 1863 echoed this motto. A sketch of the "temporary" burial of Colonel Garesche, chief of staff to General William S. Rosecrans, accompanied a short article on his interment during the battle of Stones River. Whereas Chaplain Hallock voiced regret over the lack of attention given to the dead, the correspondent in this article contrasted the absence of ceremony with the glories of the war cause itself. With no coffin, shroud, or pall, the grave for Colonel Garesche was dug next to a "disfigured and headless corpse." This interment took place with no "procession of plumed officers, no rolling of muffled drums, no parting volley of rattling musketry, none of the rites and ceremonies of religion." In fact there were clearly more important duties drawing the soldiers away from what would have been a reverent, dignified rite in peacetime. "Alas! the living comrades of the dead hero are too terribly in earnest. They cannot even turn aside to give a farewell glance at their departing friend. The fate of the battle, possibly of the republic, hangs upon the swing of an arm, the glance of an eye. To-day is for action — to-morrow for regret. 'Let the dead bury the dead' is the silent impulse of even his dearest friends."[7]

Although many soldiers were buried on or near the field of battle without ceremony, in the Union camps and hospitals away from the fighting the dead were more likely to receive more traditional treatment. This was not because there were fewer bodies to inter in these locations — disease, remember, was the primary killer in this war — but rather because hospitals and army camps had the resources for more satisfying forms of disposal. They could afford, for example, to spare men and women to engage in these activities, and many had cemeteries nearby, offering an ordered, accessible space for their disposal. The conditions of these cemeteries and the treatment provided for the dead in the camps and hospitals, uneven early in the war, gradually improved as the federal government demonstrated a growing commitment to the responsibilities involved in the disposition of the Union martyrs.

Some cemeteries were close to encampments, and at least one journalist suggested that it would be "remarkable to a stranger, when first visiting the army, to notice the proximity of the burial grounds to the tents of the soldiers."[8] The relative calm of the camps and the free time that many Union soldiers had when not fighting made funeral services possible in some instances. General Robert McAllister, an officer from New Jersey involved in nearly every engagement of the Army of the Potomac, gave details of one collective funeral ceremony. Writing from Camp Fitzugh Farm, Virginia, on June 4, 1863, McAllister described the sober occasion in a letter home:

> The coffins were . . . laid on two caissons, each drawn by eight horses. The coffins were covered by the national colors. An escort of about fifty men, armed, led the column with a fine band of music playing the slow and solom "Dead March." We followed the corpses; then came the Surgeons — seventeen in number, then the officers, followed by the privates. . . . We moved along at the dead march until we arrived at Division burying ground. A hymn was sung, the caskets lowered, muskets fired, and we bid adieu to the remains of these brave men.[9]

The conditions in the general hospitals — those facilities set up in large towns and cities — were even more conducive to the observance of funeral ceremonies than the army camps. Hospital nurses, along with members of the Sanitary Commission and the Christian Commission, tried to make sure that fallen soldiers received a proper burial. Charles Page, reporting for the *New York Tribune,* wrote near the end of the conflict from City Point, Virginia, that "all burials from hospitals the last forty days, from Belle Plain to City Point, have been made by the [Sanitary] Commission, always with a decent interment, and generally with religious services by a clergyman."[10] He went on to say that those involved in the interments gave each grave site a headboard, "properly and indelibly marked," and that the Hospital Directory of the Commission at Washington contained all the pertinent information about the deceased. As the general hospitals away from the heat of battle began to function with more efficiency, the treatment and disposal of the dead began to improve as well. Burial rites at hospitals for most of the conflict included the registration of the death, the placement of the corpse in a coffin with some form of written identification, a small military escort from the hospital to the grave, the presence of an army chaplain to perform a brief service, the firing of arms, the playing of the "Dead March" if a band was available (a fife or drum would do if not), and the erection of a headboard at the grave site.

In regimental hospitals closer to the fighting, burial could be just as crude and impersonal as interment on battlefields. Many Union hospitals were woefully ill equipped to dispose of the dead, and the potential for pain, disease, and death made them oppressive and hideous places for the living. Descriptions of what soldiers had witnessed in these places frequently appeared in their letters and diaries. Edward King Wightman, a member of the Hawkin's Zouaves, Ninth New York, saw action at Antietam, South Mountain, and Fredericksburg. Writing to his brother from a camp near Falmouth, Virginia, after the battle of Fredricksburg, Wightman related: "Other regiments, you know, suffered terribly. There is a camp of hospital tents and ambulance wagons on our right, overburdened with cripples; heaps of unburied limbs and a large newly-filled grave yard adjoining, thickly packed with cracker-box headboards, speak in plain terms of the numbers and suffering of the wounded."[11]

Greater care and more traditional forms of reverence could be exercised when deceased soldiers had enough concerned survivors close by them after death to smooth their journey to the grave. In *Hospital Sketches,* Louisa May Alcott referred to a dead soldier who was laid in state for a half-hour in the hospital before attendants transported his body to a burying ground.[12] Moreover, in addition to providing dead-houses that stored the corpses of soldiers before burial, hospital cemeteries sometimes employed their own sextons. In one engraving from *Harper's New Monthly Magazine,* "Jacob," the black grave digger at the military hospitals at Fortress Monroe, stood in a newly dug grave, with the image of Washington's monument behind him. Although identifying Jacob as "a relic of by-gone days," the short poem under the illustration indicated that he performed an integral function at the hospital. As Jacob himself informed the reader: "I gather them in! I gather them in!"[13]

Burial of Union soldiers in southern prisons took place according to another set of procedures, obviously less ceremonial than what occurred in camps and hospitals. Solon Hyde devoted a chapter of his memoirs to the cemetery in the prison at Andersonville, Georgia, and provided a fairly graphic account of the scenes of death and the treatment of the dead there. After fellow prisoners pinned a name to the dead soldier's shirt, they brought him to the prison deadhouse. From here, according to Hyde, twenty-five to thirty bodies at a time were transported on a wagon to the prison cemetery, "here an arm and there a leg dangling over the side, . . . sometimes a head rolling from side to side over the footboard." The superintendent of the burial ground, Minnesotan Alonzo Avery, presided over his duties "morning till night, rain or shine." With the help of a group of black prisoners, Avery made sure the dead were buried as adequately as possible. Hyde described their activities: "The manner of burying was to dig long trenches, six feet wide and four feet deep, with a six-foot space between trenches. The bodies were placed side by side without any coffin, and generally naked or nearly so. As each one was placed in position, the paper containing his name was inscribed with the number of his grave and the date of death. At the same time a stake was numbered to correspond, and laid on the ground opposite or above the body, and when the trench was filled this stake was driven in at the head."[14]

Whether thrown in trenches in Confederate prisons or interred with military honors in a Union hospital, most northern soldiers who died during battle were buried under southern soil. This fate added to the anguish and grief of the soldier's family and was highly disruptive to the normal patterns of thought and behavior established in northern Protestant communities for the disposal of the dead. The desire to make sure death took place in the home, that loved ones viewed the body, and that the burial of the deceased occurred with appropriate ceremonies in a space containing relatives and friends had become essential features in northern Protestant death rituals. The battles of the Civil War, however, were fought primarily in the South. Transporting a body north was generally not feasible for the majority of families who experienced the loss of a close relative during the conflict. But in spite of an imposing set of obstacles, individuals in northern communities endeavored to retrieve the remains of fallen soldiers in the South. For those who could pay, innovative technology for preserving the corpse for transportation allowed certain bodies to make the long journey home.

One of the most highly publicized journeys of dead soldiers north occurred immediately after the conflict began. When the Sixth Massachusetts Regiment had to walk through Baltimore to switch trains for Washington, a crowd of hostile Confederate sympathizers confronted them. A riot broke out as the regiment made its way to the train station, and by the time the fighting ended four soldiers and numerous citizens of Baltimore had been killed.[15] The bodies of the soldiers were returned at the behest of the governor of Massachusetts, and when the train brought them back to the state thousands of citizens welcomed them home. The metallic coffins that bore the corpses were taken from the train, placed on biers, and covered with American flags. While the hearses carried the soldiers during the public ceremony, the "military marched with arms reversed, and the band played solemn dirges as the funeral cortege passed along the streets, which were crowded with people, all preserving a religious silence."[16]

As the war persisted and the number of dead increased, states became progressively less likely to get involved in retrieving corpses from the South. For dead Union soldiers to return to their families, the determined friends or relatives had to intervene. Sometimes fellow soldiers contributed to the costs of sending the remains home, though this may have occurred more frequently early in the war when bonds between comrades were strongest. George W. Woodward wrote to his sister in February of 1862 that when one of the new recruits died, the "boys were all in favor of sending his remains home and we made up a purse of 45 or 50 dollars, and ere this he is buried in Vermont."[17] James Edward Glazier from Salem, Massachusetts, wrote his parents that when "a member of our company dies we pay a dollar a piece and send the remains home."[18]

Occasionally families and friends back home would raise the necessary sum to pay for transporting the body home. The longing to bring the deceased home was so strong that in many cases it hardly mattered if the family was poor or that the corpse had already been buried months before. In a letter dated November 11, 1864, M. H. Mills sent General Larkin Dickason in Washington seventy dollars and requested that a soldier who died in an Alexandria hospital in August be sent home: "Will you be kind enough to see that the body is properly exhumed and forwarded to my address. . . . The sum enclosed has been raised here by [the soldier's] friends out of respect for him and his relatives who are poor."[19]

Many rural citizens in the North were unaware of the realities of battle and the new necessities for interment even though they were often and so graphically described in newspapers and magazines in cities. H. Clay Trumball, an army chaplain in the Union forces, related the story of a mother in Connecticut who inquired about the possibility of sending the body of her dead son home. He had died and been buried "some six to eight months before" in North Carolina. Before Trumball arrived to investigate, the soldier's regiment had moved from the state, so he could not locate the burial site. Instead of explaining the "unnecessary details" of her son's burial, "which would have grieved her heart," Trumball simply told her that it was impossible to find the remains of her son. She wrote back surprised that a chaplain was "unwilling to do this small service for a soldier's mother." She continued: "Why, Chaplain, if you don't know just where my John is buried, you might ask the sexton. He'll tell you."[20] Trumball observed that this woman and many citizens in the North were "in the dark" about how the Union forces disposed of their dead.

While some civilians seemed confused about the details of burial, many northerners made impassioned efforts to retrieve the remains of federal soldiers. Family members of a deceased soldier often took matters into their own hands and searched the battlefields, camps, and hospitals in order to find husbands, fathers, sons, and brothers and bring them home. Louis C. Duncan, captain of the Union Medical Corps, wrote that after the second battle of Bull Run the 139th Pennsylvania Volunteers were sent out under a flag of truce to bury the dead. Unfortunately, those on burial duty could identify few of the soldiers before their interment. A number of civilians came to the battlefield after the fighting had ceased determined to discover the remains of loved ones. Duncan wrote that the Washington newspapers had to publish a notice warning that identification would be impossible for most: "Our dead there were necessarily buried in trenches containing from one to three hundred corpses each, and by persons unable to identify one of them. In some few cases they were identified, a stake marked with a pencil with the name of the deceased directs where his remains may be found."[21]

On the other hand, individuals sometimes went on their own solitary missions to find their dead or dying relations. Both men and women undertook the search for the bodies of those they loved; what they often found were bureaucratic complications and displays of tremendous human suffering. A noncombatant's experience of the latter could be especially debilitating to her or his search. Walt Whitman, perhaps more than any other American artist, found a way to write about how death and bodily torment dominated the landscape after a battle: "Of all harrowing experiences, none is greater than that of the days following a heavy battle. Scores, hundreds, of the noblest young men on earth, uncomplaining, lie helpless, mangled, faint, alone and so bleed to death or die from exhaustion, either actually untouched at all, or with merely the laying of them down."[22] Confronting these scenes for the first time, as well as the fear that one of the men could be the object of your search, made the journey particularly daunting.

Wives and mothers on battlefields or, more commonly, in hospitals, often provided reassuring comfort to the soldier who lived a while before succumbing to an illness or to his wounds. If the soldier had died before the visit, the mourners might receive assistance from generous hospital personnel in transporting the body home. Sophronia E. Bucklin, one of many nurses who wrote memoirs of their work in Civil War hospitals, related various stories about visitors trying to make sure their dying relatives had a good death and burial. In one case, Bucklin described the plight of a woman who had four children back home in Philadelphia. She arrived at the hospital only to see her husband die of chronic diarrhea: "He died, and her case was laid before the surgeon in charge of the hospital, Dr. Higgins, and the story wrought for itself considerable hearing. He gave her transportation for herself and the body home. A good coffin was procured, the body well laid out."[23]

Missions to find the location of a soldier's grave and to ensure that the remains traveled north required perseverance, the right contacts, and good investigative skills. Stillman King Wightman resolved to find, collect, and ship home the remains of his son, Edward King Wightman, who had died at Fort Fisher in January 1865. The elder Wightman, who obviously knew some important officials, wrote about his experiences two months after he returned to New York with the body of his dead son.

After receiving a pass from his old friend and Secretary of the Navy Gideon Welles, Wightman made the long and torturous journey to Fort Fisher, near the mouth of the Cape Fear River in North Carolina. Plagued by doubts whether he could ever find his son and exhausted from the rigorous journey south, Wightman finally arrived at the fort. In a short time he found Edward's marked grave and began to make preparations for the journey home. A surgeon suggested that the only way to transport the body safely was to use a lead coffin, which might take a number of months to procure. Wightman responded that he would not leave without the body, so the surgeon reconsidered and said that it would be possible to transport the body "in tolerable safety" if he used a regular coffin and filled all the spaces with salt and rosin.

Acquiring all the materials he needed took time and energy, but Wightman finally was able to see to the exhumation of his son. The body was wrapped in tent-cloth with pitch applied on the outside, then deposited in a coffin. The coffin was nailed shut and then placed in a larger box. Both the coffin and the outside box were sealed shut with additional pitch. From the harbor at Cape Fear, Edward Wightman saw the remains of his son shipped back to New York. The Whitman family held the funeral on February 10, 1865, and interred the body next to his sister's remains in the family burying ground at the local cemetery.[24]

As Wightman's story suggests, there were imaginative and technological limits to sending a body north. Wightman found a way to bring his boy home that was not terribly complex: he wrapped the remains in a strong fabric and enclosed them in a secure, sealed wooden coffin. But there were many dangers associated with this method, particularly during summer months, when humidity and blistering hot days accelerated decomposition. The spread of disease, the putrid effluvia, the physiological processes that could lead to an exploding corpse — these and other threats required that extra precautions be taken. One fairly common technique for transporting corpses before the war, but used infrequently during the conflict, was to pack the body in a cask of whiskey, a useful and highly accessible preservative.[25]

A lead or metallic coffin, alluded to in Wightman's story, might also be purchased to transport bodies. As we have seen, the middle decades of the nineteenth century brought a proliferation of innovative coffin designs made from an array of materials, such as metal, cement, marble, and iron. These containers not only had a certain aesthetic appeal, they also could preserve the remains for an extended period of time, a detail that was not lost on marketers or consumers. But metallic coffins were expensive and hard to find in the South during the war, so for those who had the time and money, arrangements had to be made in Washington or larger cities in the North. The *Army and Navy Journal* contained an advertisement in September of 1864 that gave a clear account of a metallic coffin's purported benefits: "Fisk's Metallic Burial Caskets and Cases Are manufactured of Cast Metal, in imitation of rosewood, as well finished and highly polished as the best Rosewood Piano. They are perfectly AIRTIGHT, INDESTRUCTIBLE, and FREE from ENCROACHMENTS of VERMIN or WATER. We disclaim all connection with the VARIOUS IMITATIONS manufactured of SHEET IRON and other materials."[26]

The most radical and resourceful method for safely transporting the corpse during the Civil War was a technique that offered the military as well as northern citizens what seemed like a pragmatic, hygienic, and rational choice: embalming. The appeal of the procedure to northerners who desired the remains of their loved ones superseded earlier prejudices. If bodies were going to be shipped north, new forms of preservation would have to be accepted by the public.

Embalming was carried out through arterial injection, with chemicals prepared by the embalmer himself. These chemicals included "arsenicals, zinc chloride, bichloride of mercury, salts of alumina, sugar of lead, and a host of salts, alkalies, and acids." If the body could not be embalmed in this fashion, other means were employed, including filling the eviscerated trunk with such substances as sawdust, powdered charcoal, or lime.[27] A Washington correspondent described what he saw of the process and commented on some of the related economic and military developments associated with it in a May 1862 article in *Frank Leslie's Illustrated*:

> The body is placed on an inclined platform, the mouth, ears, nose, &c., are stopped with cotton; if wounded, cotton is put in the wound, and a plaster is put on; an incision is made in the wrist, the attachment is made from an air pump, and fluid is injected into the arteries. The wound is then sewed up and the body is hoisted up to dry. To save some eyes from sinking in, wax is put under the eyelids. The hair I found to come out very easy, but after the embalming it could not be removed. The bodies take on an average about seven quarts. There were some eight bodies on hand; some had been there 30 days. The operators say in four months the body will become solidified like marble, but no chance has yet been had to prove it. . . . Dr. Holmes, late of Williamsburg, Long Island, is the oldest in the business here, and I am informed he has made $30,000. Messrs. Brown & Alexander are trying to get a bill through Congress for the exclusive right to embalm bodies, and to have Congress authorize a corps of embalmers for each division. The charges are $50 for an officer, and $25 for a private, and I must say the bodies look as lifelike as if they were asleep.[28]

In antebellum America embalming had not been associated with the burial of the dead, though serious attempts had been made to preserve corpses through such methods as refrigeration, encasement in air-tight compartments, and chemical applications to the flesh. Although it rarely entered the minds of most citizens in this period, the practice of embalming had become current for the U.S. medical community with the 1840 translation into English of *The History of Embalming*, by the French chemist Jean Nicolas Gannal. Until the outbreak of the war, this practice was used only for the preservation of cadavers for dissection in medical schools. Embalming was of importance to the study of medical pathology and was of interest to those professionals associated with medicine, including physicians, anatomists, chemists, pharmacists, and druggists.[29] The Civil War not only introduced the public to the viability and usefulness of embalming, it also helped to determine which professionals would be associated with it in the future.

As the war dragged on and the death tolls climbed higher, the demand for a way to transport bodies north increased and led to the appropriation by a group of enterprising undertakers of what had been heretofore a technique exclusive to the medical profession. Few of the undertakers who worked independently or who were contracted by the government had sufficient knowledge of embalming to preserve bodies effectively on their own at the beginning of the war. They either learned the basics, improvised, or hired "embalming surgeons" from the field of medicine. In any case, undertakers began offering family members a more sensible method of preservation then what was currently available; ice and specially designed containers could not guarantee a suitable corpse for the familiar and final rite of passage.[30] Although a sense of patriotic duty motivated many of these men, some of whom had served in the Union army before assuming their new roles, the financial rewards for providing the service were undeniably attractive to most.

Embalming was expensive, limiting the market that could afford these services. Some undertakers had special prices for enlisted men, but the majority of embalmed soldiers were either officers or from wealthy families. Oliver Wendell Holmes commented on the class differences affecting the treatment of the dead in his observations after the battle of Antietam: "The slain of higher condition, 'embalmed' and iron-cased, were sliding off on the railways to their far homes; the dead of the rank and file were being gathered up and committed hastily to the earth."[31] Still, embalming proved to be a lucrative business, and near the end of the war the federal government sanctioned this method of preservation. In fact, by the last year of the war all those soldiers who died at the Armory Square Military Hospital in Washington were embalmed before interment in the event that a family should request the body be shipped north.[32]

During the course of the war, Washington became the nation's embalming capital. Many observers remarked on the number of embalming establishments in and around the city. Julia Ward Howe wrote in her reminiscences that when visiting the city, she "saw the office of the 'New York Herald,' and near it the ghastly advertisement of an agency for embalming and forwarding the bodies of those who had fallen in the fight or who had perished by fever."[33] By 1863 at least four "embalmers of the dead" listed their services in the Washington directory, with one advertising the following:

Bodies Embalmed by Us NEVER TURN BLACK! But retain their natural color and appearance; indeed, the method having the power of preserving bodies, with all their parts, both internal and external, WITHOUT ANY MUTILATION OR EXTRACTION and so as to admit of contemplation of the person Embalmed, with the countenance of a one asleep. . . . Surgeons and all interested are cordially invited to call and examine specimens after Embalmed. . . . N.B. Particular attention paid to obtaining bodies of those who have fallen on the Battle Field.[34]

Other embalming undertakers opened businesses close to major army hospitals and camps in Virginia, particularly near Alexandria and City Point. Edward Colyer, a guard at an Alexandria hospital, wrote home to his mother that he "stopped at two places where they embalm the dead, they had a corpse at each place and going through the operation."[35] From a hospital near City Point, Samuel Webster wrote in his diary on Thursday, December 22, 1864, that after a "council" with a doctor and two nurses, they decided that a woman who had died of dysentery would be embalmed. The next day a larger group of hospital personnel reaffirmed the decision: "The ladies concluded, after much solicitation to order the body embalmed, and unless heard from to the contrary to have the Doctors (Bunn and Heintzleman) on the hill near here who attend to that business call at eight o'clock this p.m."[36] "That business," which had grown so prominent during the years of fighting, offered northerners another alternative for the disposal of close loved ones.

Soon undertakers began to venture ever closer to the action. Just as sutlers followed the movements of the Union army to provide goods and services to the living, embalmers began to travel with the very soldiers who could end up on their embalming tables. Because there were few northerners to sell to in and around Virginia, at least one entrepreneur targeted the men who could be both consumer and commodity in this transaction. Near the end of the conflict, a visitor to the Army of the James reported that outside of Richmond, Virginia, General Butler and his men passed by a row of trees with embalming advertisements posted on them. The officers did not appreciate his resourcefulness in drumming up business: "The chief of the medical staff pointed out their demoralizing influence; and the General sent the embalmer a civil order to desist from this method of advertising."[37]

In another example of the embalmer's presence at or near the front, Chaplain H. Clay Trumball wrote in his memoirs that in the last year of the war two rival embalmers operated near other "firms" providing goods and services to Union soldiers close to the Richmond and Petersburg lines. He claimed that both would send teams out to the lines "advertising their business, and asking for patronage." In Trumball's view, the "seductive" handbills that began with the words "The Honored Dead" seemed to combine sentimentalism with the economic realities of the work of these specialists. Embalmers were clearly attempting to exploit the emotions of soldiers who were likely to know someone about to die or who themselves might not make it through the battle. For a price, the precious remains could be assured a safe passage north, out of the perceived degradation and filth of the South and into the secure and comforting care of loved ones back home.[38]

Embalmers offered another critical service in addition to the actual preparation of corpses: they could be engaged to search for the bodies of deceased soldiers in hospitals and on battlefields. A family from rural New Hampshire sent a photograph of their deceased relative to those who were involved in the search. Two undertakers were paid seventeen dollars, but no body arrived. The family grew concerned but wrote to a middleman involved in the transaction that the undertakers had reassured them of their willingness to follow through on the deal: "The letter that we received . . . says, that the body was not delivered to them, consequently they could not embalm it, but they added, that they were ready and willing to get the body and send it home."[39]

At the very outset of the war, embalming was thrust into the public eye with the death and funeral of Colonel Elmer Ellsworth. A double-barreled shotgun blast to the chest killed Ellsworth as he was taking down a Confederate flag from the Marshall House Hotel in Alexandria, Virginia, on May 24, 1861. Despite the severity of this blast, Ellsworth's body was successfully embalmed by a Dr. Thomas Holmes, one of the earliest chemical embalmers in the United States. Holmes went on to embalm — so he claimed — more than four thousand soldiers.[40] According to one account, the preservation of Ellsworth's body had an impact on northern attitudes toward the new procedure: "Colonel Ellsworth's embalming and viewable appearance were widely and favorably commented on in the press and did much to familiarize the previously uninformed public with embalming."[41] The defining moment in the public awareness of the cosmetic and technological advantages of embalming, however, came at the end of the conflict with the assassination and funeral journey of President Abraham Lincoln.

John James Barralet, "Apotheosis of George Washington" (1802). The Metropolitan Museum of Art, Gift of William H. Huntington, 1982.

FISK'S PATENT METALLIC BURIAL CASES.

THE PRICE GREATLY REDUCED.

The above Cases, air-tight and indestructible for protecting and preservidg the Dead, for ordinary interments, for vaults, for transportation, or for nny other desirable purpose, are made of iron and other metal—are just what has been long wanted, for preserving in the most secure and appropriate manner, the remains of the dead from sudden decay, from water, from vermin and from the ravages of tee dissecting knife.

The price has been recently so much reduced as to place them within the reabh of the entire respectable portion of community, being no more expensive than other good coffins, and they will never decay. Being air-tight, the remains can be kept in them in dwellings for weeks, without any offensive smell, even in the warmest weather. They are not cumbersome, as the largest sizes weigh but about 100 pounds. The attention of the public is directed to them, and they are requested to call and view them at the Warerooms of WM. W. ROBERTS, No. 1 Pratt street, who is the authorized agent for their sale, and where they can always be had ready for immediate use.

Also, a complete assortment of WOOD COFFINS always onhand.   1yd   nov 4

Hartford, Conn. *Times*
March 29, 1850

"Fisk's Patent Metallic Burial Cases" (advertisement, 1850). From the private collection of Edward C. Johnson and Melissa Johnson Williams.

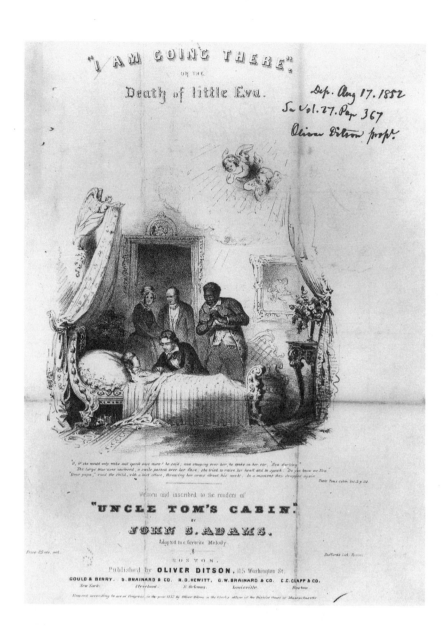

Death bed of Little Eva (music cover lithograph, 1852). Library of Congress, Prints and Photographs Division.

"A Death Scene" (illustration in Andrew Jackson Davis, *Death and the After-Life*, 1874). Library of Congress, Rare Book Division.

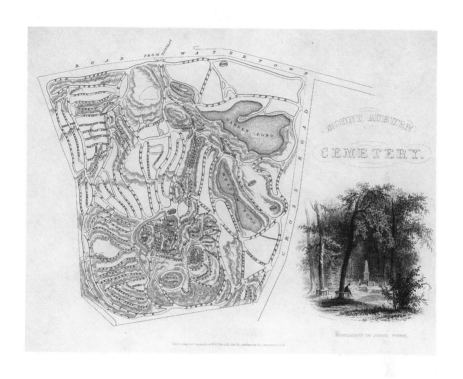

Mount Auburn frontispiece (From Cornelia Walters, *Mount Auburn Illustrated*, 1847).
Library of Congress, Prints and Photographs Division.

William Sidney Mount, "Jedediah Williamson" 1837 (posthumous portrait). The Museums at Stony Brook; Bequest of Ward Melville, 1977.

Ambrotype of Mrs. Timothy Bigelow and her dead daughter, 1857. From the collections of
the Worcester Historical Museum, Worcester, Massachusetts.

Jarvis Hanks, "Death Scene" (1841–1842). The Ohio Historical Society, Camus Martius Museum, Marietta.

"Rebel Lady's Boudoir." *Frank Leslie's Illustrated* 14, no. 342 (1862): 64. Library of Congress, Prints and Photographs Division.

Jacob, the black grave digger. *Harper's New Monthly Magazine* 24, no. 171 (1864): 316. Library of Congress, Prints and Photographs Division.

"A Burial Party, Cold Harbor, Va., April 1865." Library of Congress, Prints and Photographs Division.

Posed "dead" soldiers at Gettysburg, 1863. Library of Congress, Prints and Photographs Division.

"Dr. Burr on the Battlefield." Library of Congress, Prints and Photographs Division.

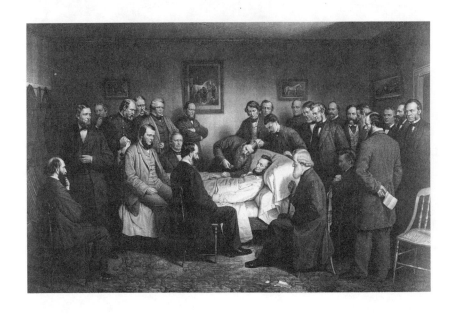

Lithograph of Lincoln deathbed, 1865. Library of Congress, Prints and Photographs Division.

Photograph of Lincoln funeral cortege, Philadelphia, 1865. Library of Congress, Prints and Photographs Division.

Lithograph of Lincoln lying in state at City Hall, New York, 1865. Library of Congress, Prints and Photographs Division.

National Interests

The government never contracted with embalmers for their services, but near the end of the conflict federal regulations were established to scrutinize the work of these new death experts. By the close of the first year of the war, political, military, and religious leaders in the North understood the symbolic value of the dead and claimed to share in the pain of citizens who were losing so many of their close relations. The federal government also came to understand its responsibilities for the physical remains of Union soldiers and began to intervene in their disposal. The North could not simply rely on rhetoric and images that glorified and redeemed the physical sacrifices of northern soldiers; the surfeit of bodies produced by this war required some form of political action. Under these circumstances, the army began to contract with some undertakers to bury the Union dead.

In one contract, signed by Frank T. Sands, an undertaker in the city of Washington, and Edward L. Hartz, assistant quartermaster of the U.S. Army, Sands agreed to bury deceased soldiers "that may die within three miles of the City of Washington, and North of the Potomac River," and for each burial Sands would "receive the Sum of Seven Dollars and Fifty Cents." The contract further stipulated that Sands would prepare the body for burial, furnish necessary coffins that were "well and substantially made, and . . . stained in imitation of Cherry or Walnut"; "dig the grave," which should "not be less than

Five feet, Six inches in depth"; and ensure a "suitable means of transportation to the grave."[1] Other contracts were drawn up between the federal government and various undertakers from such major urban areas as Chicago, Boston, and Cincinnati to provide the dead with the best and most appropriate treatment possible.[2]

But government interest in the dead went beyond hiring undertakers. The level of governmental concern for the dead rose sharply during the war, translating into vast improvements in burials of army personnel compared with previous national conflicts. The War Department issued a series of general orders at various points during the conflict bearing on the dead and the creation of national cemeteries for Civil War soldiers. A policy with respect to military burials had begun to take shape with the Mexican War in the 1840s. Shortly after this conflict, Congress appropriated funds for a cemetery to be established in Mexico City for the reinterment of soldiers' remains. The passage of time had rendered identification of these remains impossible, but more than a decade before the creation of a national cemetery on American soil, the government had taken action to provide for the disposal of American soldiers in a foreign land.[3]

Before the Civil War broke out, the Quartermaster Department had assumed responsibility for handling the military dead without any official directive. According to Erna Risch, historian of the department, from 1775 to the time of the Civil War the quartermaster's office supervised the burial grounds in many of the army posts throughout the nation and provided the material resources, such as coffins and headboards, for the interments.[4] This system of managing the dead at army posts reflected popular attitudes of the time, which required individualized graves and a marked, delineated space for the disposal of corpses; the department kept records as accurate as for the civilian frontier populations. The Mexican War was the first major test of the quartermaster's mortuary responsibilities. The department proved unprepared for the demands of broader warfare and had difficulty arranging and organizing the interment of soldiers.[5]

Within two months of the first battle of Bull Run the War Department realized that the dead from the civil contest — who died on the nation's *own* soil — would require immediate and special attention. Though leaders in the federal government could not predict the coming slaughter, they demonstrated a genuine administrative concern for the disposal of Union soldiers. Of primary importance to the state at this early point was the maintenance of reliable records; military officials wanted to be sure they know who died and where bodies were located. General Order 75, issued on September 11, 1861, commanded the quartermaster general to supply army hospitals with the necessary forms to preserve "accurate and permanent records of deceased soldiers and their place of burial."[6] The order also insisted that headboards be placed on all military graves. In addition, the commanding officer of a military post or company had to transmit any and all mortuary records to the adjutant general at Washington.

Instructions from the state became more complex when the War Department issued another order relating to the appropriate actions the military must take to bury those who died in service of the country. War Department Order 33, released on April 3, 1862, required commanding officers to secure ground "in some suitable spot near every battlefield" for the interment of soldiers. Officers were ordered to procure land as soon as possible and to ensure that thorough records be maintained by the necessary military personnel. Each dead soldier should have a headboard with a number and, "when practicable," a name.[7] Although these orders were rarely observed in the field, the gesture by the War Department at least acknowledged the shortcomings of military policy in past conflicts.

It also led to the establishment of a unit that was critical to many subsequent American conflicts, the Graves Registration Service.[8] Until July 1862, even after such battles as Bull Run, Fort Donelson, and Fair Oaks, the government had no means to purchase land for military cemeteries. Some assistance came from cemetery associations formed in the North, often in conjunction with groups connected to the growing "rural" cemeteries that wanted to do their patriotic duty. These associations either managed the burial grounds themselves or turned over land to the government. But such private efforts were insufficient to the challenge of disposing of bodies in the vicinity of Washington, let alone on southern fields of battle.[9]

Congress turned to the question of burials in July 1862 and authorized that land for a national cemetery could be purchased on the president's command and "securely enclosed . . . for the soldiers who shall die in the service of the country."[10] Twelve such cemeteries were created by the end of the year, located at various forts, near Union camps and hospitals, and on major battlefields. To assist in the organization and management of the dead late in the war, an act of July 4, 1864, officially instructed the Sixth Division of the Quartermaster General's Office to look after the physical remains of Union soldiers. Among other accomplishments during the war, this arm of the government, under the direction of Quartermaster General Montgomery Meigs, created Arlington National Cemetery on Robert E. Lee's old estate across the Potomac. According to Edward Steere, military historian of the Graves Registration Service, "an improvised grave registration unit" operated for the first time in 1864 during a "skirmish at Fort Stevens," where "this unit made a perfect score, identifying every body on the battlefield and correctly registering each grave."[11]

Finally, before the close of the war in April 1865, the United States Army issued General Order 39, which specifically addressed the presence of embalmers in the field and near major Union camps and hospitals. The directive — in effect a government sanction of the practice — stated that all embalming undertakers had to operate under the "special license of the Provost Marshal of the Army, department, or district which the bodies may be." These provost marshals were to decide during which seasons disinterments would occur, distribute licenses only to those individuals who could prove their technological acumen as embalmers, set prices for the service, and take whatever additional action might be necessary for the protection of "the interest of the friends and relatives of deceased soldiers." Each applicant for a license was required to submit "in distinct terms the process adopted by them, materials, length of time its preservative effect can be relied on and such other information as may be necessary to establish their proficiency and success." In addition, the order stipulated that provost marshals could rely on medical directors for assistance in reviewing the applications.[12]

After the war the government assumed responsibility for the burial of all Union soldiers who died during the battles, making sure that as many of them as possible were interred in federally owned national cemeteries. In the name of democracy, liberty, and Christian morality, identifying the remains of individual soldiers and ordering them in an accessible space became national imperatives; the lifeless bodies of "common" soldiers would find a place in the revived social body.[13] Land was appropriated — much of it southern — and permanent grave markers began to be installed in the new cemeteries, often replacing the less durable wooden or cardboard markers erected during the conflict. One of the first sites chosen after the war for a national cemetery was Andersonville prison in Georgia. Seventy others were soon established, and within roughly a decade 299,696 bodies were reinterred in national cemeteries.[14]

The national cemetery at Gettysburg, located near some of the worst fighting in the war, is a portion of the battlefield that was converted for the purpose of reinterring the Union dead within a month of the battle (though not officially turned over to the government for several years). The Pennsylvania governor put David Wills, a Gettysburg attorney, in charge of burying the dead. Wills submitted a report to the state House of Representatives in March 1864 that outlined the steps that were taken in this process. Initially a local cemetery association suggested that, for an agreed-upon price, the dead could be buried in land it owned next to Evergreen Cemetery, close by the battlefield. After this proposal failed to win political support, the same individuals from the association argued that they should maintain "control, supervision, and management" of an enclave within the confines of the larger, established cemetery. This plan was also rejected by state representatives, who were advised by Wills.[15]

Instead the local politicians decided that a separate plot of land under the supervision of a collection of interested states would be used for the establishment of a national cemetery. Wills purchased five lots on Cemetery Hill, situated on "one of the most prominent and important positions on the whole battle field," and consulted with William Saunder, an "eminent landscape gardener," on the layout of the grounds. Next, Wills had to engage a contractor to collect the dead from the field and reinter them in the new cemetery. Thirty-four bids were submitted, ranging from one dollar, fifty-nine cents to eight dollars per body. The lowest bidder was awarded the contract and, according to Wills, performed his duties satisfactorily. Wills gave most of the credit to a Samuel Weaver, who was hired as superintendent of the exhumations. The black laborers who did the physical work of exhuming and reinterring the bodies must also have contributed to the success of this venture.[16]

The most difficult and demanding component of the work was probably identification of the dead. Few of the grave markers used by the soldiers who originally buried these bodies were helpful; when Weaver and his men found unmarked graves, "letters . . . papers, receipts, certificates, diaries, memorandum books, photographs, marks on the clothing, belts, or cartridge boxes" were examined for clues that might lead to proof of the soldier's identity. As Wills observed, however, this unappealing task could yield a poignant reward:

> Words would fail to describe the grateful relief that this work has brought to many a sorrowing household! A father, a brother, a son has been lost on this battle field, *supposed* to be killed, but no tidings whatever have the bereaved friends of him. Suddenly, in the progress of this work, his remains are discovered by sure marks, letters probably, photographs, &c., and they are deposited in a coffin with care, and buried in this very appropriate place. . . . There his grave will be properly cared for and permanently marked. The friends, who have probably written me several letters of inquiry, are immediately informed of the discovery. What a relief from agonizing hope and despair such certain information brings![17]

Weaver also detailed his part in the creation of Gettysburg National Cemetery. In a report submitted to Wills, Weaver wrote that from October 27, 1863, to March 18, 1864, his workers reinterred 3,512 bodies, of which 979 remained nameless and could not be identified even by state. He also cited his determination to oversee every minute detail of the reburial process, claiming that he "saw every body taken out of its temporary resting place" and recorded any and all information that was gathered from the bodies. Even before Weaver began to collect the bodies, many of the graves had apparently been opened by friends and relatives searching the only battlefield located in the North for loved ones. In Weaver's view, some undertakers involved in these disinterments were careless, often leaving "particles of the bones and hair lying scattered around." He made a point of insisting that contractors never engage in such sloppy work and that "every particle of the body [be] gathered up by them."[18]

According to detailed reports from the field, bodies seemed to be better preserved when they were located in clay soil or in marshes. But because the Confederates controlled much of the battlefield at Gettysburg early on in the fighting, the deceased were often left unburied until their comrades could give them a shallow grave or place them in a trench. A body thus exposed to the air rapidly decomposed, leaving nothing but a "dry skeleton." Nonetheless, Weaver concluded, no Confederates were mistakenly identified as Union soldiers. In the course of the reburial process, more than three thousand corpses were examined. Many were ultimately buried in trenches that contained as many as two hundred bodies each.

How did Weaver distinguish between Union and Confederate soldiers? Mainly, he told, by the clothing on the dead soldier's body. If the deceased had a United States coat on, he was probably a northerner, for rebels, unwilling to wear Union colors, typically stole only pantaloons from enemy dead and not their coats. Rebel clothing was also generally made of cotton, while Union soldiers wore wool. The shoes of rebels were also different from those of northern forces. If all of these indicators failed, "then the underclothing was the next part examined." A cotton undershirt proved—to Weaver, at least— that a corpse belonged to the Confederate army. Based on evidence of this sort, Weaver was absolutely certain that no bodies of rebel soldiers had mixed with those of Union heroes.[19]

On November 19, 1863, more than three months after the fighting at Gettysburg, President Abraham Lincoln gave a short address at the dedication of the national cemetery. Surrounded by the living who were witnessing the ceremonies and the dead who had not yet been taken up by Weaver and the black laborers, Lincoln spoke of the obligation to finish what remained undone. His famous speech was an attempt to give meaning to the fighting that was destroying the country and to make sense of the violence, suffering, and death experienced by Union soldiers and northern citizens. Although questions about the nature of government, the abolition of slavery, and reconciliation of the two sides dominated public discussions of the conflict, the number of dead soldiers in hospitals, camps, and battlefields made the costs of war painfully obvious. Lincoln, like so many others during the fighting, knew that the war would have a tremendous impact not only on relations among the living but also on relations between the living and the dead.

10

"Resurrection Days" and Redemptive Blood

During the Civil War, bodies of dead soldiers could not be integrated into the established rituals normally employed by survivors to remove them from the living community. The funeral journey, so ingrained in Protestant culture before the war, was impossible for most soldiers who lost their lives in the conflict. Expiration in the home, surrounded by family members, friends, and neighbors; the final opportunity to view the remains before burial; the solemn procession from the home to the grave; and the careful, attentive rituals of corpse disposal — all of these traditions were shattered when soldiers fell in battle. In spite of enormous obstacles, efforts were made to adapt to the new circumstances and offer the dead as much respect and consideration as possible. Of course, Confederate soldiers who died during the war did not demand the same kind of efforts; these fallen soldiers represented southern degradation and corruption to many in the North. Their bodies were unworthy of any special treatment, and the symbolism of these remains — often demonized and linked to acts of barbarism — served to reaffirm the Union mission.

But whether or not they received "proper" burials by antebellum standards, the dead began to be understood in ways that were appropriate, practical, and emotionally and symbolically satisfying to family members and friends in the North, at the same time they advanced the goals of the federal government. To meet these sometimes incompatible demands, new standards of propriety had to be established for understanding, and undertaking, the obligations toward the dead; most, though not all, of the solutions were linked to the circumstances of war. In addition to the national imagery associated with the war dead, some of the dominant and most familiar symbol systems used by Protestants to make sense of and respond to death during the fighting were connected to the domestic family unit and to personal relationships with Jesus. When bodies could be brought into a familiar ritual setting, either by making the voyage home or through the ceremonies performed in camps and hospitals, the interpretive task for the living was less difficult. Unfortunately, most soldiers who died during the war received a lonely, impersonal burial in southern soil, thus making the imaginative work by survivors to account for their dead more problematic.

The rhetorical strategies for making sense of all the suffering and death had to address a series of conditions that were particular to the Civil War. First, of course, was the matter of sheer numbers: far more Union soldiers lost their lives in this war than in any previous one. Then, too, northerners who died on southern battlefields were far away from their living families, but not so far away that retrieval of their bodies was impossible, at least for those who could afford the great expense. And finally, for the sake of the stability and perpetuation of the Union, the sacrifice of young men would have to continue indefinitely. In order to alleviate the anxieties and grief of northern citizens, religious and political leaders and much of the popular media imaginatively transformed the destruction of life into something heroic; their message inevitably returned to the sacred life of the nation and the promise of a "good death" in the service of the Union.[1]

At the same time, challenges to the patriotic imaginative representations circulated in the North during the war. These counternarratives and alternate interpretations disrupted the dominant collective strategies for constructing meaning and subverted the religious and political justifications for mass sacrifice. Although many citizens — and Union soldiers themselves — linked the bodies littering the battlefields with the destiny and regeneration of the nation, others pursued unconventional interpretive strategies that were based on a conflicting set of interests, experiences, and values. The overwhelming number of bodies on battlefields, in hospitals, and near camps, for example, led to a growing public indifference to the corpse — especially among the combatants themselves. In addition, a new realistic portrait of death, available in photographs, in newspaper stories, and in accounts from many associated with Union medical units, contributed to the ongoing domestication and objectification of the corpse. And finally, in the midst of the slaughter, a new and thoroughly modern death specialist emerged; the embalming undertaker could manipulate the physiological processes of decomposition and preserve the body for the journey north without facing the strong opposition that had been prevalent in antebellum society.

In the domain of Protestant public culture, on the other hand, the symbolic meanings associated with the corpse retained a vital importance to the Union social body. One of the clearest and most authoritative interpretations of the dead during the Civil War was expressed by Abraham Lincoln in the Gettysburg Address. This speech, which has become one of America's most sacred documents, contained many of the themes and images that others used to articulate an understanding of the relation between the dead, the war, and the nation.[2] As Lincoln stood on the ground where Confederates had made their deepest penetration into northern territory, dedicating a portion of the battlefield to the dead, he transfigured the carnage around him into a symbol of northern national unity and the glory of the Union cause. Although many in subsequent generations have felt deep reverence for the document, its worth was debated immediately after it was read. Most observers and reporters praised Lincoln's speech, but others dismissed it as an embarrassment. The *Chicago Times,* for example, wrote that "aside from the ignorant rudeness manifest in the President's exhibition of Daedalism at Gettysburg and which was an insult at least to the memory of part of the dead . . . it was a perversion of history so flagrant that the most extended charity cannot view it otherwise than willful."[3]

In the brief speech Lincoln did not mention the institution of slavery, the recently issued Emancipation Proclamation, or the general direction of the war, and he alluded only once to God. Instead, Lincoln chose to address the reason for the occasion — the burial of the war dead — with language and imagery he hoped was straightforward, meaningful, and reassuring to northern citizens. As the historian Allan Nevins has written, Lincoln had "a duty to say something that might assuage the grief of the kinsfolk of the slain and uplift the spirit of the nation."[4] There is no question that in the few words spoken at Gettysburg, Lincoln succeeded in incorporating the Union dead in the shared history, destiny, and physical landscape of the nation; he also found a practical use for their remains — inspiration for the living to continue fighting and dying.

More important than the deaths of individual soldiers was the life, the rebirth, of the Union, the reconstitution of the fragmented body politic. More than a year after the death of his own son, Willie, who succumbed to disease while battles raged, Lincoln encouraged his fellow citizens to put personal grief aside and strengthen their commitment to the war effort. Sounding a millennial theme that looked both to the past, when a chosen nation was "conceived in liberty," and to the future, when "the great task remaining before us" would lead to the regeneration of that nation, Lincoln made the present violence and bloodshed justifiable and necessary. Lincoln noted that the living must draw inspiration from the dead, not as individual citizens but as Union martyrs. This understanding would help to preserve and uphold the democratic ideals upon which the country was founded and ensure "a new birth of freedom" for citizens throughout the land — presumably regardless of skin color.[5]

The ground of the first national cemetery, Lincoln suggested, was consecrated not because of any inherent value in the land, nor because of any discursive manipulations wrought by his words or the words of other speakers. Rather, the straightforward acts of Union soldiers who prevented a Confederate victory — and the presence of the remains of those men who died in this noble cause — transformed the soil at Gettysburg. Lincoln's reference to "what they did here" was double-edged: the soldiers fought to save the Union, but they also lost their own lives in the effort. While he may have thought that the words commemorating their struggle would soon be forgotten, Lincoln realized that a national cemetery on Union soil would inscribe their sacrifice into national space as well as collective memory.

As the historian Garry Wills notes, Lincoln's address drew from nature imagery associated with the "rural" cemeteries that had grown in popularity in the northeast before the war. In addition to the biblical language and classical rhetorical style, the speech was characterized by a natural symbolism that linked the placement of the dead in nature with a new form of pedagogy. The language of nature in this setting, what Wills identified as "Lincoln's fertility-language of conception and rebirth," evoked a range of emotions and images, often relating to moral development, societal regeneration, and spiritual renewal. Although individualized monuments testifying to personal or familial achievements were absent here, the entire space of the cemetery communicated the message that collective sacrifice could rehabilitate the broken, divided nation. But the natural imagery was critical to the message, as Wills points out: "In the context of rural-cemetery rituals, the contrasts [in the text] are those mediated by nature — life springing from death, from the soil, in the circle of seasons."[6]

In the Gettysburg Address, Lincoln acknowledged the national debt the living owed to the dead. While the latter had attained immortality through their sacrifice and as objects of collective memory, for Lincoln it was up to the survivors to "take increased devotion to that cause for which they gave the last full measure of devotion." He did not praise individual heroes, or single out any units that had demonstrated truly exceptional courage; all were united as the silent dead who "gave their lives that that nation might live." The public's veneration of the fallen soldiers depended not on how they imagined the spiritual condition of their souls, nor was it based on a belief that they communed with God in heaven; the honor of the living resulted from the material presence of the dead in a delineated, purified national space on the field of battle. But it also depended on the future victory of Union forces. Only with that idea in mind could the exchange of blood for ideology, human life for political meaning be viably negotiated.[7]

Other northern Protestant leaders and spokespersons, like Lincoln, stressed the millennial nature of the conflict over the political — or, more accurately, understood the political crisis in theological terms. The dead and wounded were devastated by a conflict that was larger than the sectional fighting engulfing the land. In this interpretive context, Protestants subsumed individual deaths within a larger cosmic framework and understood the blood of slaughtered soldiers as a sign for past sins and future glories. The American historian James H. Moorhead notes that the war "reinvigorated the jeremiadic tradition" and that many religious observers saw the wrathful judgment of God, as well as the possibility for purification, at work in the conflict.[8] The cultural critics of the period believed that the country had broken its covenant with God and the price for the nation's sins, which included violating the Sabbath, intemperance, lack of discipline, material greed, and most importantly the toleration of slavery, was being paid for with the lives of both northern and southern soldiers.

Many in the North also believed that the nation was involved in an apocalyptic battle of epic proportions. This battle had consequences not simply for the future of the United States, but for the salvation of the world. Millennial ideas about progress, the coming Kingdom of Christ, and America's role in the destiny of the world did not diminish as a result of the terrible destruction of the war but grew in symbolic potency. In the midst of suffering and death, sinfulness and degeneration, northern Protestant leaders found cause for optimism and hope. In a discourse near the end of the war W. H. Furness, a leading Unitarian minister, articulated the belief that with proper religious reform the consequences of the war would yield profound spiritual benefits beyond national boundaries: "We all have faith that the giant curse is to be removed from the land. But, friends, this is but the beginning of the good that will come. . . . The imagination cannot begin to depict the glories of the new Era which will open upon Christendom, let this revolution have its rightful termination, as we have faith now that it will."[9]

Whatever future glories were promised to the nation as moral leader of the world and prime instigator of "the coming of the Lord," many understood and agreed with the equation being offered in northern public culture: the price for regeneration and remission of sins was to be paid in blood. No one expressed the urgency and gravity of this exchange better than the evangelical Congregationalist Horace Bushnell. Bushnell decried the Enlightenment ideals found in the Declaration of Independence and lamented the absence of clear moral and religious principles in American government. For him the war signaled both God's disapproval with the direction of the country and the need to return to more traditional forms of religious authority. After the first battle of Bull Run in 1861, Bushnell warned his listeners of the sacrifices that would be necessary to correct the nation's faults in forceful language that was as graphic as it was compelling. "Without shedding of blood there is no such grace prepared. There must be reverses and losses, and time of deep concern. There must be tears in the houses, as well as blood in the fields; the fathers and mothers, the wives and dear children, coming into woe, to fight in hard bewailings. . . . In these and all such terrible throes, the true loyalty is born. Then the nation emerges, at last, a true nation, consecrated and made great in our eyes by the sacrifices it has cost."[10]

Even members of the theologically liberal New England Transcendentalists used an orthodox imaginative strategy similar to that found in the speeches of evangelicals like Bushnell for understanding the meaning of the violence, suffering, and death brought on by the war. Such Transcendentalist figures as Channing, James Freeman Clarke, and Cyrus A. Bartol identified the nation's sinfulness as a primary cause for the fighting and proposed that the sacrifice of human life was the only way to atone for these sins. Purification and salvation — again, for the world as well as the nation — would be enacted through a baptism of blood.[11] Emerson himself voiced a disturbing though prevalent view that a human slaughter might bring positive, moral revitalization to the country. In a letter to the parents of a Union soldier who died fighting the southern enemy, Emerson wrote that "one whole generation might well consent to perish, if by their fall, political liberty & clean & just life could be made sure to the generations that follow."[12]

The logic of this equation was as simple as it was unavoidable in the Protestant imagination. Many religious and political leaders in the North instructed their brethren to remain steadfast and calm in their confrontation with violence and mass death, and never to lose sight of the larger issues at stake. Even as the bodies of loved ones were being left uncared for or haphazardly buried on southern battlefields, many asserted that the virtuous nature of the Union effort — equal in gravity to the revolutionary cause that had brought the country into existence — transformed the dead into national heroes and ensured victory for the northern forces. As Byron Sunderland affirmed in his sermon at the First Presbyterian Church in Washington on the observation of National Fast, April 30, 1863:

> [T]he same power that brought our fathers through the bloody baptism of the Revolution, and gave to them, to bequeath to us, their children, this glorious inheritance, will thunder for us along all our lines of battle, and put our enemies to rout and confusion forever. . . . We cannot any longer trifle before God. These are days of sacrifice — the days of heroic suffering — the days of many and most noble martyrdoms. . . . Let us compose and prepare ourselves for the sacrifice; let us look defeat, disaster, and even death, if need be, steadily and calmly in the face.[13]

The language of martyrdom, of tremendous numbers of sacrificed soldiers suffering a noble death for a just cause, in part served to compensate for — if not entirely erase — the material reality of the majority of bodies left unattended or given minimal ceremonies in the South. Looking at the "sublime whole" rather than the individual tragedy — a young soldier dying of diarrhea in a Union hospital, a mortally wounded officer expiring on a field of battle, a corpse left rotting and unburied on southern soil — focused the northern population on abstract principles and national ideals.[14] Conceptualizing the dead as a monolithic totality was useful to the rhetoric of societal redemption and the symbolism of Union religious nationalism; it also allowed the bodies of soldiers to be reimagined according to a different set of principles and ideals than those that were dominant in northern society during the antebellum period.

Once again the words of Bushnell illustrate the point. In an address given shortly after the end of the war, he discussed the meaning of the dead and the nation's "obligations" to them. The blood of the war dead not only demanded that the country "see that every vestige of slavery is swept clean," it also "cemented and forever sanctified" national unity. While the dead contributed to the birth of a new age in history and a renewed commitment to Jesus, Bushnell realized and asserted that they were also the pillars at the foundation of American nationhood.[15] In many ways for Bushnell the organic life of the nation required the destruction of human life; the spiritual bonds of nationhood relied on the real, material blood of individual soldier-martyrs.

Octavius Frothingham, an antislavery minister in Boston, expressed the linkage between soldier-martyrs and national enrichment in a sermon preached early in the war. In Frothingham's theological reading, dying soldiers were like seedlings from plants that were "dropped or thrown out by the breaking of the shell, to take root in the earth and reproduce their kind." In one of the few sermons that specifically addressed the question of the corpse, Frothingham's natural symbolism echoed the rhetoric of those antebellum burial reformers who sought to legitimate the "rural" cemetery. But, like Lincoln and Bushnell, he made the connection between the dead in American soil and the strengthening and rejuvenation of national character more explicit, arguing that the "Spirit of Liberty" is nourished by the blood of Union soldiers soaking the physical landscape.

> These deaths of noble young men in battle, which, on our first hearing of them, make us shudder so and ask why this dreadful waste of life, are the snapping open of so many brave caskets, and the dropping into the fruitful soil of humanity of the quick seeds of a new national and human life. . . . These are the great resurrection days of American character; and there is no resurrection without a grave. The Spirit of Liberty is increasing in power and truth, and the volume of it, the purity of it, are swelled by the souls of these young martyrs, who give their dust to the dust whence it came, and their life to the country whose ideas were its sustenance and inspiration.[16]

Interpretations that subsumed individual deaths into a larger perspective that encompassed national and world history dominated the public arena and the speeches of many northern Protestant leaders. But in spite of the endeavor to keep northern citizens focused on the heroism and the sacrifices of the collective Union forces, there was a countervailing tendency to remember, personalize, and glorify the deaths of single individuals as well. While establishing images of the sublime whole, many northern Protestants fixed also on individual soldiers who were losing their lives to save the Union — an effort to locate noble sacrifices in real flesh-and-blood examples of individual heroes who died illustrious, patriotic, Christian deaths. The sentimentalization of death, so strong and persistent in the antebellum period, found reinforcement in personal accounts of redemptive deaths described in newspapers, letters and diaries, and songs and poems.

Whether or not the martyr was explicitly compared to Jesus or simply characterized as dying a Christian death, the glorification of a soldier's demise often hinged on perceptions of his courage and spiritual preparedness, especially early in the war. For the survivors back home this was particularly important and could have a bearing on the emotional response to the news of a close relation's death. In the words of one historian, "If the soldiers were sent home dead — or, more likely, buried where they fell — those at home hoped desperately for last words that would confirm that their soldier had preserved his decency. The dying were most concerned to fix their courage, but families were equally anxious for reassurance of the soldier's purity."[17] Perhaps the worst possible fear for soldiers and citizens with loved ones in uniform was a sudden and anonymous death, with no one to record heroic last acts or pious last words. Most of the soldiers fighting in this war were raised in a culture that valued the presence of close friends and relations when someone made the transition from life to death. In the midst of battle, soldiers could be killed in an instant and left on the field while their comrades continued fighting; or, if wounded, they might be abandoned and left for dead as others fought for their own survival.

For these reasons dying in hospitals sometimes offered soldiers a greater degree of solace. These institutions served as important sites for death because witnesses, particularly nurses, were available to see how a soldier died, comfort him and assist in his spiritual preparation, and, if possible, assuage his fears with encouragement about the triumphant Christian death to come. Although women had begun to lose their intimacy with the dead in the decade before the war broke out, some found themselves in an especially important relationship with the dying as nurses during the war years.[18] Thanks to the efforts of Dorothea Dix, appointed superintendent of female nurses in 1861, Clara Barton, instrumental in the creation of the American Red Cross, and various women working with the Christian and Sanitary commissions, nursing became a highly respectable and valued profession in America during the Civil War.[19]

In addition to the critical medical assistance they provided, nurses also fulfilled the role of surrogate mothers to wounded and dying soldiers. Under these circumstances, nurses who comforted and cared for soldiers in field hospitals frequently gave expression to an interpretation of death that was different from the predominant millennial views espoused by many politicians and clergymen in the North. Their close interaction with the dying, and with bodies violently transformed by the circumstances of war, did not always offer them a vision of the sublime whole and national salvation. Surrounded by some of the most graphic reminders of the war — amputated limbs, maggot-filled wounds, and lifeless corpses — nurses often viewed the suffering and mortality in individualized, personal terms that remembered each soldier's dignity and valor.

Many of the nurses who recorded their observations and thoughts during the war paid more attention to stories of individual suffering and death than to the cosmic implications of the battle. As one biographer of Clara Barton remarked, "She was too busy to note each day's events in the small pocket diaries she always carried with her, but they are filled with the names of dying men and last messages, each one too precious at that instant to be overshadowed by the larger reality of war."[20] In the middle of the destruction, images of the good death were invoked by many nurses. Rather than gloss over the individual loss of life or focus on the anonymity of a battlefield strewn with corpses, many women expressed a sensibility that valorized dying soldiers' private sufferings and employed a combination of familial and Christian imagery to convey martial courage, Union patriotism, and spiritual redemption.

In *Hospital Sketches* (1863), a volume based on letters written during her brief time as an army nurse, Louisa May Alcott described life and death in military hospitals. Alcott highlighted a vision of death that brought the individual Union soldier into the foreground; by domesticating, personalizing, and beautifying specific cases of wounded soldiers who expired in her company, Alcott reminded her readers of the northern, Christian virtues that could be found in the transition out of life — even in the most horrific circumstances. In her account of a soldier laid in state, Alcott, like Stowe before her, emphasized both the tender affections aroused by those who knew the deceased and the therapeutic benefits of viewing and having contact with the corpse:

> But a universal sentiment of reverence and affection seemed to fill the hearts of all who had known or heard of him; and when the rumor of his death went through the house, always astir, many came to see him, and I felt a tender sort of pride in my lost patient; for he looked a most heroic figure, lying there stately and still as the statue of some knight asleep upon his tomb. The lovely expression which so often beautifies dead faces, soon replaced the marks of pain, and I longed for those who loved him best to see him when half an hour's acquaintance with Death had made them friends. . . . After I had cut some brown locks for his mother, and taken off the ring to send her . . . I kissed this good son for her sake.[21]

The impulse to sentimentalize death, to envision order and beauty in what was clearly a chaotic and repulsive set of circumstances, was not limited to the imagination of women nurses. Soldiers themselves attempted to gloss over the scenes in front of them and convey spiritual victory in the face of bodily devastation. A soldier dying of diarrhea wrote home to his wife that he was prepared to die and eager to see her in heaven. While it is difficult to ascertain the degree of this soldier's religious convictions before entering the war, he asserted that "religion seems more precious and valuable to me now than ever before" and that he had "no doubts about heaven." In spite of his physical ailments, he did his best to maintain a calm and optimistic disposition: "I never felt so happy before. All is bright and clear." Even concerns about the fate of his body after death were expressed with a seeming nonchalance. "If you choose, come and take my remains home."[22]

The promise of heaven was a constant source of hope and optimism for many survivors and dying soldiers. Instead of the regeneration of the nation, the turn toward heaven provided a valuable form of encouragement and consolation for many Protestants affected by the ravages of the war. The belief in the afterlife — and that the soul or spirit immediately ascends there while the body remains here on earth — was expressed in a variety of contexts, including letters, diaries, war songs and poems, and journal articles. In a column of the Methodist journal, *Zion's Herald,* for example, a woman related her response after receiving the sad news that her brother died in a recent battle. Although her brother was now absent from all those who loved him and had been buried on a southern battlefield, the sister would not feel sadness: "And though I love that brave manly form that now lies mouldering in dust, I will not sorrow for him. For though his body lies low in the grave, his spirit lives in heaven."[23]

The strategy of countering mass, anonymous death with individual stories and testaments of heroism and/or promised spiritual rewards found institutional expression in the United States Christian Commission. The initial motivation for this organization came from the Young Men's Christian Commission in the summer of 1861; throughout the course of the war, however, it grew into a broad, interdenominational volunteer operation. Although the volunteers performed some military assignments, they were primarily concerned with the spiritual status of the soldiers and engaged in activities that promoted an evangelical agenda. Their activities included distributing religious tracts and bibles, working revival meetings in camps, writing letters home for the wounded and dying or to notify families of a loved one's death, and preparing soldiers for their own death.

The presence of death and a keen awareness of the possible ways of dying in this conflict — sometimes suddenly, often accompanied with excruciating pain, and generally without the consolation of burial rituals — frequently made the task of conversion easier for volunteers of the commission. On the one hand, part of its mission was to increase the number of identifiable Christian soldier-martyrs who would contribute to the redemption of the nation; on the other hand, commission members also tried to remind them that their own spiritual trajectory in the next life depended on their immediate decision for or against Jesus in this one. Regardless of the emphasis placed on individual cases, however, numerous accounts of deathbed conversions and the apparent successes of revivals in northern armies assisted in the overall legitimation and perceived righteousness of the Union cause throughout the war.[24]

Protestants in the commission remained focused primarily on addressing the spiritual needs of individuals, especially because these individuals were constantly confronted with the reality of their own impending death. In a pastoral letter presented at the Massachusetts General Association of Congregationalist Churches in June of 1864, the institutional imperative for the spiritual care of Union soldiers was clearly articulated:

And, dear brethren, let us never forget, that the soldier's claims on us are *high and peculiar*. . . . All we have his valor makes our own. And, oh, at how stern a sacrifice! Every endurance on the field and in the hospital, every torture in the rebel prison, life itself, — this is the cost to him. The man who dies for us! Can the claims of any other be compared with his? Passing in a moment away, shedding his blood for us, are we not solemnly bound, if we can, to make sure that for the soldier the precious blood of Jesus shall avail in the last solemn day?[25]

The sentimental ethos that pervaded most discussions of the work of the commission and many accounts of dying and dead soldiers was animated by a triad of symbols: Jesus, country, and home. This constellation of images and ideas was firmly entrenched in the imagination of many Protestant soldiers, and of their relatives and friends in the North; the commission and its members sought to ensure that no death occurred without an appropriate link to this trinity. Each one of these terms resonated with citizens and soldiers, and all worked together to disguise the violence enacted on individual bodies. Protestant culture in both the antebellum period and during the war was saturated with biblical symbolism and assertions about the saving power of Jesus. As we have seen, the relation between national destiny and Christian ideology was confirmed and clarified during the course of the war. And while the rhetoric produced by this fusion of symbol systems justified the spilling of blood and sacrifice of large numbers of northern men, the final element in the sentimental trinity — home — contributed to the personal and familiar face of death and consoled both dying soldiers and grieving survivors.

Home could mean many things to Union soldiers; it clearly had popular appeal as a feminized symbol, frequently associated with women and set against the masculine world of war. Sometimes it was represented by a wife, occasionally by a sister, but most commonly it was as a mother that home became a routine symbol in the death imagery surrounding the fallen Union soldiers. References to the kind and loving presence of "dear mom" served a reassuring and morally significant function for soldiers who were far away from home and constantly in danger — not only of physical death but of the corrupting influences of army life.[26] The few women that soldiers encountered during their fighting — primarily nurses in hospitals — served as substitutes for the moralizing, comforting, and spiritually nurturing mothers who were absent from their lives during their tenure in the army. In songs, poems, and letters the reverence and humility evoked by an imagined maternal figure indicated an unwillingness to give oneself over to the "national family" completely. The presence and memory of individual mothers, as embodiments of the safety and security of home, contributed to the symbolic counteroffensive against meaningless, chaotic death. One member of the Christian Commission spoke of this sentiment in an address delivered at a Washington conference in February, 1864:

> O, mothers who are here to-night, let me say to you that whatever else a soldier forgets, he never, *never*, NEVER forgets his mother. And I will tell you, my friends, that is one of the things I have noticed in an American army that I believe is a great characteristic of the American heart, that it cling to home and mother. I have stood by the cot of a dying soldier, and stooping down to catch his last breath, have heard him whisper 'mother.' I remember passing over a battle-field and seeing a man just dying. . . . I stood and looked upon the poor fellow. A smile passed over his face — a smile, O, of so much sweetness, as, looking up, he said, 'O mother, O mother! I am *so* glad you have come.' . . . He turned over and passed sweetly to his rest, and he was borne up to the presence of God on the wings of a pious mother's prayers.[27]

The desire to find death meaningful under war conditions relied on this symbolic triad of Jesus, country, and home. For death to be "good," to be "triumphant," to work the moral regeneration of the country, it had to be linked to one, two, or all three of these symbols in the collective Protestant imagination. The apparent contradiction between the sublime whole and the sentimental death of the individual — two of the predominant interpretive strategies employed by northern Protestants during the conflict — was resolved in the appropriation and utilization of this symbol system. Soldiers and civilians alike could draw from the reservoir of familiar messages and images that were suggested by each symbol in the triad and reconsider their understanding of all the destruction and death.

Because corpses were not receiving the careful attention they had previously and because their treatment was based on principles of expediency, routinization, and military victory, the living fixed the imagined spiritual destiny of Union soldiers on a different sort of "solid ground" — either in the comfort of a heavenly home or the security of a regenerated nation. To look at the carnage without recourse to these options could threaten morale, lead to despair, or, what many considered worse, cause uncertainty about the effectiveness of the Union effort. Yet many were affected by the scenes of destruction and the loss of life in ways that challenged those very strategies that were considered so instrumental to Union success. These people, many of whom exhibited an abiding commitment to the northern cause, could no longer fall back on older models or authoritative, institutionalized directives for understanding the significance of death and the meaning of the corpse.

11

Disenchantment with the Mortal Remains

As William Gable's letters revealed, encounters with the dead on and off the battlefield did not always lead to an appreciation of the "resurrection days" for the American spirit, nor did they necessarily lead to consoling thoughts of domestic security and Christian triumph. Instead, Gable and many others divested the body of all emotional and symbolic significance; they began to feel increasingly indifferent to the mortal remains and unlikely to draw meaning from them. The condition of Union corpses and the hurried, pragmatic manner in which they were buried forced many northern Protestants to modify traditional categories of understanding death and to alter conventional standards of communal responsibility in their disposal. Compared with his refusal to touch a dead body before the war — an indication of the liminal, overdetermined status it had for him then — Gable learned to treat the physical remains of his comrades during the war as nothing more than "sticks of wood."

For some people the Civil War diffused the shock value of the corpse and restructured its meaning in ways that were antithetical to notions of sacrifice and regeneration, of triumph and redemption. The barrage of severed limbs, lifeless bodies, and anonymous graves accelerated the turn away from the spiritual significations of the corruptible body and toward a greater admiration for emotional and intellectual detachment from it. Instead of emphasizing the life of the spirit, the memory of the deceased, or the glory of the Union cause, imaginative and emotional disengagement from the sight of the dead body had pragmatic value. This kind of response, however, which essentially demolished the religious symbolic edifice constructed around the corpse, was not unique to the Civil War. It had roots in the Enlightenment and could be distinguished in the antebellum period, when the inclination to link death with natural processes—what James Farrell associated with the rise of "scientific naturalism"—was one expression of the tendency to deflate theological readings of the corpse.[1]

Over the course of the Civil War the adoption of a detached, unemotional attitude toward the physical remains of the dead became a reasonable, some would argue even patriotic, sensibility. As the Civil War historian Reid Mitchell points out, the process of growing "hardened" by the war experience "also included becoming accustomed to death and violence."[2] Whether or not soldiers believed that the spirits of their fallen companions survived while their uniformed bodies began to decompose, whether they thought that human blood enriched the spiritual life of the nation, for some the sight of corpses simply did not engage the imagination or the emotions at all. Instead, severing the body from any spiritual and symbolic associations allowed the machine of war to operate more smoothly and efficiently. When a soldier grew inured to the gruesome scenes of death on and near battlefields, he was less likely to be distracted from his primary duty: destroying the Confederate army.

Some northerners who witnessed the fighting, of course, were able to maintain a perspective that fell somewhere between pious veneration and utter disregard in the face of death and physical suffering. Confronting scenes of death and destruction in such a politically significant moment of national history led them to find a way to imaginatively reconcile the two extremes by expressing an "engaged indifference" toward the victims of war. For these individuals it was counterproductive to become too emotionally invested in the dead, but they nonetheless demonstrated a genuine concern about the loss of life—if only because the fate of the Union hung in the balance. This vision of battlefield carnage emphasized collective suffering over individual sacrifice, and although the degree of human wreckage aroused anguish and bewilderment, the observer would not succumb to the emotional weight of such scenes.

Robert McAllister, the general from New Jersey, was involved in the fighting around Spotsylvania Court House in Virginia during the winter of 1863–1864. In seven days of fighting, which included the battles in the Wilderness and near the court house, the Army of the Potomac suffered severe losses. McAllister's brigade became embroiled in the infamous conflict at "Bloody Angle"—fourteen hours of what the historian James McPherson has called "some of the war's most horrific fighting," including one of the few outbreaks of hand-to-hand combat.[3] In a letter home a few days after the battle McAllister wrote to his family: "We lost very heavily; the North will be in mourning. . . . I have never witnessed such scenes. At a point where I stood for at least 14 hours, urging the men forward and to stand firm, the slaughter was terable. . . . Such a sheet of fire and storm of leaden hail the historian has never yet recorded."[4]

McAllister's steady and composed description demonstrated a combination of restraint and wonder at what he had witnessed. The distant "point" from which he gave orders and viewed the fighting — a common position for officers and other elites during the war — allowed him to be both dispassionately removed from and intimately involved with what transpired. Those who beheld the spectacle of battle and its aftermath from afar often assumed a more imperturbable disregard for the state of the dead. While soldiers and nurses might adopt this attitude because of their close contact with actual corpses, many Protestant leaders in the North who remained focused on the sublime whole frequently displayed an ambivalent reaction to the sufferings of their fellow citizens. The knowledge that large numbers of Union men lost their lives on the fields of battle could be tolerated with the slightest disruption in emotional composure when the imagination remained fixed on more pressing issues, such as national destiny and military prowess.

Emerson's sympathy with the suffering of others hardened and grew subservient to the necessity for national moral regeneration, even though he remained compassionate toward those soldiers who were in pain. Nathaniel Hawthorne, who seemed to have a more complex and critical response to the sectional conflict than many of his famous contemporaries in the North, appreciated the consequences resulting from the exaltation of the nation over the lives of individual soldiers.[5] In one letter Hawthorne wrote, "Who cares what the war costs, in blood or treasure? People must die, whether a bullet kills them or no. . . . Emerson is a breathing slaughter, like the rest of us; and it is really wonderful how all sorts of theoretical nonsense, to which we New Englanders are addicted in peaceful times, vanish in the strong atmosphere which we now inhale."[6] As the war continued and the death tolls climbed higher, the necessity of crushing the South overshadowed all the humane considerations associated with individual Union soldiers dying in camps and hospitals and on battlefields.

In contrast to those who were comforted by religious discourse, or to those who could maintain distance from the carnage while still committed to the Union cause, many soldiers grew emotionally numb to the suffering and death going on around them and disenchanted with traditional responses that made such common scenes bearable. The tone of soldiers' letters, so optimistic and full of hope in the early part of the war, tended to demonstrate greater cynicism and insensitivity as the war dragged on. Notions of courage, valor, and even sacrifice gradually became subverted by the unrelenting fear of one's own death, the likely prospect of dying anonymously, and the possibility that one's body would be abandoned on southern soil. The duration of the war and the length of service in the Union army inured some soldiers to the horrors of war; what many others had interpreted as glorious and redeeming was seen by these soldiers as simply the profane excess of the business of war.[7]

Messages from the government, ranking officers, and relations back home about the urgency of saving the Union, combined with ugly, brutal scenes of human destruction, contributed to the general disenchantment with death among many of the soldiers doing the fighting. Soldiers self-consciously referred to their changing attitudes toward the sights and sounds of death in their diaries and letters home. Oliver Wendall Holmes Jr. mentioned his own acquired "aristocratic" sensibility that resulted from the frequent exposure to the surfeit of bodies on battlefields and in hospitals: "But it's odd how indifferent one gets to the sight of death — perhaps, because one gets aristocratic and don't value much a common life — Then they are apt to be so dirty it seems natural — 'Dust to Dust' — I would do anything that lay in my power but it doesn't much affect my feelings."[8] Elisha Hunt Rhodes conveyed a similar perspective after witnessing one of many military burials, writing that "death is so common that little sentiment is wasted. It is not like death at home."[9]

Just as troop movements, control of the battlefield, and position of the enemy could determine the level of attention paid to the corpse, the imaginative involvement in the dead grew increasingly subordinate to military considerations and issues of individual survival. Rather than initiate a process through which an individual discovered some profound spiritual or moral truth, the sight of the dead only heightened awareness of the dangers at hand. When Napolean Radcliffe, fighting with the Army of the Potomac near Antietam Creek in September 1862, came upon an open field full of the dead and wounded, he wrote that he "did not mind it anymore than if no one was there, stepping over dead & wounded as I would over a log; I had too much to think about shot & shells."[10]

Insensitivity to the realities of death and human devastation was often couched in gendered language during the war.[11] Notions of self-discipline and courage circulating throughout the camps as well as in the print media set up a dichotomy between the masculine strength of soldiers in the field and the feminine vulnerabilities of women in the domestic realm back home. According to many observers in the North, these two characteristics had to be separated — even with regard to death — if the Union was to achieve victory. In fact, the very presence of death, and the common displays of human suffering and bodies destroyed by disease and Confederate guns, were believed to eradicate any trace of feminine sensibilities. One reporter from *Leslie's Illustrated* described a scene of a Union camp graveyard. In the course of his article he made a point of reassuring readers that the soldiers' familiarity with death did not make them less masculine nor willing to die. Rather than engendering a "sepulchral gloom," the prevalence of death "rubbed that fine sentimental and womanly enamel from their hearts, and they stand ready to take their places in the same spot at the call of duty."[12]

The imaginative and emotional detachment from the dead was reinforced by another wartime benevolent association that, although frequently working in conjunction with the Christian Commission, exhibited striking philosophical and ideological differences with the popular religious organization. Established early in the war, the United States Sanitary Commission, like the Christian Commission, depended greatly on women working the fields of battle; indeed, what Lincoln referred to as the "fifth wheel to the coach" grew out of the Women's Central Association of Relief for the Sick and Wounded of the Army. But with institutional legitimacy came a decided paternalism that reflected the elitist, conservative ideas of its ranking male members. Henry Bellows, George Templeton Strong, and Frederick Law Olmstead, New York aristocrats who ran the commission, valorized military discipline over softhearted humanitarian rhetoric.[13] At the heart of their patriotic agenda was the obligation to ensure that there were strong, healthy male bodies available to the federal forces who could destroy the South — or die trying.

The Christian Commission's primary goal was the salvation of souls. The Sanitary Commission, on the other hand, made questions about soldiers' spiritual condition secondary to the immediate national objective: military victory. And leaders in the commission realized that the most practical way to improve the military machine was to improve the health and hygiene of individual soldiers animating it. While the enterprise to mobilize around the physical well-being of Union soldiers and supplement the work of the Army Medical Bureau was initially resisted by some in the military, the Sanitary Commission soon became a crucial and highly appreciated volunteer relief agency. By coordinating the activities of civilians, raising money at "sanitary fairs," and distributing everything from food and clothing to medical supplies and hospital boats, the commission eventually became a powerhouse in governmental politics and a model of government efficiency in a time of crisis.[14]

As the historian George Fredrickson has observed, though, the organization's ideology was "from the outset . . . not concerned with the relief of suffering as an end in itself. . . . Brutally stated, this meant that the commission saved the soldier in the hospital so that he could die a useful death on the battlefield."[15] The commission assumed that the highest patriotic duty it could perform, one that would be remembered with honor and distinction by the American public, related to its ability to make sure that the soldiers who literally gave their physical bodies to the perpetuation of the body politic were healthy, strong, and disciplined. Indeed, maintaining the health of Union soldiers who might ultimately be cut down by a sniper's bullet or buried in a ditch did not signal a humanitarian act of compassion and benevolence. It was rather a civic duty of the highest order. *The Soldier's Friend,* a pamphlet distributed by the commission during the war, articulated this perspective: "What the people have thus far done for their soldiers will long be held in honorable remembrance as a magnificent National act, not only of humanity and charity, but of Patriotism also, for by preventing disease and speeding convalescence, it has materially strengthened the National forces, contributed to the success of the National cause, and added a certain number of thousand bayonets to the available strength of the Army during every month of the past two years."[16]

The meaning of death and the emotional reaction to it had to be modified if the commission was to achieve its goal. Those who worked for the commission advocated a disciplined disinterest in dead bodies and a regimented pragmatism in their disposal. Any sentimental affection or pious reverence shown to the physical remains, they thought, could detract from the work of the living and thus endanger the larger Union goal. This attitude did not represent an absence of concern for the spirit of a fallen soldier, only a subjugation of the symbolism and treatment of the corpse to the ordered regulation of military practice. In *The Soldier's Friend,* hymns that glorified the spirit in heaven after a noble death were only a few pages removed from a section titled "The Dead." Here the mortuary duties of agents working for the Sanitary Commission were spelled out — burying the dead with proper markers, keeping accurate records, and so on. The commission also realistically assessed the difficulties posed by the conditions of war: "This [burial] cannot be done systematically with a moving campaign, but at Post hospitals, &c, it is done wherever practible."[17]

In the field camp and general hospitals many nurses and doctors assumed this attitude by closing themselves off emotionally from the carnage surrounding them and the pain exhibited by Union soldiers. At a time when amputation was the favored procedure for many bullet wounds and castor oil and calomel the standard approach to dysentery, these individuals were confronted with some of the worst scenes of human suffering in American history. The degree of physical torment experienced by sick and wounded soldiers and the unsophisticated medical techniques used in the treatment of injury and disease demanded an emotional disengagement so that the endeavor to heal them, or relocate their remains after life had expired, could be carried out as routinely as possible. Many thought that only with the most stoic, dispassionate, even dehumanized sensibility could they meet the task of tending the destruction of human bodies.

Katherine Prescott Wormeley, working with the Sanitary Commission during the Peninsula Campaign of 1862, expressed the hard-hearted realism she found necessary for optimum efficiency in the medical corps: "We are here with health, strength, and *head*. To think or speak of the things we see here would be fatal. No one must come here who cannot put away all feelings. Do all you can and be a machine—that's the way to act; the only way."[18] As Fredrickson suggests, the long-term cultural significance of this attitude—legitimated and encouraged by the national government and the medical community—also called into question dominant humanitarian values entrenched in political and religious discourse before the war.[19] Rational, systematic, and utilitarian actions in the service of the Union began to take precedence over the merciful, soul-serving actions of many benevolent volunteer associations.

By focusing on the sanitary conditions of army life and the vitality of individual soldiers, many commission officers, surgeons, and nurses tried to make death as prosaic and uneventful as possible. This is not to say that they and others who sought to detach themselves from the corpse were irreverent or disrespectful. If they were religious they simply did not imagine that the soul could be associated with the carnage on the battlefield. Beliefs about the soul, as we have seen, depended on a series of symbolic clusters and recurring themes drawn from Christianity, national history, and the memories of family and friends. The corpse, on the other hand, was an inevitable product of war that lost all of its symbolic value as soon as the "vital spark" had escaped. Under these circumstances, the federal government, doctors and nurses, and many soldiers attempted to move the bodies of the dead to a predictable, ordered environment. Burial assignment determined which men would be on the front lines of that environment, managing their fallen comrades.

Burial duty, as outlined earlier, was an odious charge that aroused feelings of indignation and resentment. As the Civil War historian James I. Robertson Jr. writes, "the gruesome and nauseous job was done with haste rather than reverence."[20] Many of those on burial detail had neither the time nor inclination to ponder the relation between the body and the spirit; they were either too pressed or too sickened by the conditions of the dead to engage in spiritual contemplation. Unless they were from the same unit as the dead or knew who they were burying, these soldiers saw their work as a necessary but unfortunate responsibility they were stuck with. Perhaps that is one reason why there was no resistance to assigning burial detail to African Americans, who were often employed by the Union armies as manual laborers to dig trenches, construct fortifications, and build latrines. Although this may at first be taken as a sign of rudimentary acceptance of blacks by white soldiers, it may in fact simply indicate a lack of concern with the fate of the dead and increasing indifference to the treatment of corpses. That blacks were involved in handling some of the dead when federal forces controlled the field after a battle or when fallen soldiers were reinterred in national cemeteries reflected the decline in symbolic value of the physical remains of fighting men for many northern Protestants.

For many during the war the human form became insignificant when it ceased to function as an embodiment of Union ideology. Even an amputee had the potential to instill feelings of patriotism and righteousness among the living who viewed his scarred body. The corpse, on the other hand, became a sign of failure and vulnerability and was, to many, incapable of any symbolic recuperation. This is one reason why the collective integration of the dead into sacred, symbolic national spaces was so effective — without losing any of their spiritual fecundity, the symbolic power of the dead could be dissociated from the individual human frame and organically linked to the life of the nation. While the spirit continued to be glorified in the imagination of the Protestant North, the individual material trace grew less and less problematic in some circles, ultimately signifying nothing but battlefield curiosities, occupational burdens, or "sticks of wood."

12

Looking Death in the Face

If the conditions brought on by the Civil War contributed to the expansion of a heretofore marginal cultural attitude of indifference toward the dead, the conflict also encouraged a contrary but historically familiar tendency: submission of the dead to an enveloping gaze that kept them fixed in the imagination and — at least for a short period after death — close at hand and under the control of the living. For families searching for lost relations, for photographers trying to capture the essence of battle and the audiences who flocked to see their pictures, and for individuals in the federal government and medical profession who showed a keen interest in the details of morbid anatomy, the dead body acquired a peculiar value. That value was determined by certain sensibilities and interpretive strategies that had been developing in the antebellum period and that became especially prominent as a result of a series of new circumstances that were unique to the Civil War.

The corpse continued to be an object of fixation, fascination, and curiosity to many Protestants in the North throughout the war. Some citizens thought the bodies of fallen Union soldiers too important to be left on southern battlefields, even if they could believe that their fathers, sons, husbands, or brothers were receiving a respectful burial or that those fields would eventually be transformed into national cemeteries. As we have seen, some family members either undertook arduous journeys to retrieve loved ones or hired undertakers who knew how to suspend decomposition long enough for the bodies to be shipped north, seen one last time, and interred securely in local cemeteries. In addition, the popular attraction to images of battle led an industrious group of professional men to present these scenes in the most authentic way they could — with photographs of the dead on the field after fighting had ceased. Finally, the confluence of interest by doctors and army officials in the scrutinized corpse led to the further legitimation of state, rather than familial or religious, control over the bodies of the dead and the fragmented body parts of wounded soldiers.

During the war the integrity of the body, so cherished by northern Protestants before the conflict, became less important than other concerns — medical intervention to save the life of a soldier, improvement of medical knowledge for greater military effectiveness, and transportation of the remains to family members back home. In the antebellum era the practice of dissection, or any kind of postmortem examination of the cadaver, was considered an offense to religious and communal sensibilities. However, with numerous bodies requiring medical attention and large numbers of corpses requiring disposal, some northerners became increasingly tolerant of a perspective that elevated the pedagogic usefulness of the cadaver over any personal or collective value placed on it. Although this perspective had limited reach, the banality of death during the war and the common indifference to the sight of severed limbs and bloodied, decomposing corpses signaled an opportunity to give credence to and public sanction of such a position. The federal government, in conjunction with medical officers in the army, took advantage of the trend and began to seek bodies and body parts of soldiers for the good of the Union.

The clearest expression of this interest can be found in the efforts by Surgeon General William A. Hammond to institute an Army Medical Museum and in the subsequent work of the initial curator for the museum, Dr. John H. Brinton. In early August 1862, less than two months after the Seven Day's Battle, in which nearly ten thousand Union soldiers were killed or wounded, Hammond sent an order to Brinton regarding the creation of this museum. Brinton, who graduated from medical school in 1852, had served for a time early in the war as General Grant's medical director. He was in Washington when Hammond contacted him about the museum, sitting on the examining medical board and doing research for a surgical history of the Union army. In Hammond's view, an Army Medical Museum, devoted to the exhibition of "specimens of morbid anatomy, both medical and surgical," could be associated with the establishment of a school of medicine for army medical officers.[1]

The order sent by Hammond directed Brinton "to collect and properly arrange" such specimens and to "take efficient measures for the procuring hereafter of all specimens of surgical and medical interest." If any medical officers resisted or neglected to contribute such items to the museum, Brinton was to report the name of the officer to the surgeon general's office. The government's desire to catalog and display wounded bodies, body fragments, and the history of disease in bodies was cast in terms of its utility for the general advancement of medical science as well as for "future generations of military surgeons."[2] There were many lessons to be learned from the conflict, and a better understanding of the violence of war, as it was inscribed on the bodies of Union soldiers — alive or dead — became a priority to Hammond and other officers preoccupied with improving military and medical effectiveness in wartime.

As curator of this museum, Brinton was primarily interested in specimens — bone fragments, projectiles, severed limbs — that illustrated some surgical procedure or pathological curiosity. Brinton had ample assistance in his work; one hospital steward "was an admirable bone cleaner and working anatomist," and photographers and artists were later engaged to visually represent the incoming material.[3] According to the government order regarding the preservation of specimens, bones or other body parts removed during a surgical operation were to be immersed in a keg full of salt water, alcohol, or whiskey. Compliance was common among army surgeons in city or general hospitals, but procurement was much more difficult for medical personnel who worked in field hospitals. In many cases Brinton went directly to battlefields when the fighting had ended to show the doctors how to prepare and send specimens to the museum as efficiently as possible.

For many witnesses to Brinton's work, a mound of severed and mutilated limbs piled near surgery tents provoked revulsion. His fastidious attention to this detritus of human carnage seemed eccentric at best. Yet Brinton declared that his interest in these relics aroused a cooperative spirit in corps hospitals that furthered his mission: "Many and many a putrid heap have I had dug out of trenches where they had been buried, in the supposition of an everlasting rest, and ghoul-like work have I done, amid surrounding gatherings of wondering surgeons, and scarcely less wondering doctors. But all saw that I was in earnest and my example was infectious. By going thus from corps hospital to corps hospital, a real interest was excited as to the Museum work, and an active co-operation was eventually established."[4]

In one of what were surely many "strange scenes" during his search for material, Brinton heard about a "remarkable injury of a lower extremity."[5] Convinced that the exhibition of this injury would be a worthwhile addition to the museum, he was committed to finding the body in question. Unfortunately, when the soldier who suffered the injury died, he was buried by soldiers in his unit. When Brinton arrived at this unit's camp, these soldiers blocked his access to the grave. After explaining his purpose, however, and the "glory of a patriot having *part* of his body at least under the special guard of his country," Brinton persuaded the soldiers to permit the body to be disinterred: "My arguments were conclusive; the comrades of the dead soldier solemnly decided that I should have the bone for the good of the country, and in a body they marched out and dug up the body. I gravely extracted the bone and carried it off carefully; the spokesman of the party remarking gravely, 'that John would have given it to me himself, had he been able to express his opinion.' "[6]

Brinton's scientific interest in mortality led him to investigate various theories about the physiological details of death during his searches for museum artifacts as well. When he visited the corpse-strewn field at Antietam roughly one month after he received his orders from Hammond, he not only collected specimens for the museum, he also conducted a study of the "rigor of instantaneous death." By examining the corpses he was able to characterize the muscular action at the moment of death and account for the body position of many of the soldiers — and horses, for that matter — on the battlefield. The medical observations he made there may not have been particularly useful to the museum, but they were eventually published in the *American Journal of Medical Sciences* and subsequently republished in European medical journals.[7]

Near the end of the war, the museum was still soliciting useful corporeal artifacts from medical officers. These officers were directed by the surgeon general's office to "diligently collect and preserve . . . all pathological surgical specimens which may occur in the hospitals under their charge." Objects of interest to the museum included "fractures of the cranium," "diseased bones and joints," "wounded viscera," and "photographic representations of extraordinary injuries, portraying the results of wounds, operations, or peculiar amputations."[8] Part of the directive was intended to ensure that doctors also sent a careful history of each specimen as well as the name and rank of the person supplying it so that due credit could be given when the complete surgical history of the war was compiled.[9]

According to Brinton, the museum was a popular attraction when it opened in the Washington area: "The public came to see the bones, attracted by a new sensation."[10] In addition to the civilian public, maimed soldiers also visited the museum, often in search of missing limbs. Many soldiers who survived the conflict literally gave of themselves to the Army Medical Museum, but the dead also contributed to its success. Whether they died after a particular operation, during a surgical procedure, or before any medical intervention could be carried out, they were able to serve a valuable function for those who were interested in collecting, cataloging, and examining specimens of morbid anatomy. As Brinton's account of the creation of the museum suggests, the bodily remnants of warfare and the exhibition of human relics ultimately served a patriotic purpose. But medical specialists and government officials weren't the only ones to gain by exposing the dead to a detached, scrutinizing gaze.

Rather than displaying body fragments dissociated from battle in an antiseptic museum setting, certain photographers sought to represent the immediacy and realism of war in all of its gruesome detail to the American public through photographic exhibitions. What better way to bring the war home, to convey to civilians throughout the North the human wreckage that resulted from military combat, than by providing them with photographic representations of scenes of destruction? Technological advances in visual representation irrevocably altered how war was conceptualized by northern Protestants. The glories of battle and the noble deaths of fighting soldiers traditionally envisioned in literature and painting were undercut by the appearance of the photographic war image.[11] This new medium ensured that the realities of war could never again be fully disguised with poetic language and creative visual techniques.

In October of 1862 a series of photographs were exhibited in a New York City gallery owned and operated by Matthew Brady, one of the most famous photographers of the period. Some of his assistants, including Alexander Gardner (who would eventually break from Brady and go into business for himself), had traveled to the Antietam battlefield after the Union victory a month earlier and had begun photographing what they saw there—an area devastated by some of the worst fighting in the war. According to William A. Frassanito, a historian of Civil War photography, the photographers' access to the newly dead on the field was unprecedented: "Antietam was the first battlefield in American history to be covered by cameramen before the dead had been buried."[12]

"The Dead of Antietam," the photographic series that resulted from the work of the cameramen, was an unusual, disturbing, and popular photographic exhibition. According to an October 20, 1862, report in the *New York Times*, crowds constantly moved in and out of the gallery, with patrons examining scenes of bloated, decaying, and unburied bodies. The reporter added that along with repulsion, there was a "terrible fascination [that] draws one near these pictures, and makes him loth to leave them."[13] But in spite of the ambivalence that these scenes of human slaughter aroused, the *Times* reporter and other commentators observed that the photographs had an uncanny ability to "bring home" the war. As a result of viewing the pictures, of confronting images of bodies left on the field of battle, northern citizens could finally get a glimpse of what so many of them had been reading about: the real-life horrors of warfare.

Photographs of corpses strewn across a killing field may have served as unparalleled testimony to the violence and bloodshed wrought by war, but their appeal had a subtler element as well. Visitors seemed to be interested in scrutinizing the "face" of death, in examining the particulars of lifeless corpses. A reviewer for *Harper's Weekly* presented a detailed description of each image in the photographic exhibition and, at one point, suggested that a closer look would yield even more fascinating realism: "Minute as are the features of the dead, and unrecognizable by the naked eye, you can, by bringing a magnifying glass to bear on them, identify not merely their general outline, but actual expression."[14] There was something unique and unprecedented in the appreciation of such scenes of destruction, an aesthetic of death that did not necessarily rely on any conventional system of symbols associated with mortality.

An enduring commentary on this group of photographs was written by Oliver Wendell Holmes, in the pages of the *Atlantic Monthly*. Holmes spent only a small portion of the essay, "Doings of the Sunbeam," exploring the photographs from Antietam. They aroused no fascination in him, no desire to gaze more closely at the dead. Holmes had been to Antietam, searching for his son. He had seen corpses, and the photographs made him want to conceal rather than unmask their secrets. Instead of using a magnifying glass to enhance his vision of all the gory details, Holmes preferred to "bury" such images so the deadly specifics of human warfare could be erased from personal as well as national memory. "Let him who wishes to know what war is look at this series of illustrations," he wrote. "It was so nearly like visiting the battlefield to look over these views, that all the emotions excited by the actual sight of the stained and sordid scene, strewed with rags and wrecks, came back to us, and we buried them in the recesses of our cabinet as we would have buried the mutilated remains of the dead they too vividly represented."[15]

As the cultural historian Alan Trachtenberg notes, the sentiment expressed in this piece "is a compelling moment of discomposure on the part of perhaps the most composed, the most properly buttoned and self-possessed of the Boston Brahmins."[16] Holmes, like his Brahmin brother Emerson, overcame what was represented in the images by shifting from the visual realities to abstract ideological themes like martyrdom and national redemption. Holmes was not alone in clinging to the heroic and romantic ideals of war and militarism; his field of vision—the "sublime whole"—would not allow him to isolate a soldier's mutilated corpse from larger political realities. Although photography could convey the scenery of war, Holmes and various other

Protestant elites in northern culture preferred to turn a blind eye to graphic depictions of individual corpses and instead stay focused on national goals.

Photographers may or may not have been as motivated by politics or patriotism as Holmes. But they certainly knew their trade, and it was clear that capturing the dead in striking, graphic images could be a profitable enterprise. According to Frassanito, "it appears that the sale of Gardner's Antietam views continued at a steady pace throughout the war. . . . The series provided cameramen with an example to be followed, and its financial success provided the incentive to make extraordinary efforts to reach the sites of carnage before the ugliest scars had been covered."[17] Gettysburg offered another opportunity for these cameramen to memorialize the mortal consequences of warfare, explore the aesthetics of dead bodies, and cash in on the public's desire to bring the war into their field of vision and closer to their own lives.

Once again Gardner and his cameramen were the first photographers to arrive at the field; once again they made sure to appear before the dead disappeared. After surveying the content of the photographs taken there — 75 percent of the series focused on "bloated corpses, open graves, dead horses, and related details of wholesale carnage" — Frassanito draws the obvious conclusion about Gardner's interest in the scenery he chose to capture on film: "Considering both the rapidity with which Gardner and his men reached the Gettysburg battlefield and the type of view they spent most of their time taking, it is apparent that Gardner was fully aware of the potential market value such views possessed."[18] In the period before the Civil War, sensational literature was the only popular expression that capitalized on people's fascination with the "ugly" side of death and provided cultural forms that rejected the beautification of the corpse. Now the public had the opportunity to see and ultimately purchase visual representations of "real" dead bodies in all of their macabre glory.

But on closer inspection it is evident that the realism these photographs promised — a realism celebrated for its ability to share the truth of warfare with civilians far away from the battles — often disguised artifice and illusion. At Gettysburg Gardner and some of his associates took artistic liberties with the corpses to endow their photographs with a much more suggestive, aesthetically intriguing narrative. The dead, in effect, became props that were useful for evoking specific, often patriotic responses.[19] Whatever ideological impulses were behind this manipulation, cameramen realized how appealing posed corpses could be to the public. And these aesthetic concerns with the "look" of the bodies of the dead already had a certain cultural legitimacy: recall the memorial photographs and posthumous portraiture that were popular in northern communities before the war.

The staging of death on battlefields proved to be of particular interest to wartime photographers. In one instance of macabre orchestration, Gardner and his assistants seem to have moved the body of a young Confederate soldier at Gettysburg forty yards to a position they wanted to photograph — a position that they felt had greater potential for the composition of the image than where the corpse actually was found on the blood-soaked field. In "Dead Confederate soldier at sharpshooter's position in Devil's Den" (6 July 1863), they transformed an abandoned rebel position behind a stone wall in Devil's Den from a banal, unexceptional battlefield scene into a highly evocative, memorable visual representation of the human costs of war. To effect this transformation the cameramen apparently transported the body of a young soldier to the spot, placed a rifle near him — a type not used by sharpshooters — and put a knapsack under his head.[20]

Another illustration of the signifying power of manipulated bodies in photography was a series of six *carte de visite* views recorded by the Weavers of Hanover, Pennsylvania. They are also from the area of Devil's Den at Gettysburg, though apparently taken a few months after the conflict. According to Frassanito, these scenes of bodies on or near a rock formation are utterly unreal. Everything about the photographs had an artificial quality; they were created for what must have been an audience eager for battlefield carnage. In fact, Frassanito doubts whether the bodies in the image were really dead at all; the "corpses" may have been soldiers masquerading for the photographers on the field. Where did photographers find soldiers to volunteer for their scenes of death and destruction? As Frassanito suggests, "Likely they were participants in the dedication ceremonies [for the Soldiers National Cemetery at Gettysburg], coaxed by fun or profit to accompany the photographers into Devil's Den."[21] If so, then on the very day that Lincoln sacralized the ground in which the dead were buried, photographers and the honored dead's living comrades were conspiring to capitalize on the public's fascination with representations of the slaughter.

Public hunger for glimpses of the dead, as well as governmental efforts to draw medical knowledge and political capital from the remnants of mutilated and lifeless bodies, were ostensibly at odds with another sentiment circulating in northern Protestant culture: the resolute attachment to the bodies of soldiers who died in battle or in hospitals far from friends and families. But in fact the impulses were related, if uneasily so. Like the establishment of the Army Medical Museum and the success of photography, the urgent desire to bring the dead home was linked to a deeply rooted longing to control and gaze upon the physical remains before they disappeared from sight for good. But while the museum had the organizational backing of the federal government and photography was driven by technological progress, survivors had to rely on their own resources to seize the dead from hospitals and battlefields in the South and return them to caring relations in the North.

In spite of government efforts to exploit the ideological symbolism of the war dead, many northern families simply refused to sacrifice their loved one's soul *and* body to the state. The retrieval of the corpse was a heartfelt, compelling matter for civilians who did not believe that such abstractions as national martyrdom or blood baptism legitimated abandonment of the remains of a father, husband, brother, or son. Stillman Wightman, who made the long, formidable journey to find the remains of his son and transfer them home, articulated the sentiments of many northerners who insisted on controlling the fate of their dead: "I came away feeling that all my care and toil was nothing, compared with the satisfaction of knowing that his remains had been taken up from a grave in an enemy's land, and had been safely transported to the land of his birth, and peacefully buried in our family cemetery."[22]

As we have seen, some families enlisted specialists with the expertise and entrepreneurial skills to aid them in their endeavor to locate and retrieve their dead. Embalmers, America's new death specialists, were able to supply mourners in the North with the corpses that were necessary for a relatively normal farewell to the loved one. The procedure remained inaccessible to some and unacceptable to others. The poorer classes could not afford it, and many people clung to a viewpoint common in the United States from the beginning of the republic: embalming was disgusting and uncivilized even in the most desperate circumstances. Yet many commentaries allude to the growing popularity of this form of bodily preservation during the war. Adelaine W. Smith, a nurse with the Union army, disparaged the impulse behind this growth industry after a day spent visiting camps around City Point Hospital with other army personnel: "Returning [from an excursion], we stopped only at the embalmer's, where many bodies were daily prepared to be sent to friends at home. The morbid fancy which is manifested by so many to possess dead bodies, especially those which have long laid buried, seems one of the most barbarous customs permitted in a civilized country."[23]

Without calling into question the patriotism or sincerity of those whose livelihood depended on the dead, it would be difficult to deny that the war brought them substantial business opportunities. One embalmer, who handled only the bodies of high ranking officers, did not disguise the fact that he could charge different prices for soldiers depending on their military status. After the battle of Gaines Mill, he was reported to have said: "I used to be glad to prepare private soldiers. They were wuth a five-dollar bill apiece. But, Lord bless you, a colonel pays a hundred, and a brigadier-general two hundred. . . . I might as a great favor, do a captain, but he must pay a major's price. I insist upon that! Such windfalls don't come every day. There won't be another killing for a century."[24] Other embalmers expressed a greater degree of ambivalence about the source of their income. After a particularly fierce battle that left him with a number of profitable corpses, one embalmer remarked to Army Chaplain H. Clay Trumball, "Chaplain, I should be glad to have this terrible war end, even though peace would greatly interfere with my business."[25]

While some judged the trafficking in cadavers to be vulgar and unchristian, many others were grateful for a profession that could give them their dead, at any and all costs and in whatever condition short of complete decay. Concern for the internal integrity of these bodies, whether based on theological notions about the resurrection or sentimental feelings about proper treatment, was suppressed in light of other considerations. It was important to some, for example, simply to have some degree of control over the management and fate of their dead—to ensure that the remains were located in sacred northern soil rather than in the impious South, and to have one last opportunity to see the corpse before its interment. Abandoning the body of a family member in the profane soil of the southern states or giving it over to the federal government was anathema to many Protestants in the North. The only appropriate way to bury the dead—indeed for some the only way to assure the loved ones' salvation—was to keep them close to both living and dead relations. If the body could be removed from the South and buried in the North, it would share the ground with departed ancestors and remain protected by surviving relatives and friends. Embalming became one of the primary means of enabling northern citizens to give meaning to their dead.

As one historical account asserts, "It seems clear that, by the time the last shot had been fired, this mode of preservation had secured for itself a permanent place in the American funeral customs."[26] In the span of roughly five years, embalming was transformed from a practice almost exclusive to the emerging professional medical field—peripheral to the public arena and resisted by northern Protestants—to an accepted, highly visible, and desired treatment for the dead. In places like City Point, Alexandria, and the Union capital itself, embalming had begun to insinuate itself into the deathways of American society. Even out on the field of battle, traveling civilian embalmers would set up shop next to or near the fighting Union soldiers. And as the outrage and disgust evoked by embalming were replaced by the gratitude of comforted survivors, the status, location, and meaning of the dead in northern Protestant culture underwent considerable change. The new visions of death, and the rituals that were employed to usher corpses out of the land of the living, defused the ambiguous power associated with the dead.

By the end of the war — and, even more pointedly, with the death and funeral train of Abraham Lincoln — the public image of death had been recast. The desire to preserve bodies so that they could be moved from foreign territory to the comfort of home and the watchful eyes of close family and friends signaled an endorsement of the process of embalming and contributed to its future success as a basic feature in the burial of the dead. With the public acceptance of this practice, the dead required specialists who could mediate between them and the living — people who could, in effect, domesticate the corpse for the public imagination and assume managerial responsibilities for its disposal. But in order to legitimate their enterprise, the disparate local undertakers in the North would have to transform their services into a "profession"; the carnage of the war and the tragedy of President Lincoln's assassination represented a watershed for a new death industry.

The Birth of the Death Industry

Abraham Lincoln's Hallowed and Hollowed Body

By the time John Wilkes Booth shot Abraham Lincoln in the back of the head in Ford's Theater on Good Friday, April 14, 1865, the citizens of the divided nation were beginning to establish a new relation with the dead. The treatment of Lincoln's body and the ceremonies surrounding it signaled some of the changes that would come in northern Protestant culture. Before the Civil War, family relations, close friends, and community members prepared the corpse for its disposal and escorted it from living society; during the war, when young men died far from home, other individuals — often strangers with no personal connection to the deceased — were involved in the essential task of disposal. The most important class of mediators to emerge during the war comprised the embalmers and embalming undertakers — professionals who offered their services to anyone who could afford them.

The experiences of Mary Todd Lincoln after the assassination of her husband also bear on the transformation of American deathways in the post–Civil War period. By the end of the century women would no longer play a major role in the preparation of the dead for burial; instead, they were often separated from the physical remains and replaced by male professionals with technical expertise in the treatment of the dead.[1] Mary Todd, like many other bereaved family members in the postbellum North, left the physical remains in the hands of experts, who took charge of the body in the intermediate period between death and burial. In turn, the body, and memory, of her martyred husband became the focus of unprecedented celebration, commemoration, and memorialization—in brutal contrast to Mary's destiny as the wife of the first murdered president in American history.[2]

In the weeks after the assassination, Lincoln's corpse became visible and accessible to the nation; from the moment he was shot until the interment in Springfield, Illinois, his body was considered public property, given to the citizens who made up the Union body politic. The president's translucent and legible body was quickly prepared for and exposed to the scrutiny of the masses. The funeral journey, which began in Washington and stopped in numerous northern cities, ended twenty days after the murder. Throughout the course of the journey citizens of the North had unprecedented access to Lincoln's corpse, and the popular desire to gaze upon the body at each stop suggests that a well-preserved, mobile, and visible corpse did not arouse public indignation or challenge traditional concerns about bodily integrity.

In the nation's capital the accessibility of the body began almost instantly. Roughly twenty-five soldiers, doctors, and bystanders carried the mortally wounded president from the theater to a room across the street. Numerous men moved in and out of the small room where the president was to die, including family members, friends, doctors, and politicians; the president's body was always in sight, and every breath, sound, or facial expression was subject to analysis. At the moment of death a few of the men cried, though the majority of them remained silent.[3] A short time after Lincoln died, the Reverend Dr. Phineas Gurley was asked to say something. He responded with a patriotic appeal, that "we and the whole nation might become more than ever united in our devotion to the cause of our beloved, imperiled country."[4]

But before the body could be given over to the people as a symbol of this national unity, it had to be taken apart and then reassembled for public presentation. At the moment of death, the president's body was given over to professionals who specialized in death and the dead. Doctors from the newly created Army Medical Museum performed an autopsy in the guest room on the second floor of the White House. During this examination the top of the president's head was sawed off and the brain removed. As the surgeons withdrew the brain, the bullet that had been lodged there fell onto the floor.[5] At the conclusion of the autopsy another set of specialists took over, and the embalming of the body began.

Undertakers from the firm of Brown and Alexander drained the blood from the jugular vein.[6] A chemical preparation was injected through the femoral artery, giving the corpse what some subsequently called a statuesque, marblelike appearance. The postmortem interventions of these specialists were frequently reported in various newspapers, offering the public general information about the technological innovations being discovered in bodily preservation along with specific details about the procedures used on the deceased president. The Pittsburgh *Daily Post,* for example, printed the following account from a correspondent for the New York *World:*

> There is now no blood in the body, it was drained by the jugular vein and sacredly preserved, and through a cutting on the inside of the thigh the empty blood-vessels were charged with a chemical preparation which soon hardened to the consistence of stone. The long and bony body is now hard and stiff, so that beyond its present position it cannot be moved any more than the arms or legs of a statue. It has undergone many changes. The scalp has been removed, the brain scooped out, the chest opened and the blood emptied. All this we see of Abraham Lincoln, so cunningly contemplated in this splendid coffin, is a mere shell, an effigy, a sculpture. He lies in sleep, but it is the sleep of marble.[7]

When these specialists were finished with the body, War Secretary Edwin M. Stanton selected the clothes that the president would wear on his journey—the same black suit he wore for his second inaugural. The coffin was placed on an elaborate catafalque constructed in the East Room at the White House. On Tuesday, April 18, the embalmed corpse of the sixteenth president was presented to the public. A line stretching more than a mile long, six or seven people across, had formed by midmorning.[8] Citizens were allowed to mount the catafalque and file past the body; they were given an opportunity to glance at the face of the late president and pay their last respects.

The next day was reserved for people who had special passes to attend the funeral. Some five hundred people crowded into the East Room for the official religious services—conducted by representatives of the Episcopalian, Methodist, Presbyterian, and Baptist churches. But all across the North people attended memorials for the dead president. Unlike the obsequies for an absent Washington, many northern citizens would have the opportunity to see the passing funeral train bearing Lincoln's body or to visit and worship near his actual remains. Before the funeral train left on its journey, however, a grand funeral procession transported the body from the White House to the Capitol.[9] Positioned on another catafalque, the corpse of the president was once again given over to the gaze of the public.

Finally, on Friday, April 21, the funeral train left Washington and headed toward Springfield, making stops in several northern cities. In each city citizens participated in ceremonies associated with the display of the fallen president's body, and tens of thousands of people were allowed to view the remains before the train left for the next destination. One reporter after another remarked on the extraordinary nature of the ceremonies and on the large numbers of people who lined the tracks to express their grief as the train passed. Although Mary Todd stayed in the background during the funeral journey, other close friends of Lincoln's, along with military personnel and other delegates, accompanied the corpse on the train. And another important figure stayed with the body all the way to Springfield: the embalmer. Working closely with local undertakers along the way, he made sure that the corpse was suitable for public consumption.

Throughout the journey there were conflicting reports about how the body was holding up. Most people remarked on the "sweet," "peaceful," "placid," and "natural" expression on the face of the president—an expression that in some instances reportedly led viewers, most of them women, to reach out and touch the president or even try to kiss his face or the coffin. Some reporters praised the work of the embalmers, one even exclaiming that "all the details were perfect."[10] Charles Page, a journalist for the *New York Tribune* during the war, remarked, "The face of the dead President bears a very natural expression, one familiar to all who saw him often. It is just the hint of a smile, and the look of benediction. I do not know to what it is attributable, but certainly the face is far more natural, more *his,* than when seen four days ago at Washington."[11]

Other accounts, though, contradicted this popular narrative of supernatural tranquility and physical composure. Instead of familiarity and peace, these reporters saw uncertainty and chaos in the facial features of the former president. The strange discoloration beginning to transform his appearance was too dramatic to overlook. In one New York newspaper a reporter suggested that the view of the remains might be "satisfactory" for those who had never seen the man up close. But, the writer went on to say, "to those who were familiar with his features, it is far otherwise. The color is leaden, almost brown; . . . the cheeks, hollow and deep pitted; the unnaturally thin lips shut tight and firm as if glued together." This journalist, pessimistic about the presentability of the corpse for the remainder of the journey, questioned whether it was appropriate or prudent—despite the "cunning workmanship"—to "tempt dissolution much further."[12]

Upon reaching Springfield, the body of the former president was clearly beginning to lose the illusion of solidity and tranquility; the irrepressible onset of putrefaction threatened its statuesque, marblelike appearance. The undertakers who opened the coffin before its exposure to the public were dismayed at what they saw and what they were having difficulty controlling: the increasing darkness on the face, signaling decay. Throughout the journey attendants had tried to disguise the signs of death, but their efforts were no longer effective. Frustrated in his attempts to make the body presentable, the traveling embalmer gave in to the request of the local undertaker and let him try to conceal the progress of decomposition. With the help of thick applications of rouge chalk and amber, the undertaker seemed to be able to hide the marked discoloration.[13]

Unfortunately, the applications did not hold when the body was exhibited in the State House the next day. In addition to the usual remarks about his serene countenance and peaceful features, there were also the more candid comments about the wholly unnatural appearance of the face and the disconcerting impression this left with many of those who filed by.[14] But despite the formation of a marginal counter-narrative describing the corpse as unworthy of a last look, the president's body had been safely purified and firmly located in the hearts, imagination, and memory of the American republic as a result of its public exhibition — any signs of physical discomposure on the body became secondary to the coherent imaginative body that signified national permanence.

In a stately, ornate procession on May 4, 1865, a hearse transported the corpse from the State House to Oak Ridge, a "rural" cemetery in Springfield. The journey of Lincoln's body was finally over. As Bishop Matthew Simpson of the Methodist Church explained in his funeral oration, though the nation was paralyzed during the "mournful silence" that followed the assassination, the concentrated attention on the president's body not only obliterated all social distinctions — of class, political orientation, faith, and even race — it also encouraged social unity and collective renewal. He made it clear that the visibility of the body, the opportunity given to the public to look upon the remains, contributed to this process of healing and rejuvenating the social body. "Far more eyes have gazed upon the face of the departed than ever looked upon the face of any other departed man. . . . We ask, why this wonderful mourning — this great procession? I answer, first: A part of the interest has arisen from the times in which we live and in which he that had fallen was a principal actor. . . . Another principal is, that the deepest affections of our hearts gather around some human form, in which are incarnated the living thoughts and ideas of a passing age." Simpson went on to reiterate a common theme that was expressed during Lincoln's funeral journey: that this body was a vehicle through which God acted in history. "By the hand of God he was especially singled out to guide our government in these troublous times, and it seems to me that the hand of God may be traced in many events connected with his history."[15]

Lincoln's body also served as a vehicle for a transformation in the public image of death in northern communities. In effect there were two bodies represented during the funeral ceremonies of the murdered president.[16] On the one hand there was Lincoln's *hallowed* body, associated with the perpetuation—indeed the hegemony—of the state. Considering the terrible conflict that engulfed the nation beginning in 1861 and the unprecedented nature of the assassination at the end of the fighting, northern leaders made a concerted effort to reaffirm the integrity of the reestablished Union.[17] On the other hand, another body present during these ceremonies was Lincoln's *hollowed* body, demonstrating that new preservative techniques would allow the dead to remain in the sight of the living for a longer period of time than before.

The most convenient and historically effective interpretive strategy to disguise and reconceptualize the violence perpetrated on Lincoln's body—and carried out over the previous four years on battlefields throughout the country—was to turn to biblical themes. Lincoln was compared on one hand to Moses, for having led his people from the wilderness of slavery, but many Protestant leaders—exploiting the coincidence of the day of the assassination—used the death and resurrection of Jesus as a model to understand the national significance of the president's murder and to establish the possibility for societal redemption.[18] In concert with this interpretation of his hallowed body, the order of the state was reaffirmed in the structure of the funeral procession from Washington through other major cities and on to Springfield. The ceremonies following Lincoln's death, the long, circuitous funeral journey, and the final disposition of the body in the cemetery were rituals that represented political continuity and national order.[19] The presentation and accessibility of the body during the funeral journey at the same time represented perfect democratic egalitarianism and provided a traveling sacred center around which the government displayed its power, legitimacy, and permanence.

Besides the Christian and national meaning systems associated with the regeneration and solidity of the social body, a domestic symbolism also emanated from Lincoln's body. But the family that appropriated this body was not the nuclear family, with Mary Todd at the center, but the national family, which had lost its "father" (as well as its sons) as a result of the war. This body—hollowed out by embalming and transported by train like other bodies during the conflict—was given over to the grieving relations whose normal deathways were uprooted by the bloody conflict. Lincoln served not only as a father figure to the citizens who filed past the corpse but as a surrogate son to those parents who had lost their offspring and knew the ultimate fate of their sacrificed children—mass, anonymous burial in profane southern soil.

The spectacle of the presentation of the Lincoln corpse to his "family," less imperial than the embodiment of the national government, was based on the seemingly miraculous capacity to suspend the putrefaction and corruption of the mortal, human body and allow the living relations to behold, one last time, their lost loved one. Although the body *did* show signs of decay and disintegration, Lincoln's deification in the collective imagination of the North required the suppression of those unpleasant, disagreeable observations. In other words, the memory of Lincoln that would live long after the remains were placed in the tomb drew from the visibility of his corpse and from the positive assessments of it, which signified that the deceased had finally been relieved of the pain and suffering of this life.[20]

The extent to which Lincoln's procession immediately contributed to the popularity and respectability of the new practice of embalming is difficult to measure. But at the height of a revolution in ways of thinking about treating the corpse, the president's paraded body added to the viability of embalming as a fundamental, utilitarian, and specialized technical service for the dead.[21] It is certainly what the people wanted. In their own experiences a last gaze and the chance to see the body off was part of the conventional routine when a family member died. The Civil War disturbed that convention by increasing the distance between the dead and the living; Abraham Lincoln's body, through the perceived success of embalming, demonstrated that distance could be overcome and that the living could still view their dead—though a cost would be attached to the art of preservation.

Abraham Lincoln's hallowed and hollowed body was a major catalyst in the transformation of attitudes and practices surrounding the dead. It also served as a site where the nation could be figuratively restored and redeemed—primarily because the procedure of embalming demonstrated that even in the grips of death the president's body, like the social body, could overcome the material, physical violence enacted upon it. As the funeral procession led Lincoln's corpse through the streets of Washington and the train directed it toward its final resting place, the nation was, in the words of the former president himself, engaged in a "new birth of freedom." Although the North was in the midst of tremendous pain and sorrow after its victory, Lincoln's corpse signified national stability, integrity, and revitalization; and despite observations to the contrary, this body ensured that embalming—an unacceptable treatment before the war—would change the practice of American deathways.

13

*The Business of Death in the
Late Nineteenth Century*

The use of embalming during the war and on the president's body at its close opened the way for dramatic changes in the image of death in northern Protestant culture. In time, the new image also benefited from the consolidation and professionalization of those involved with the business of death. Social, economic, and religious circumstances conspired to appropriate the corpse and redefine its representational value for the public. The process was incomplete immediately after the war, but by the beginning of the twentieth century a new set of assumptions about the lifeless body, articulated through a new authoritative discourse, determined how Protestant society would understand its relation to the dead.[1]

After the Civil War the nation in general, and northern urban areas in particular, underwent profound social and economic transformations.[2] Among these changes was the growing legitimacy of scientific thinking in nearly all aspects of social life, including public health and anatomical studies—a development that helped redefine the meaning of the corpse. At the same time, though, the rise of a consumer culture, based in part on the emergence of a professional managerial class that guided spending habits, reestablished the value of the lifeless body for grieving survivors. Both of these trends ultimately reinforced the power of the experts who took charge of the disposal of the remains and began to manage their location in society.

In the postbellum years a cooperative effort arose among public health officials and local religious and political reformers to ameliorate living conditions and, through administrative action, decrease mortality rates. The Civil War provided northern leaders with many lessons about sanitary reform, and the impact of disease on Union soldiers alerted medical schools after the war to the importance of emphasizing the study of public health.[3] Many proponents assumed that the scientific and bureaucratic endeavor to "clean up" the social body would not only contribute to individual longevity and care for personal hygiene but would also lead to other improvements related to public safety and moral behavior.[4] Where did sanitary reformers and public health officials measure the mortal dangers and trace their effects on the social body? One of the most important sites was the corpse, which provided specialists with a translucent, concrete record of the most serious threats to public health. By reading the dead body, identifying the cause of death, and incorporating the finding into larger demographic records of mortality rates, city administrators could distinguish more accurately what social dangers posed the greatest risk to the living.[5]

As mortality figures began to provide data that could be used to improve social conditions, the science of anatomy became even more valuable in the pursuit of a medical education. Dead bodies were essential for anatomical studies, and, in the reform era of the late nineteenth century, many argued that laboratory work required cadavers for the professionalization of doctors and the legitimacy of medical schools themselves.[6] But outside the Protestant middle class, resistance to any form of bodily profanation and to the destruction of the integrity of the corpse remained firm in the popular imagination of certain groups that more often than not provided the medical profession with the cadavers for study: the working poor, immigrants, and blacks. The market for cadavers that existed before the Civil War continued to be a source of controversy in northern culture, though by the end of the nineteenth century the conflicts centered on the medical establishment, state governments, and the lower socioeconomic classes.[7] The "resurrectionists" were alive and well after the war and, despite expressions of outrage against this market and legislative attempts to thwart it, continued to find employment into the early twentieth century.[8]

Meanwhile, a number of reformers who placed a particularly strong emphasis on anatomical studies reconstituted medical education after the Civil War. In the late 1860s and early 1870s, reform-minded medical educators proposed a series of modifications in university instruction. Two subject areas they thought needed greater attention were "practical anatomy and operative surgery on the cadaver."[9] Clearly the dissection of the cadaver was still understood as an important practice for obtaining critical information about the secrets of human life and death. The analysis of the interior of the human frame at death grew more and more sophisticated as the century came to a close. Although there were still indignities visited upon corpses from the poorer classes, legislative action continued to favor the rationalizations offered by medical colleges for the pedagogic usefulness of the practice.

Embalming played a crucial role in the improvement of anatomical studies. Preservation through arterial injection not only allowed medical institutions to work on corpses acquired legally—and thus to avoid the urgency of performing dissections on "fresh" cadavers hastily—it also allowed for the accumulation of bodies over time and ensured that none would go to waste when classes were not in session.[10] The scientific knowledge offered by corpses, though championed by a relatively small elite, began to find a larger base of support, or at least toleration, in northern Protestant society by the turn of the century. As rational systems of thought and action became dominant—especially with regard to concerns about personal health and social order—the scientific perspective on the corpse advocated by men in the medical profession gradually grew more compelling to people in the middle and upper classes.

At the same time the medicalized corpse was being given a new symbolic and representational status, economic changes were having an impact on the public image and value of the dead in postbellum Protestant culture. By the last two decades of the nineteenth century an expanding consumer culture was evident in many northern cities.[11] Not coincidentally, some representatives of the emerging death industry began to market their commodities with the aim of attracting disoriented and confused customers who were no longer sure about how to handle their lost loved ones. One of the most lucrative of these commodities both before and after the war—and an integral article in the burial of the dead—was the coffin (or, reflecting the changing sensibilities in the postwar period about the precious contents contained therein, the casket).[12]

As the trappings of death were gradually modified by the demands of a consumer-oriented market, a concurrent cultural development not only located the dead within this market but also ensured that the living turned to specialists who handled every aspect of the funeral. The creation of a professional class of experts for a wide range of goods and services was an important characteristic of consumer culture in late-nineteenth-century America, contributing to the substitution of a "consumer ethic" for a "producers ethos."[13] Most consumers came to believe that these well-trained experts had the necessary knowledge to guide their spending habits.[14] By the end of the war, the arena of death also had its own professionals, known as undertakers (though in time their title would change to "funeral directors"). Through their industrious efforts to disseminate ideas about disposal of the corpse, they established authority over the funeral by the turn of the century.

Experiences on or near battlefields, camps, and hospitals in the Civil War gave many undertakers an opportunity to perfect their skills in one particular practice that proved to be indispensable to the claims of expertise: embalming the body. In an article published in 1895, the successful Pittsburgh "funeral director" W. H. Devore recounted his numerous wartime opportunities to refine the process:

> I secured the government contract for embalming and burial of all bodies from camps and hospitals then located in the section of country around Pittsburgh; also, the contract for the city, Allegheny county, and all railroads centering in Pittsburgh. These contracts were over and above my regular business. So it is readily seen that a multitude of opportunities were presented for experiment. My first experiments were during the early part of the military encampments here, and were continued with increasing success for many years, both as to the fluid used and manner of operating. Now, my methods have reached perfection, enabling me to preserve bodies perfectly an indefinite length of time.[15]

One of the best-known teachers of the art of embalming in the later decades of the century, Joseph Henry Clarke, also received his most significant training during the war. He was one of the first traveling embalmers to teach students in various northern cities the necessary skills of the procedure; he also established an embalming school in Cincinnati with Dr. C. M. Lukens, an educator in the study of anatomy.[16]

While the Civil War was critical to the acquisition of expert knowledge in the practice of embalming and the establishment of an aura of professionalism around the treatment of the dead, specific developments in the postbellum era helped to legitimate the funeral industry as a respectable and authoritative enterprise. This process of legitimation in turn alleviated customers' anxieties and concerns about giving over not only their deceased loved ones to these professionals, but sizable fees as well. One of the most important developments was the establishment of trade journals specifically focused on the business of death. These journals catered to undertakers who interacted with consumers and offered information and advice about a range of issues related to death and the disposal of the dead.

Editors at *The Casket,* one of the earliest trade journals and one of the most influential in the late-nineteenth century, geared the publication toward professionals — in the words of the magazine itself, "men of means, intelligence, taste, and refinement; reading and thinking men, who have elevated their profession" — who were trying to sell their services in an increasingly competitive market. The journal, like others that would come later, operated as a vehicle for the spread of information about recent discoveries in the field as well as about the most effective strategies for winning the patronage of middle- and upper-class consumers.[17] In addition, these journals provided one of the many contexts in which advertisements — for caskets, embalming fluids, and other materials — could find an appropriate audience.

The establishment of national professional societies for the care of the dead proved to be equally significant to the commodification of death in the northern consumer culture of the postbellum years.[18] Probably the most notable of these societies to form after the Civil War was the National Funeral Director's Association (NFDA), which from its beginning in 1882 was preeminently concerned with professional standards of conduct, the education of its members, and economic stability and growth.[19] Significantly, the question of an appropriate professional title — undertaker or funeral director — became a hotly debated topic at the organization's first national meeting. While some argued for retaining the older designation of "undertaker," the majority of the members favored the more professional sounding and broadly descriptive "funeral director." In the words of one member: "I think it will retard the prospect of progression in this business if we adhere to the old form. I hope we shall call it funeral director because it is the name which informs the public just what we are doing."[20]

Members of the new association expressed a number of concerns that were germane to the profession and its search for respectability, regarding ethics, social responsibility, and new innovations in the field. But clearly the most essential and technically sophisticated areas of knowledge discussed by the members related to the treatment of the corpse. Embalming was a practice that required expertise, and indeed this proved to be a fundamental principle in the rhetoric of the profession. The scientific acumen that was necessary for the task of burial, couched in utilitarian statements associated with preventing the spread of disease and preserving the natural appearance of the body, may have been restricted to a select few, but the social benefits of such knowledge were unmistakable — at least to the funeral directors themselves.[21]

In a paper on the "Progress of the Profession," Allen Durfee of Grand Rapids, Michigan, outlined radical changes from times past in "matters funereal." Durfee particularly emphasized how embalming "has revolutionized the methods of the profession, elevating the keeping of the human body to completeness and certainty of an exact science." He also argued that the funeral director now had complete control over all the details of burial and that "hasty burials" need not worry the living, thanks to scientific progress.[22] Members of the NFDA were as driven by their quest for profits as by their desire to attain professional, and therefore trustworthy, status in northern communities. The two goals, success and respectability, were naturally linked in the logic of consumer capitalism in the late nineteenth century. The future success of funeral directors depended in part on their ability to convince customers of their expertise in the handling of the dead and to sell these specialized services to those individuals who might not be interested in them initially.

After the Civil War and as a result of the radical changes in society before the turn of the century, the corpse had been severed from its traditional communal context and had begun to be controlled by a growing cadre of death specialists. Funeral directors were able to exploit these conditions for a number of reasons, including their expertise in the practice of embalming and, perhaps more importantly, the willingness among a significant number of northern Protestants to allow their dead to be handled by professionals who asserted they were best suited to prepare them for their exit from society. One particularly important shift in attitudes toward death, however, had to occur before the corpse could be appropriated and reconceptualized according to a rational logic that drew from scientific language and consumer culture. In order for a modern sensibility to reestablish the location, value, and status of the dead in northern society, religious Protestants had to literally and figuratively abandon the corpse and strip it of any lingering sacrality, liminality, or traces of power.

The representational value of Abraham Lincoln's body derived from interpretive strategies that deemphasized Christian authority and sanctified national, economic, and medical interest in the dead. Although linked to conventional symbol systems within northern Protestant culture, his corpse was first and foremost a national symbol with which all members of the regenerating country, at least ideally, could identify. Just as fallen soldiers were understood as martyrs in the Union cause, the material trace left by Lincoln at death served the welfare of the state, strengthening the political solidarity of the social body. But after the war ended, the dominant political symbolism of death diminished until the start of the first World War. The meanings and practices surrounding the dead in the postbellum era began to depend on new, compelling justifications emanating, as we have seen, from the medical and funeral industries.

Between 1865 and 1900, religious language in the North placed decreasing emphasis on the potential symbolic value of the corpse and increasing weight on the spirit in the afterlife — a trend that started in the antebellum period and flourished after the war. In virtually every facet of Protestant theology the physical remains of the dead were persona non grata, so to speak. While much of the dominant theology in the Gilded Age focused on the improvement of social conditions in cities, the saving of souls in this life, and the status of the spirit in the next, the corpse itself had become useless to religious instruction.[23] No longer symbolically rich with meaning — whether associated with human corruption, the character of the soul, or the sacrality of the nation — it proved to be antithetical to the values and aspirations of late-nineteenth-century Protestants in the North. What clearly mattered more than the fate of the physical body, and what held the rapt attention of religious believers, was the condition of the spirit at death.

Although Mary Todd Lincoln was originally from Kentucky, her response after the death of the president reflects one popular northern cultural strategy for making sense of death while discounting the significance of the body. As a follower of spiritualism, Mary Todd made many attempts to contact the spirit of her dead husband and sons and even had a "spirit photograph" taken, which ostensibly depicted the ethereal presence of Abraham Lincoln standing behind her seated figure.[24] She also turned to an extremely popular novel for consolation, *The Gates Ajar* by Elizabeth Stuart Phelps. This novel appeared in 1868 and expressed many of the hopes and fantasies of Protestants who, like Mary Todd, lost loved ones as a result of the bloody conflict. The annexation of heaven, and its successful colonization by sentimental consolation writers like Phelps and others, indicates the strong persistence of interest in imaginative representations of life after death in postbellum Protestant culture.[25]

Spiritualists in the Gilded Age were attracted to domesticated heavenly scenes of individual and familial continuity, and practitioners made concerted efforts to provide strict scientific evidence that validated their claims about visitations during seances. For both spiritualists and liberal-to-moderate Protestants, the spirits of the dead were present and could be accessible to the living; the corpse, on the other hand, was a rather useless, discarded covering that had value only as an object for the memorialization of the deceased. Although spiritualism began as a distinct movement in the years before the Civil War, according to the historian Sydney Ahlstrom it "reached its floodtide around 1870, when the movement claimed eleven million adherents."[26] The first national meeting of spiritualists occurred in Chicago near the end of the war in 1864.

The teachings of Andrew Jackson Davis, the philosophical leader of spiritualism, brought the movement to a peak of popularity after the war. Spiritualists allowed the living to keep the spirits of the dead close by and within reach — even if a corpse was abandoned in the South or if natural laws decreed its ultimate disintegration. They also encouraged such imaginative strategies as belief in a postmortem reality that was connected to, or, in some descriptions of heaven, a mirror of, the social world. According to spiritualists the physical remains were irrelevant to the life of the spirit, and this message found a receptive audience in a religious culture that had just experienced a massive slaughter and was turning away from intimacy with the corpse.[27]

As the historian James Moorhead argues, Protestant culture after the Civil War emphasized notions of progress and activity in their representations of heaven rather than stasis and completion.[28] This cultural sensibility, which reflected the combined postwar influences of Darwinism and postmillennialism, ultimately led to the effort to reconcile Christian teaching with the modern world. In its most extreme form, appearing at the end of the century as the Social Gospel movement, this optimistic strand of northern Protestantism sought to transform society through community action and called for cultural reform through the infusion of Christian principles into daily life.[29] Leaders in the Social Gospel movement were, like many of the reform-minded spiritualists, more concerned with the living social body than with the individual, decomposing physical body at death. They also articulated a view of the corpse that embraced a scientific naturalism that in no way affected their certainties of individual, spiritual progress.

The writing of Washington Gladden, a popular Congregationalist minister in the North who became known as "the father of the Social Gospel," illustrates the modern perspectives associated with this outlook.[30] In his essay "The Thought of Heaven," Gladden addressed the question of the fate of the body after death. The possibility that the same physical material buried in the grave would be "reanimated" was "impossible and absurd"—not only was this notion repudiated by Saint Paul, wrote Gladden, it was also rejected by "physiological science." In the next life the spirit would be clothed with another "tabernacle," similar to the earthly body in appearance, but different in substance. Gladden asserted that the afterlife would be a familiar and domestically satisfying place of cleanliness, order, extra room, and visitors:

> It is much more reasonable to suppose that we shall have in the other life bodily organisms with which our spirits will be familiar, to the uses of which they are accustomed. . . . I prefer to think that death will make no serious break in the continuity of our experience. . . . It may be something as one who comes back from a journey and finds his home improved and beautiful,— many discomforts gone, the cramped rooms enlarged, the unsightliness put away, everything arranged as he had often wished to have it, yet still the same home, with the same dear associations,—the same hearth to sit by, the same windows to look out of, all the old quiet comforts left, all the old appointments calling him back to the old ways of living.[31]

The strong affirmation of individuality in the afterlife and the equally persistent promise of reunions with loved ones were pervasive in much Protestant language at the end of the century. Gladden, like so many others, would not accept the possibility of disembodied spirits, restful inactivity, or any form of spiritual unity, and he refused to subscribe to the unscientific, orthodox proposition of a physical, bodily resurrection. Belief in the adoption of a new "tabernacle" would make the transition from this life to the next smoother, allow individuals to recognize each other there, and, perhaps most importantly, take attention away from the emotionally distracting, earthly body left behind. Perhaps this is one of the reasons Gladden advised pastors to shorten the burial service, replace the funeral sermon with a brief biographical sketch of the deceased, and direct most of their attention to soothing the emotions of the survivors.[32]

Other northern Protestant figures in the Gilded Age also argued that the physical body at death should be easily abandoned—even joyously discarded—in anticipation of the spiritual body that was to replace it. Henry Ward Beecher, the renowned evangelical liberal who attracted huge crowds to his Plymouth Church in Brooklyn, published sermons and other writings that were widely distributed in the North, where his brand of evangelicalism found a highly receptive audience.[33] He repudiated any notion of a literal physical resurrection, preferring instead to maintain a distinction between the imperfect, transient material body and the perfect, eternal spiritual form: "Some believe that this mortal body rises again. Thank God, not I! I have had enough of it. And once the earth takes it, the earth may keep it. . . . However it may be in the present, 'in the ages to come,' over the mountains, across the valleys, behind the clouds, beyond all calculable periods, there will be a state in which we shall have dropped this natural body, and shall be endued with our spiritual body, whatever that is, and shall be free from the circumscription and weariness of this mortal condition."[34]

There were, on the other hand, more conservative Protestants who maintained the orthodox line on the resurrection and the future destiny of the physical body—regardless of the natural laws of decomposition. Many of these religious leaders stuck to the principles of the Reformed tradition as they were expressed in the Westminster Confession and turned their back on the modern, scientific, and liberalizing trends in northern culture—especially the soft, sentimentalizing theologies that envisioned a domesticated heaven and progressive spiritual life. Reverend Joseph T. Smith, moderator at the Presbyterian General Assembly, wrote that "the bodies, too, which souls inhabit here, are immortal. Death is not destruction. . . . Each [the body and the soul] exists apart, during the whole period of the intermediate state, to be reunited in the resurrection of the great day."[35]

Other representatives of this position went so far as to advance the possibility of avoiding death and physical dissolution altogether. Dispensational premillennialism, nourished in the United States by the popular teachings of the British preacher John Nelson Darby, grew substantially in the post–Civil War years and its views began to permeate a variety of evangelical denominations.[36] Premillennialists focused especially on issues of biblical prophecies of the end times, and they believed that before the rule of the Antichrist a rapture would occur—literally the raising of members of the church into the air to meet Jesus. As Moorhead puts it, the saved "would never know the terrors of physical dissolution. Since dispensationalists believed that the rapture would probably occur soon, many entertained the hope that death would be for them a nonevent."[37]

But this way of imagining the afterlife and making sense of the corpse was a minority view after the Civil War. Much of the religious imagery of the period accepted the scientific evidence but deemphasized the brutal realities of corporeal decomposition. The historian James Farrell identifies this sensibility in his study of death in America: "As people accepted these naturalist assumptions and attitudes, they began to deal with death differently. They saw death as a natural phenomenon governed only by the laws of nature."[38] The Protestant religious imagination displaced the corpse from its economy of symbol and meaning systems and, continuing the trend that began before the war, chose to confront death by asserting individual spiritual continuity. This tendency ensured that the Protestant imagination would be increasingly uninterested in the lifeless body and chiefly preoccupied with the spiritualization of the dead person.

At both the elite and popular levels death, and especially the corpse, were reimagined in Protestant culture after the war. Another factor at work in this period was the gradual decline in mortality rates in many northern communities. According to one study, the death rate for whites, fairly constant at 22 or 23 per thousand between the war and 1880, dropped to about 17 per thousand by 1900.[39] People began to live longer, and the threat of disease, though still present, became less ominous in the closing decades of the century.[40] Postbellum improvements in living conditions and medical treatment for middle- and upper-class citizens mitigated the omnipresence of death in the social and imaginative worlds of Protestant society.[41]

In spite of these improvements, the dead still had to be accounted for and made meaningful. The corpse may have been devalued in the religious imagination and appropriated by professional death specialists, but this did not automatically lead to the public disavowal of the human remains. In fact, while the authoritative pronouncements over the corpse shifted from the religious community to the medical and funeral industries, grieving survivors maintained their link to lost loved ones at one critical juncture in the funeral ceremony. The significance of this moment to survivors, which persisted throughout the nineteenth century but was modified after the war, allowed the funeral industry to thrive ever since. The moment was the gaze, the last look upon the remains by the living before the physical body disappeared forever.

The desire to gaze at the body before disposal has been a consistent characteristic of attitudes toward death in America. The conditions created by the Civil War made the urgency of this act even more conspicuous, and in the case of Abraham Lincoln the centrality of gazing upon the remains was understood as a patriotic act that contributed to national healing and social regeneration. As technological advances in preservative techniques became more widely available and assurances about the hygienic value of embalming became broadly accepted, the viewing of the dead emerged as the most "natural," standard element in American mortuary rituals. Rather than turning their backs and completely giving up the dead to professionals, the living made sure they had their moment with the deceased. Unlike the communal experience with Lincoln's body, this moment grew increasingly private and personal, but it continued to be an integral moment for family solidarity and individual healing. The principal value of embalming for northern Protestants at the turn of the century was that it enabled them to look at the face of death and not be confronted by the gruesome details of decomposition and decay, or to be worried about the liminal status of the body before its final exit.

Instead, the pleasantly reposed corpse, seemingly at rest and conveying order rather than chaos, became an almost neutral object that enhanced the personal memories of the living and allowed them to bid farewell to the dead. Because there was an absence of religious symbolism and meaning projected onto the corpse, grieving relations — thanks to the work of embalmers — could create their own personal meanings and memories to counteract the pain caused by death. The funeral industry, like any consumer-oriented enterprise, simply capitalized on popular desire. Funeral directors became the new priests who presided over the corpse — that object abandoned by traditional religious authorities and community networks — and worked with the living to find a way to dispose of it adequately. In the profession's first annual meeting in Rochester, New York, funeral directors were made aware of their sacred duties by the mayor, Cornelius R. Parsons:

> In this enlightened age we have much for which to be thankful. We are taught that death is a release from bondage — a change from misery to happiness. It is now with man as it always has been. He is born to die. Even "the paths of glory lead but to the grave." But the thoughts which most naturally present themselves to us to-day, are as to the disposition of the body after the spirit takes its departure. . . . The varied improvements in your art enable you to

conceal much that is forbidding in your calling; and to you is intrusted the tender care of the precious dead.[42]

Funeral directors took their obligations seriously and gained the faith of consumers who needed guidance, support, and expert treatment in the disposal of the sacred remains of their loved ones. They, along with doctors in the medical field, supervised the disposition of the corpse and ensured that it was ushered out of society in a comforting manner for the living.

Even as the corpse became a commodity in the new funeral industry and entered a complex network of commercial activity, it was represented as a potentially valuable object that imposed sacred obligations on the living, like viewing the remains for the enhancement of memory and purchasing appropriate merchandise that reflected the aspirations of the deceased while alive. The survivors would not completely abandon their loved ones before disposal, they simply needed new authorities to assist them in their confrontation with the dead body. But intimacy with the naked truth of death, as it was embodied by the corpse, was no longer a necessary part of social life. Avoiding, rather than simply denying, this reality became a fundamental dimension of life and death in American culture during the twentieth century.

Notes

Introduction

1. Hertz, "Contributions to the Study of Death," 77–78.

2. Some of the studies informing this discussion include Huntington and Metcalf, *Celebrations of Death,* 184–211; Kearl, *Endings;* Was, Berardo, and Neimeyer, *Dying;* Charmaz, *Social Reality of Death;* Pine, *Caretaker of the Dead;* Backer, Hannon, and Russell, *Death and Dying;* Corr, Nabe, and Corr, *Death and Dying;* and DeSpelder and Strickland, *Last Dance.*

3. See Veatch, *Death, Dying, and the Biological Revolution* for a discussion of ethical issues related to death in the medical world.

4. For a recent sociological study on cremation versus burial see Dawson, Santos, and Burdick, "Differences in Final Arrangements." One study reported that roughly 17 percent of the two million deaths that occurred in the United States in 1991 culminated in cremation: Corr, Nabe, and Corr, *Death and Dying,* 223.

5. For example, see Mayer, *Embalming,* 71.

6. Ibid., 1.

7. Ibid., 19–20.

8. Kearl, *Endings,* 281. Also see Mitford, *American Way of Death,* 223–225; and Huntington and Metcalf, *Celebrations of Death,* 187.

9. For examples of the optimistic narratives see Cox, "Death Conquers Bestseller Lists." There are many manifestations of this interest in popular culture, including films (*Ghost,* for example) and personal written narratives (Betty Eadie's *Embraced by the Light* had long life at the top of the *New York Times* best-seller list).

10. Gallup with Proctor, *Adventures in Immortality*. These authors report that 67 percent agree with this assertion (see page 183 for survey results); according to Kearl and Harris's analysis of the National Opinion Research Center's General Science Survey, "more than 70 percent of the American public eighteen years of age and older believe in some form of life after death": Kearl, *Endings*, 184.

11. McDannell and Lang, *Heaven*, 307.

12. Vovelle discusses the radical changes surrounding the meaning of death and the afterlife during the Enlightenment in "Mort en question au siècle des Lumières," *Mort et l'Occident*, 367–503. Ariès identifies the "end of hell" more specifically with the rise of romanticism in the nineteenth century in *Hour of Our Death*, 474.

13. McDannell and Lang, *Heaven*, 326–332; quotation is from 327.

14. Stokes, *Major Methodist Beliefs*, 86.

15. *Service of Death and Resurrection*, 15; emphasis added.

16. Zaleski has written one of the best historical examinations of this phenomenon in *Otherworld Journeys*.

17. Zaleski, *Otherworld Journeys*; also see Kearl, *Endings*, 492–496. There is an enormous amount of literature on this subject, usually classified as "New Age" or "the Paranormal" in bookstores. Raymond A. Moody helped to popularize these narratives with *Life After Life*. Another celebrated analysis of these experiences is Ring, *Heading toward Omega*.

18. Eadie, *Embraced by the Light*, 83.

19. On the history of religion's interest in cultural fashions, see Eliade, "Cultural Fashions," in *Occultism, Witchcraft, and Cultural Fashions*, 1–17. Also, as Zaleski makes clear in her analysis, many of the themes found in near-death narratives can be identified in a variety of religious systems throughout human history: Introduction, *Otherworld Journeys*.

20. Vovelle discusses some aspects of these cultural expressions in *Mort et l'Occident*, 755–761. There are many books on the genre of the horror film, including Douglas, *Horrors!*; Halliwell, *The Dead That Walk*; and Waller, *American Horrors*. Clover engages in a stunning analysis of gender and the horror film in *Men, Women, and Chain Saws*.

21. For a recent article discussing the death of Christa McAuliffe and the *Challenger* disaster see Penley, "Spaced Out." On American memorials, battlefields, and other forms of sacred space see Linenthal, *Sacred Ground*.

22. Some of these themes are discussed in Kearl, "Politics of Death," in *Endings*, 296–343; Bellah, "Civil Religion in America," in *Beyond Belief*; Albanese on "civil religion" in *America: Religions and Religion*, 283–309; Warner, *The Living and the Dead*; and an excellent analysis of politicizing the dead in the German context, Mosse, *Fallen Soldiers*.

23. Ariès gives the most detailed and thorough account of death's taboo status in *Hour of Our Death*, 612–613.

24. Ibid., 614.

25. Looking at a much broader landscape that includes England and western Europe, Lindsay Prior quotes historian Michel Vovelle: "[the 1950s mark] the threshold of a new age in which death becomes a readily observed and much discussed object[,] an object cut free from the mask of silence which once disguised its true form": *Social Organisation of Death*, 4.

26. Gorer, a British sociologist, discusses the "silence" in an influential 1955 article, "Pornography of Death," reprinted in *Death, Grief, and Mourning*.

27. This study proceeds from the point where Stannard's *Puritan Way of Death* left off. Numerous other histories of Protestant culture in America have informed this study, including Miller, *Life of the Mind;* Ahlstrom, Introduction, *Theology in America;* Bushman, *From Puritan to Yankee;* Ryan, *Cradle of the Middle Class;* Marty, *Protestantism in the United States;* Albanese, *America: Religions and Religion,* 85–109 and 247–280; Hatch, *Democratization of American Christianity;* and Butler, *Awash in a Sea of Faith*.

28. Funeral Directors' National Association, *Proceedings of the National Convention,* 19–20.

29. Ibid., 20.

30. Stanley French, "Cemetery as a Cultural Institution"; Sloane, *Last Great Necessity,* 44–64; Linden-Ward, *Silent City on a Hill;* and Farrell, *Inventing the American Way of Death,* 99–112.

31. Kelley writes that "Over 100 American cities doubled or more than doubled in population during the 1880s": *Shaping of the American Past,* 397. Also see Wiebe, *Search for Order*.

32. The theoretical tools employed in conceptualizing this project come from a variety of disciplines, including anthropology, sociology, history, psychology, and the history of religions. Some of the specific works that have been especially important to the following study are Hertz, "Contributions to Study of Death"; van Gennep, *Rites of Passage;* Huntington and Metcalf, *Celebrations of Death;* Huizinga, *Waning of the Middle Ages;* Morin, *Homme et la mort;* Le Goff, "Mentalities: A History of Ambiguities," in Le Goff and Nora, *Constructing the Past;* Darnton, *Great Cat Massacre;* Geertz, *Interpretation of Cultures;* Richardson, *Death, Dissection, and the Destitute;* Foucault, *Birth of the Clinic;* and Hunt, *Family Romance*. In addition to these studies, the works of two French historians, Philippe Ariès and most importantly Michel Vovelle, have been absolutely critical to my research.

33. My use of the term *dechristianization* comes primarily from Vovelle's work in the history of death in the West. See *Piété baroque et déchristianisation* and *Mort et l'Occident*.

34. The French are particularly attentive to death and the dead, and quite a few of their works have been important to this study. In addition to works already cited by Vovelle, Ariès, Foucault, van Gennep, Hertz, and Morin, see Vovelle, *Mourir Autrefois;* Ariès, *Essais sur l'histoire;* Le Goff, *Birth of Purgatory;* and Thomas, *Rites de mort*. For other works on death in the European context see Gorer, "Pornography of Death," in *Death, Grief, and Mourning;* Richardson, *Death, Dissection, and the Destitute;* Camporesi, *Incorruptible Flesh;* Praz, *Romantic Agony;* Tenenti, *Vie et la mort;* and Kselman, *Death and the Afterlife*. There have been many review articles on the study of death as well, including Vovelle, "Sur la mort," in *Idéologies et mentalités;* Whaley, Introduction, *Mirrors of Mortality;* Stone, "Death and Its History"; Mitchell, "Philippe Ariès and the French Way of Death"; and McManners, "Death and the French Historians."

35. See, for example, Mitford, *American Way of Death;* Farrell, *Inventing the American Way of Death;* Huntington and Metcalf, "American Deathways," in *Celebrations of Death,* 184–211; Stannard, "Toward an American Way of Death," in *Puritan Way of Death,* 167–196; and Jackson, Introduction, in Jackson, *Passing*.

36. Stannard, *Puritan Way of Death*; Covey, *American Pilgrimage*; and Delumeau, *Sin and Fear.*

George Washington's Invisible Corpse

1. Cargill, Family Papers.
2. Hough, *Washingtoniana*, 102.
3. Schwartz, *George Washington*, 93.
4. Ibid.
5. Hough, *Washingtoniana*, 111.
6. Ibid., 138.
7. There have been some instances of popular religious activity in early American history, however, that resembled the cults of relics. After his death, the body of the Methodist revivalist George Whitefield became an object of interest and value to many individuals who venerated his remains and place of burial. See Cray, "Memorialization and Enshrinement."
8. Albanese discusses the mythology of the first president and how the nation remembered Washington after his death in "Our Father, Our Washington," in *Sons of the Fathers*, 143–181.
9. Artistic representations of Washington's death illuminated many of these themes. For a brief discussion of how artists interpreted Washington's death, see Gausted, *Faith of Our Fathers*, 70–83; on the millennial theme in early American history in general, see Tuveson, *Redeemer Nation.*
10. Schorsch, *Mourning Becomes America*, 1, 3–8.
11. "Corpse and the Beaver Hat."
12. *Report of the Case*, 2.
13. Ibid.
14. "Corpse and the Beaver Hat," 842.
15. Ibid.
16. Ibid., 845.
17. Ibid., 843.
18. *Report of the Case*, 56.
19. Ibid.

1. Signs of Death

1. "Funeral Thoughts."
2. "Elegy on the Death of Mr. Harfield Lyndsey."
3. Bode, *Anatomy of Popular Culture*, 269.
4. Garrett, *At Home*, 240.
5. Much of the research for this period has focused on Massachusetts, a state that tended to have fairly reliable vital statistics. In "Mortality Rates and Trends," 184, Maris Vinovskis addresses the question of whether or not this information can be applied to other states: "The mortality rates from Massachusetts should prove generally useful to economic historians, particularly whenever these rates can be broken down by the type of

town for estimating rates in other states after adjusting for differences in the degree of urbanization and industrialization."

6. Shryock, *Medicine in America*, 14.

7. Vinovskis, *Fertility in Massachusetts*, 35; Yasuba, *Birth Rates of the White Population*, 82, 100; also, see Daniel Scott Smith, "Differential Mortality in the United States," 759: "Farmers had the lowest mortality in places with populations under 2,500, which suggests that rural isolation had its health advantages."

8. On rural death rates see Vinovskis, "Mortality Rates and Trends," 205. The lack of solid statistical data yields a wide range of interpretation. See Florin, *Death in New England*, fig. 22, p. 49; Yasuba, *Birth Rates of the White Population*, 89–91; Jaffe and Laurie, "Abridged Life Table"; and Shryock, *Medicine in America*, 128.

9. Fischer, *Growing Old in America*, 3.

10. Vinovskis, "Jacobson Life Table of 1850," 720.

11. Smith, "Differential Mortality in the United States," 735.

12. Nugent, *Structures of American Social History*, 56.

13. Larkin, *Reshaping of Everyday Life*, 75.

14. Stone, Diaries, 1847.

15. Sarah Walker to David Hamant, 19 August 1837, Walker Letters.

2. From the Place of Death to the Space of Burial

1. Saum, *Popular Mood*, 94. For a comprehensive history of the deathbed scene in Western history, see Ariès, *Hour of Our Death*.

2. Written account of Harriet Peck's death, Peck, Perez Family Papers, 1821. Also see, for example, letter from James H. Sargent to Mary Sargent Lyman, 13 September 1854, Bullard Family Papers, and journal entry of Louisa Adams Park, Park Family Papers, May, 1801.

3. Saum, *Popular Mood*, 82.

4. This effort to combat bodily decomposition has a long history in Western civilization. For recent discussions of prevalent strategies in European and American history, see Ariès, *Hour of Our Death*; Vovelle, *Mort et l'Occident*; and Thomas, *Rites de mort*.

5. Farrell, *Inventing the American Way of Death*, 147; Larkin, *Reshaping of Everyday Life*, 98–99; Pike and Armstrong, "Custom and Change," in *Time to Mourn*, 15; Habenstein and Lamers, *History of American Funeral Directing*, 235–236; and Mitford, *American Way of Death*, 199.

6. Stone, Diaries.

7. Ulrich, *Midwife's Tale*, 39.

8. Ibid., 47.

9. Habenstein and Lamers, *History of American Funeral Directing*, 237.

10. Authors who assume that the task was left exclusively or almost exclusively to women include Pike and Armstrong, "Custom and Change," in *Time to Mourn*, 15; Habenstein and Lamers, *History of American Funeral Directing*, 235–236; and Rumford, "Role of Death." Also see Runblad's dissertation, "From 'Shrouding Woman,' to

Lady Assistant," which provides a sociological analysis of women and the treatment of the dead in American history.

11. Clark, Journal.

12. Letter from Samuel Smith to Susan Eleanor, Smith Collection.

13. Richardson, *Death, Dissection and the Destitute,* 17.

14. Larkin, *Reshaping of Everyday Life,* 99.

15. Coffin, *Death in Early America,* 104; and Rumford, "Role of Death," 77–78.

16. For discussion of this activity see Rumford, "Role of Death," 37; and Mitford, *American Way of Death,* 199.

17. There are numerous references to this activity in the regional oral histories collected by the WPA Federal Writers Project in the New England area, many of which describe the years before the Civil War. This report comes from Mrs. Frank Webber of Bowdoinham, Maine, 1938. See also Rumford, "Role of Death," 37.

18. Farrell, *Inventing the American Way of Death,* 147.

19. Sargent, *Dealings with the Dead,* 1: 13.

20. Ibid.

21. Letter from Samuel Smith to Susan Eleanor, 17 September 1837, Smith Collection.

22. Cole, "New England Funerals," 217; see also Larkin, *Reshaping of Everyday Life,* 100.

23. Davis, Diary, 1839.

24. Rumford, "Role of Death," 57; also see Dwight, *My Native Land,* 20; Cole, "New England Funerals," 220; and Coffin, *Death in Early America,* 116.

25. Habenstein and Lamers, *History of American Funeral Directing,* 356–357.

26. Cole, "New England Funerals," 220; and Rumford "Role of Death," 60–61.

27. West Bridgewater Hearse Books, Massachusetts, 1812–1813.

28. For another example of the eventual acceptance of the use of hearses, see Smith, *History of Peterborough, New Hampshire,* 226.

29. Mesick, *English Traveller in America,* 87; on this practice in English popular culture see Richardson *Death, Dissection, and the Destitute,* 23–24.

30. Cole, "New England Funeral," 218; Larkin, *Reshaping of Everyday Life,* 100; and Farrell, *Inventing the American Way of Death,* 147.

31. Bond, Journals, 1817.

32. Anderson, *Recollections,* 160. There are numerous descriptions of funeral processions in published writings from the period. For further descriptions of funerals in the North see, for example, Niemcewicz, *Under Their Vine Tree,* 117–118, 234–235.

33. Park, Journal.

34. Rumford, "Role of Death," 7–8; Farrell, *Inventing the American Way of Death,* 147–148; and Mitford, *American Way of Death,* 199.

35. "Funeral Scene," 231.

36. Larkin, *Reshaping of Everyday Life,* 102.

3. Simplicity Lost

1. Rosenberg, *Cholera Years,* 1; Larkin, *Reshaping of Everyday Life,* 82–83; and Shryock, *Medicine and Society in America,* 161.

2. John Sherwood to Ann Getz Leech Lake, 4 July 1849, Ann (Getz) Lake Correspondence.

3. Rosenberg, *Cholera Years*, 112. For a firsthand account of this experience see Thorburn, *Forty Years' Residence*, 56–57.

4. Scharf and Westcott, *History of Philadelphia*, 3: 2357.

5. Hone, *Diary*, 848.

6. Duncan, *Travels Through the United States*, 312–313.

7. Fisher, *Philadelphia Perspective*, 164–165.

8. Duncan, *Travels Through the United States*, 313.

9. Fisher, *Philadelphia Perspective*, 19.

10. Ibid., 210.

11. Ibid., 330. Gender discrimination might also work in the reverse, most often in the case of the death of an infant, when, except for the father, only women would be involved in the funeral. See Duncan, *Travels Through the United States*, 314.

12. King, *Handbook*, 465.

13. See, for example, the short discussion of Mount Auburn in an early history of another famous "rural" cemetery, *Allegheny Cemetery*, 13.

14. Dearborn, *History of Mount Auburn*, 52.

15. Sargent, *Dealings with the Dead*, 1: 46.

16. Histories of the funeral director can be found in Habenstein and Lamers, *History of American Funeral Directing*; Pine, *Caretaker of the Dead*; and Farrell, *Inventing the American Way of Death*, 146–183.

17. Two receipts that furnished this information came from the Bullard Family Papers and the Smith Collection.

18. Habenstein and Lamers, *History of American Funeral Directing*, 357–364.

19. Ibid., 251–310.

20. Ibid., 265.

21. "In the Board of Health, 1810."

22. Ibid.

23. Ibid.

24. Ibid.

25. Stannard, *Puritan Way of Death*.

4. The Great Escape

1. Many books have been written on death in the Christian tradition. Some of the most useful for this research have been Ariès, *Hour of Our Death* and *Western Attitudes Toward Death*; Vovelle, *Mort et l'Occident*; McDannell and Lang, *Heaven*; and Hick, *Death and Eternal Life*. For a recent discussion of Christian perspectives about bodily resurrection in the ancient and medieval West, see Bynum, *Resurrection of the Body*.

2. The most comprehensive study on death in Puritan culture is Stannard, *Puritan Way of Death*. Also see Geddes, *Welcome Joy*; Fischer, "Death Ways," in *Albion's Seed*, 111–116; and Covey, "Destination Death," in *American Pilgrimage*, 11–25.

3. Willard, *Mourners Cordial*, 62–63; quoted in Geddes, *Welcome Joy*, 26. Also,

Vovelle explores these themes, and their eventual demise, in New England graveyard epitaphs in "Century of American Epitaphs."

4. Fischer, "Death Ways," in *Albion's Seed*, 114.

5. Stannard, *Puritan Way of Death*, 89.

6. Many works explore the preoccupation with sin and punishment in Puritan history, including Stannard, *Puritan Way of Death*; Covey, *American Pilgrimage*; and Delumeau, *Sin and Fear.*

7. For discussions of the change in Protestant theology during this period, see, for example, Ahlstrom, *Religious History*, 385–454; Albanese, *America*, 85–109; Miller, *Life of the Mind*; and McLoughlin, *Revivals, Awakenings, and Reform*, 98–140.

8. *Complete Sermons of Emerson*, 1: 309. This quotation is from Emerson's sermon on Psalm 23:4, "Though I walk through the valley of the shadow of death."

9. This movement in American Protestant theology was skewed toward Catholicism and a romantic return to "historic" traditionalism. Nevin and others sought to reinvigorate the Protestant church through a renewed interest in liturgical and sacramental practices, valorizing a corporate understanding of worship over an individual one. See Ahlstrom, *Religious History*, 615–632; Nichols, *Romanticism in American Theology*; and Hudson, *Religion in America*, 160–164.

10. Nevin, *Mystical Presence*, 4: 169.

11. Ibid.; emphasis in original.

12. Ibid. Also see a letter written by Nevin expressing his condolences to a couple who had lost their son, quoted in Appel, *Life and Work of Nevin*, 765. For another example of how High Churchmen interpreted the meaning of death, see the writings of John Henry Hobart, Episcopal bishop in New York, including *Christian's Manual of Faith* and *Funeral Address.*

13. *Constitution of the Presbyterian Church*, 195–196.

14. On the history of evangelicalism in America see Ahlstrom, *Religious History*; Hudson, *Religion in America*; McLoughlin, *Revivals, Awakenings, and Reforms*, and Introduction, *American Evangelicals*; Sweet, *Evangelical Tradition*; and Schneider, *Way of the Cross.*

15. Many studies investigate the changing religious and cultural landscape of the antebellum period. See, for example, Douglas, *Feminization of American Culture*; Johnson, *Shopkeeper's Millennium*; and Ryan, *Cradle of the Middle Class.*

16. Ariès subsumes these trends under his category "the death of the other" in *Hour of Our Death*, 410–556. On the domestication of death in general during the nineteenth century see Douglas, *Feminization of American Culture.*

17. Ariès, *Hour of Our Death*, 410–474; quotation is from 473.

18. For a psychoanalytic analysis of this scene and its relationship to sexuality, see Fiedler, *Love and Death*, 264–269.

19. Stowe, *Uncle Tom's Cabin*, 295.

20. Dwight, *Sermon*. For another example of how evangelicals in this period understood the meaning of death see Lyman Beecher's reflections on the death of his son in *Autobiography*, 346.

21. Dwight, *Theology Explained and Defended*, 4: 435.

22. Numerous studies explore the religious revivals of the first half of the nineteenth

century. Two works that have been especially useful are McLoughlin, *Revivals, Awakenings, and Reform;* and Weisberger, *They Gathered at the River.*

23. For discussions of Finney's life, work, and impact, see Cross, *Burned-Over District;* McLoughlin, *Revivals, Awakenings, and Reform,* 122–130; Weisberger, *They Gathered at the River,* 87–126; and Harman, *Charles Grandison Finney.*

24. On the death of the self see Ariès, *Western Attitudes Toward Death,* 27–52, and *Hour of Our Death,* 95–293.

25. Finney, "How to Change Your Heart," in *Sermons on Important Subjects,* 56.

26. Finney, "Eternal Life," in *Promise of the Spirit,* 36.

27. Tuveson presents a thorough discussion of millennial themes in American history in *Redeemer Nation;* also see Ernest R. Sandeen, "Millennialism" in Gausted, *Rise of Adventism,* 104–118.

28. Moore, *Religious Outsiders.* For more specific discussions of Miller and this movement, see the collection of articles in Numbers and Miller, *Disappointed,* especially Ruth Alden Doan, "Millerism and Evangelical Culture"; and Rowe, *Thunder and Trumpets.*

29. Doan, *Miller Heresy,* 78.

30. "Scene of the Last Day," in Bliss, *Memoirs of William Miller,* 413.

31. For a discussion of these and other elements of Unitarian liberalism, see Howe, *Unitarian Conscience;* and Wright, *Beginnings of Unitarianism.*

32. As the leader of one of the dominant religious movements in New England society in the nineteenth century, Channing had an impact on many areas of American culture, including literature and humanitarianism. See Ahlstrom, *Theology in America,* 194.

33. "Heaven" in *Memoir of William Ellery Channing,* 2: 22.

34. "Future Glory of the Good," in *Memoir of William Ellery Channing,* 2: 27. For another example of Unitarian interpretations of the meaning of death see Gannett's funeral sermon for Channing, *Sermon Delivered.*

35. Douglas *Feminization of American Culture;* and Ariès, *Hour of Our Death,* 450–454.

36. For one of the most recent examinations of spiritualism in America, and of the relation between women and this movement, see Braude, *Radical Spirits.* Also see Moore, *In Search of White Crows.*

37. Davis, *Great Harmonia,* 1: 157.

38. Ibid., 1: 166; emphasis in original.

39. Ibid., 1: 171.

40. Cole presents a similar process relating to changing attitudes toward aging and perceptions of old age in *Journey of Life.*

5. "The Law of Nature"

1. Vovelle writes that a "fundamental rupture" in attitudes toward death occurred at the turn of the eighteenth century, when Christian strategies of interpretation offered only one series of meanings among a host of other possible socially legitimate options: *Mort et l'Occident,* 532.

2. On Emerson and Transcendentalism see Ahlstrom, *Religious History,* 599–609; Albanese, *Corresponding Motion;* and Boller, *American Transcendentalism, 1830–1860.*

3. *Young Emerson Speaks,* 138.

4. "Cape Cod," in *Walden and Other Writings,* 442.

5. Ibid., 446.

6. Brief discussions of representations of death in American art can be found in Wolf, *Romantic Re-Vision;* and Davidson, *Eccentrics.*

7. On the "dark romanticism" that flourished in Europe as well as England, see Praz, *Romantic Agony;* and see Vovelle's discussion of art, literature, and philosophy in nineteenth-century Europe in the chapter "Des inquiétudes aux certitudes" in *Mort et l'Occident,* 575–604.

8. Harris, *Artist in American Society,* 117. Studies of Cole and his work can also be found in Novak, *American Painting,* 61–79; Powell, *Thomas Cole;* and Davidson, *Eccentrics.*

9. Miller, "Nature and the National Ego," in *Errand into the Wilderness,* 214; also see Bode's brief discussion of Cole's works in *Anatomy of American Popular Culture,* 70–71.

10. Albanese provides a discussion of nature and republican religion in *Nature Religion in America,* 47–79.

11. Hawthorne, "Roger Malvin's Burial." Another literary example of this theme can be found in Cooper's *Last of the Mohicans.*

12. For some fascinating and diverse critical readings of this short story, see Fredrick C. Crews, "The Logic of Compulsion of 'Roger Malvin's Burial,'" in Bloom, *Nathaniel Hawthorne,* 71–83; McIntosh, "Nature and the Frontier," 188–204; Frank, *Hawthorne's Early Tales,* 192–200; and Slotkin, *Regeneration Through Violence,* 475–485.

13. Hawthorne, "Roger Malvin's Burial," 85. McIntosh also discusses the connection between Native peoples and frontiersmen in this story, commenting on the irony of Malvin's body position when Bourne left him to die: "Reuben leaves Roger sitting upright in the posture of Freneau's Indian hunter and warrior dressed for burial; in effect he has buried him alive as if he were an Indian": "Nature and the Frontier," 194.

14. On the history of cemeteries in the West see Ariès, *Hour of Our Death;* and Vovelle, *Mort et l'Occident.* For discussions of the American scene see Sloane, *Last Great Necessity;* Linden-Ward, *Silent City on a Hill;* and Stanley French, "The Cemetery as Cultural Institution: The Establishment of Mount Auburn and the 'Rural Cemetery' Movement," in Stannard, *Death in America.*

15. Allen, *Documents and Facts,* iii.

16. [Coffin], *Dangers and Duties of Sepulture,* 27.

17. Other examples include Atticus, *Hints on Interments;* and *Report on the Subject of Interment.*

18. For a comprehensive discussion of these rationalizations in connection with the rural cemetery movement see Linden-Ward, *Silent City on a Hill.*

19. French discusses these sentiments in "Cemetery as Cultural Institution."

20. Story, *Address at Mount Auburn,* 13.

21. Walter, *Mount Auburn Illustrated,* 9.

22. Jacob Bigelow, "Interment of the Dead," in Walter, *Mount Auburn Illustrated,* 29.

23. Ibid., 34, 35.

24. The quoted phrase is from the subtitle and work of Linden-Ward, *Silent City on a Hill: Landscapes of Memory and Boston's Mount Auburn Cemetery.*

25. For further discussion of the relationship between scientific naturalism and death see Farrell, *Inventing the American Way of Death.*

6. Morbid Obsessions

1. Louisa Jane Trumball Diaries, 7 February 1833, Trumball Family Papers, 1773–1896.

2. Ibid., 30 June 1833; emphasis in original.

3. Journal of Louisa Park, May 1801, Park Family Papers, 1800–1890.

4. Ibid.

5. Josiah Stone Diaries, Old Sturbridge Village Library.

6. Bentley, *Diary,* 2: 372.

7. Sargent, *Dealings with the Dead,* 1: 45–46.

8. Emerson, *Journals,* 4: 7.

9. Phoebe Lloyd, "Posthumous Mourning Pictures," in Pike and Armstrong, *Time to Mourn.*

10. Richardson, *Painting in America,* 174.

11. Frankenstein, *William Sidney Mount,* 285.

12. Ibid., 142.

13. Ibid., 335.

14. For a complete discussion of this form of portraiture see Lloyd, "Posthumous Mourning Pictures."

15. Ibid., 71, 73.

16. Ruby, "Post-Mortem Portraiture in America."

17. Meinwald, "Memento Mori," 8. Burns has published a fascinating collection of postmortem photography in American history in *Sleeping Beauty.*

18. Rinhart, "Rediscovery," 80.

19. Ruby, "Post-Mortem Portraiture in America," 208–209; also see Meinwald, "Memento Mori."

20. Fiedler, "Male Novel."

21. For a discussion of this form of romanticism in Europe see Praz, *Romantic Agony.* Michel Vovelle presents a full discussion of dark romanticism in England and Europe in the chapter "Des inquietudes aux certitudes" in *Mort et l'Occident,* 575–604.

22. Reynolds, *Beneath the American Renaissance,* 178.

23. Ibid., 188 ff.; for a discussion specifically focused on the literature and mythology of the frontier see Slotkin, *Regeneration Through Violence.*

24. Reynolds provides an insightful analysis on the "sensational" literature of the period as well as on Lippard himself in *Beneath the American Renaissance.* Also see Reynolds's *George Lippard.*

25. Lippard, *Quaker City,* 3–4.

26. Fiedler, "Male Novel," 80.

27. Lippard, *Quaker City,* 304.

28. Review quoted in Reynolds, *Beneath the American Renaissance,* 91.

29. Lippard, *Quaker City,* 437.

30. Ibid., 438.

31. Foucault, *Birth of the Clinic*. This book provides an analysis of the relationship between death and the beginnings of modern pathology in France.

32. For a thorough examination of this practice in England see Richardson, *Death, Dissection, and the Destitute*.

33. Humphrey, "Dissection and Discrimination."

34. This account is found in Waite, "Grave Robbing in New England," 287.

35. There have been numerous short studies on the history of anatomy and anatomy laws, including a chapter entitled "Body-Snatching: Anatomy Laws" in Harrington's *Harvard Medical School*; Waite, "Development of Anatomical Laws"; Bardeen, "Anatomy in America"; and Marks and Beatty, *Story of Medicine in America*, especially chapter 6, "Dissection and Anatomy," 73–97.

36. *Report of the Select Committee.*

37. Ibid., 47; emphasis in original.

38. Ibid., 54.

39. Ibid., 70.

John Brown's Body

1. One of the best historical accounts of Brown's life is Oates's *To Purge This Land*.

2. Sanborn, *Life of John Brown*, 613.

3. Oates, *To Purge This Land*, 318–319.

4. Ibid., 344.

5. Abels, *Man on Fire*, 369–370; Oates, *To Purge This Land*, 356–357.

6. Drew, *John Brown Invasion*, 71.

7. Wiley wrote in *Life of Billy Yank*, 159, that "the number-one song in Federal camps was 'John Brown's Body.'"

8. McPherson, *Battle Cry of Freedom*, 212–213.

9. To Martha and Elizabeth Gable, 23 August 1864, William Morton Gable Collection. Although another account (see note 16) mentions distant Charleston, Gable was doubtless actually buried near neighboring Charles Town, West Virginia.

10. To Martha and Elizabeth Gable, Gable Collection.

11. Letter to Martha and Elizabeth Gable, 28 April 1862, Gable Collection.

12. To Gable family, Gable Collection.

13. To Gable family, Gable Collection.

14. To Gable family, Gable Collection.

15. To Gable family, Gable Collection.

16. Rev. Samuel W. Gehrett, quoted in Farrar, *Twenty-Second Pennsylvania Cavalry*, 341. For a geographical clarification of Gable's burial site see note 9.

17. To Elizabeth Gable, 27 October 1864, Martinsburg, West Virginia, Gable Collection.

7. Death During Wartime

1. Vinovskis provides a wealth of information on mortality rates during the Civil War as well as comparative data with other wars in "Have Social Historians Lost the Civil

War?" in *Toward a Social History,* 1–30; quotation is from 5. Vinovskis's data do not include the relatively light casualties of the Persian Gulf war.

2. Ibid., 7, 29. According to Herman Hattaway ("The Embattled Continent," in Davis, *Touched by Fire,* 1: 46), roughly "18 percent of the slightly more than 2,000,000 individuals who served as Federals perished. . . . In the Union army 1 out of approximately 30 men was killed in action, 1 of 46 died of wounds. . . . 1 of 7 captured died in prison." In one of the earliest and most comprehensive analyses of military losses, William F. Fox calculated the percentages of men who were killed within specific regiments. Throughout the course of the war more than 10 percent of Union soldiers from any given regiment were killed immediately on the field of battle or died of wounds inflicted during combat. In the Fourteenth New Jersey, Sixth Corps, for example, around 11 percent of the unit were killed; in the 141st Pennsylvania, Third Corps, just over 16 percent; and in the First Maine, Second Corps, just under 20 percent. Fox also estimated the percentage of total deaths by state based on War Department statistics compiled in 1885. According to his figures, Rhode Island lost roughly 10 percent of its soldiers; New Hampshire almost 17 percent; and Vermont nearly 20 percent (*Regimental Losses,* 10–14; 526).

3. These statistics are taken from Livermore, *Numbers and Losses.*

4. Adams, *Doctors in Blue,* 224. McPherson writes, "twice as many Civil War soldiers died of disease as were killed and mortally wounded in combat," *Battle Cry of Freedom,* 485.

5. On disease in the Civil War see Adams, *Doctors in Blue;* Wiley, *Life of Billy Yank,* 124–151; Steiner, *Disease in the Civil War;* Robertson, *Soldiers Blue and Gray,* 145–169; and McPherson, *Battle Cry of Freedom,* 485–489.

6. Paluden, *"People's Contest",* 37.

7. McPherson, *Battle Cry of Freedom,* 557.

8. Humphreys, *Field, Camp, Hospital, and Prison,* 50.

9. Radcliffe, *Journal of the War,* unpaginated.

10. Ibid. For a description of execution by firing squad, see Wiley, *Life of Billy Yank,* 206–207; also, see Masur's examination of the history of executions in the United States, up to and including the Civil War, in *Rites of Execution.*

11. Webster, *My Diary in Field and Camp,* Webster Collection; emphasis in original.

12. Page, *Letters of a War Correspondent,* 10. Also see Wiley, *Life of Billy Yank,* 347.

13. Illustration from *Frank Leslie's Illustrated* 14, no. 342 (1862): 64.

14. "On Antietam Battle," *Harper's Weekly* 6, no. 302 (1862): 655.

15. McPherson, *Battle Cry of Freedom,* 686–687.

8. *"Let the Dead Bury the Dead"*

1. "130th Pennsylvania Regiment," *Frank Leslie's Illustrated* 15, no. 368 (1863): 53.

2. Rhodes, *All for the Union,* 71.

3. "Battlefield of Bull Run," *Frank Leslie's Illustrated* 17, no. 424 (1863): 124.

4. Wilkinson, *Mother, May You Never See the Sights,* 262–263.

5. Johnson, *Muskets and Medicine,* 111.

6. Hallock, *Letters from a Pennsylvania Chaplain,* 8 and 24.

7. "Burial of Col. Garesche," *Frank Leslie's Illustrated* 15, no. 387 (1863): 366.

8. "Graveyard in the Camp," *Frank Leslie's Illustrated* 15, no. 390 (1863): 401.

9. McAllister, *Civil War Letters,* 319.

10. Page, *Letters of a War Correspondent,* 181.

11. Wightman, *From Antietam to Fort Fisher,* 95

12. Alcott, *Hospital Sketches,* 58.

13. "Military Hospitals at Fortress Monroe," *Harper's New Monthly Magazine* 24, no. 171 (1864): 315–316.

14. Hyde, *Captive of War,* 262.

15. McPherson, *Battle Cry of Freedom,* 285.

16. "Massachusetts Dead Returned Home," *Frank Leslie's Illustrated* 11, no. 286 (1861): 14.

17. Letter to sister, 7 February 1862, Woodward Collection.

18. Letter to parents, 1 August 1862, Glazier Collection.

19. M. H. Mills to Gen. Larkin Dickason, 11 November 1864, New Hampshire Civil War Collection.

20. Trumball, *War Memories,* 208.

21. Quoted in Duncan, *Medical Department in the Civil War,* 45–46.

22. Whitman, *Walt Whitman's Civil War,* 103–104.

23. Bucklin, *In Hospital and Camp,* 208.

24. Wightman, "In Search of My Son."

25. This is mentioned in Bradford, "Military Order of the Loyal Legion."

26. Advertisement in *Army and Navy Journal* 2, no. 5 (1864): 79.

27. Mayer, *Embalming,* 41.

28. "Miscellaneous," *Frank Leslie's Illustrated* 14, no. 340 (1862): 30.

29. Habenstein and Lamers, *History of American Funeral Directing,* 311–352; also see Edward C. Johnson, "The Origin and History of Embalming," in Mayer, *Embalming.*

30. Mayer, *Embalming,* 41–48; also see Habenstein and Lamers, *History of American Funeral Directing,* 337.

31. Holmes, "My Hunt After 'The Captain,' " 29.

32. Mayer, *Embalming,* 45; Johnson, "Brief History," 8.

33. Howe, *Reminiscences, 1819–1899,* 270.

34. Habenstein and Lamers, *History of American Funeral Directing,* 330.

35. Letter to mother, 20 May 1863, Colyer Collection.

36. Webster, *My Diary in Field and Camp.*

37. "Visit to General Butler," 438.

38. Trumball, *War Memories of an Army Chaplain,* 224–225.

39. R. B. Neal to Mr. Mason, 8 November 1864, New Hampshire Civil War Collection.

40. Dr. Thomas Holmes, who claimed to be the father of modern embalming, is a critical figure in the history of the practice in the United States. There does seem to be some discrepancy, however, surrounding many of his claims. See White and Sandrof, "That Was New York"; Habenstein and Lamers, *History of American Funeral Directing,* 323–328; Mayer, *Embalming,* 41–42; and Johnson, "Civil War Embalming."

41. Mayer, *Embalming,* 41; also see Habenstein and Lamers, *History of American Funeral Directing,* 324.

9. *National Interests*

1. Articles of Agreement, 5 May 1862.

2. Habenstein and Lamers list some of these undertakers in *History of American Funeral Directing*, 333.

3. Steere, *Graves Registration Service*, 3. For other brief histories of national policy for burying the military dead see MacCloskey, *Hallowed Ground*, 17–45; and Risch, *Quartermaster Support of the Army*, 462–468.

4. Risch, *Quartermaster Support of the Army*, 462.

5. MacCloskey, *Hallowed Ground*, 18.

6. General Order No. 75, *General Orders of the War Department*, 1: 158.

7. General Order No. 33, *General Orders of the War Department*, 2: 248.

8. Steere, *Graves Registration Service*.

9. Risch, *Quartermaster Support of the Army*, 465; and Steere, *Graves Registration Service*, 4.

10. Quoted in MacCloskey, *Hallowed Ground*, 24.

11. Steere, *Graves Registration Service*, 7.

12. General Order No. 39, 15 March 1865, quoted in Mayer, *Embalming*, 44.

13. Sloane, *Last Great Necessity*, 114.

14. Risch writes about the increasing popularity of these cemeteries for war veterans in the decades following the war. Risch, *Quartermaster Support of the Army*, 467.

15. Wills, *Revised Report*.

16. Wills, *Revised Report*, 8; on black workers at Gettysburg see, for example, Cole and Frampton, *Gettysburg National Cemetery*, 5.

17. Wills, *Revised Report*, 9; emphasis in original.

18. "Report of Samuel Weaver," 19 March 1864, in Wills, *Revised Report*, 149.

19. Ibid., 150–151.

10. *"Resurrection Days" and Redemptive Blood*

1. Two recent studies that address the construction of meaning in the face of devastating human losses during the Civil War are Mitchell, *Vacant Chair;* and Sweet *Traces of War.*

2. The "sacred" quality of Lincoln's address is based not only on its centrality in American mythology, but also—like many sacred objects—on its economic value in the marketplace. At a Civil War Round Table Association meeting in November 1993, Dr. Lloyd Ostendorf, who claims to have one of the few original versions of the address, relayed the great interest auction houses like Sotheby's and Christie's have in this document.

3. This example, as well as other negative quotations, can be found in Warren, *Lincoln's Gettysburg Declaration*, 145–148.

4. Nevins, *Lincoln and the Gettysburg Address*, 7.

5. Thurow, *Abraham Lincoln*, 84–86.

6. Wills, *Lincoln at Gettysburg*, 77–78.

7. For more on this principle of exchange see Allen Grossman, "The Poetics of Union

in Whitman and Lincoln: An Inquiry toward the Relationship of Art and Poetry," in Michaels and Pease, *American Renaissance Reconsidered*; and Sweet, *Traces of War*, 27–34.

8. Moorhead, *American Apocalypse*, 45.

9. Furness, *Voice of the Hour*, 14–15. For a more comprehensive discussion of these themes see Moorhead, *American Apocalypse*; and Shattuck, *Shield and a Hiding Place*, 14–18.

10. Bushnell, *Reverses Needed*, 23.

11. For a comprehensive study of the Transcendentalists during the Civil War see Albrecht, "Theological Response of the Transcendentalists."

12. Letter of Emerson to Benjamin and Susan Rodman, 17 June 1863, cited in Fredrickson, *Inner Civil War*, 80–81.

13. Sunderland, *Crisis of the Times*, 34–35.

14. "The sublime whole," which Fredrickson uses in his analysis of "the individual response to suffering" during the Civil War, appeared in the diary of Josephine Shaw, daughter of Francis George Shaw: "One loses sight of the wounds and suffering, both of the enemies and one's own forces, in thinking of the sublime whole, the grand forward movement of thousands of men marching 'into the jaws of death,' calmly and cooly." Quoted in *Inner Civil War*, 84.

15. Horace Bushnell, "Our Obligations to the Dead," in McLoughlin, *American Evangelicals*.

16. Frothingham, *Seeds and Shells*, 3, 7–8.

17. Linderman, *Embattled Courage*, 87.

18. Mitchell provides an interesting analysis of the role women played during the war in "Men Without Women," in *Vacant Chair*, 71–87.

19. McPherson, *Battle Cry of Freedom*, 483–484; and Rosenberg, *Care of Strangers*, 216–217.

20. Pryor, *Clara Barton*, 94.

21. Alcott, *Hospital Sketches*, 58–59. Fredrickson also discusses Alcott's sentimentality and this particular death in *Inner Civil War*, 88.

22. Letter no. 4, "The Dying Soldier's Letter to his Wife," in Billingsley, *From the Flag to the Cross*, 114.

23. Smith, "My Absent Brother," *Zion's Herald and Wesleyan Journal* 34 (January 1863): 72.

24. Moss, *Annals of the U.S. Christian Commission*; also see Shattuck, *Shield and a Hiding Place*, 85–86. For an analysis of the content of many evangelical sermons, see Quimby, "Recurrent Themes and Purposes," 425–436.

25. Moss, *Annals of the U.S. Christian Commission*, 202; emphasis in original.

26. On the prevalence of these corrupting influences, see Wiley's discussion of religion in the Union ranks in *Life of Billy Yank*, 247–274. For an examination of the contrasts between the masculine world of war and the feminine world of home see Mitchell, *Vacant Chair*.

27. Quoted in Moore, *Anecdotes, Poetry and Incidents*, 515; emphasis in original.

11. Disenchantment with the Mortal Remains

1. Farrell, *Inventing the American Way of Death*, 44–73; also see Vovelle's discussion of the various changes in attitudes toward death during this period in *Mort et l'Occident*, 367–503; and McManners, *Death and the Enlightenment*.

2. Mitchell, *Vacant Chair*, 8.

3. McPherson, *Battle Cry of Freedom*, 730.

4. McAllister, *Civil War Letters*, 420.

5. Fredrickson discusses the reactions of Emerson and Hawthorne, as well as many other leading cultural figures, in *Inner Civil War*.

6. Hawthorne to Henry A. Bright, Concord, 14 November 1861, in Masur, "... *the Real War*," 165–166.

7. For excellent discussions of the effects of the war experience, see Linderman, *Embattled Courage;* and Mitchell, *Civil War Soldiers*.

8. Holmes, *Touched with Fire*, 78.

9. Rhodes, *All for the Union*, 84.

10. Radcliffe, *Journal of the War*.

11. Mitchell discusses the gendered characterizations that were pervasive throughout the war in *Vacant Chair*.

12. "Graveyard in the Camp," *Leslie's Illustrated Newspaper* 15, no. 390 (March 1863): 401.

13. Maxwell, *Lincoln's Fifth Wheel;* and Fredrickson, *Inner Civil War*, 98–112.

14. See Maxwell's *Lincoln's Fifth Wheel* for a complete history of the commission.

15. Fredrickson, *Inner Civil War*, 102–103.

16. United States Sanitary Commission, *Soldier's Friend*, 12–13.

17. Ibid., 33.

18. Quoted in Fredrickson, *Inner Civil War*, 90.

19. Fredrickson, *Inner Civil War*, 90. This book is an excellent examination of cultural and ideological shifts in the North that resulted from the war.

20. Robertson, *Soldiers Blue and Gray*, 225.

12. Looking Death in the Face

1. Brinton, *Memoirs*, 179; also see Adams, *Doctors in Blue*, 34.

2. Brinton, *Memoirs*, 180, 181.

3. Ibid., 181, 188.

4. Ibid., 188.

5. Ibid., 190.

6. Ibid., 190–191; emphasis in the original.

7. Ibid., 207.

8. Circular letter from the surgeon general's office, Washington, D.C., 24 June 1864. Reprinted in Barnes, *Medical and Surgical History*, vi.

9. Such a compilation was put together in 1866: Woodhull, *Catalogue of the Surgical Section*.

10. Brinton, *Memoirs,* 189.

11. There have been a number of valuable works on visual representation in the Civil War, including Thompson, *Image of War;* Sweet, "Some Versions of Pastoral," in *Traces of War;* Trachtenberg, "Albums of War"; and especially the work of Frassanito, *Antietam* and *Gettysburg.*

12. Frassanito, *Antietam,* 17.

13. Quoted in ibid., 288.

14. "Battle of Antietam," *Harper's Weekly* 6, no. 303 (October 1862): 663.

15. Holmes, "Doings of the Sunbeam," 266–267.

16. Trachtenberg, "Albums of War," 8.

17. Frassanito, *Antietam,* 286.

18. Frassanito, *Gettysburg,* 27–28.

19. Sweet explores the "pastoral" sensibility that can be found in many of these photographs: *Traces of War,* 107–137.

20. For a full discussion of this photograph see Frassanito, *Gettysburg,* 191; Sweet engages in a much more interpretive reading of the photographic series produced from Gettysburg in *Traces of War,* 107–137.

21. Frassanito, *Gettysburg,* 185.

22. Wightman, "In Search of My Son," *American Heritage* 14, no. 2 (February 1963): 77–78.

23. From a letter dated 8 November 1864, in Smith, *Reminiscences of an Army Nurse,* 123.

24. Townsend, *Campaigns of a Non-Combatant,* 180–181.

25. Trumball, *War Memories of an Army Chaplain,* 208.

26. Habenstein and Lamers, *History of American Funeral Directing,* 338.

Lincoln's Hallowed, Hollowed Body

1. Runblad, "From 'Shrouding Woman' to Lady Assistant."

2. For a more thorough discussion of Mary Todd Lincoln's life after the assassination, see Baker, *Mary Todd Lincoln;* Turner and Turner, *Mary Todd Lincoln;* and Randall, *Mary Todd Lincoln.*

3. Kunhardt and Kunhardt, *Twenty Days,* 1, 80.

4. Quoted in ibid., 80.

5. Ibid., 93.

6. This was the same firm employed by the Lincolns when, in the midst of war, their young son Willie died of fever: ibid., 95; also see Shea, *Lincoln Memorial,* 111.

7. Pittsburgh *Daily Post,* 22 April 1865, 2.

8. Kunhardt, *Twenty Days,* 120; and Sandburg, *Abraham Lincoln,* 1: 735.

9. For one account of many of the activities around the country, see Shea, *Lincoln Memorial.*

10. Philadelphia *Daily Evening Bulletin,* 24 April 1865, 1.

11. Page, *Letters from a War Correspondent,* 364; emphasis in original.

12. *New York Times,* 25 April 1865, 1. Also see remarks in Sandburg, *Abraham*

Lincoln, 739; and the commentary by a visitor from England, who said, among other things, that the "process of embalming had been unsuccessful. . . . They had to resort to the hideous trick of puffing out the cheeks and painting them before they could expose it to view": Kean, *Death and Funeral of Lincoln,* 22.

13. Kunhardt, *Twenty Days,* 256.

14. Ibid., 256–257.

15. Quoted in Shea, *Lincoln Memorial,* 230–231. For a recent analysis of the religious discourse that appeared in the North after the assassination see Chesebrough, *"No Sorrow Like Our Sorrow."*

16. My discussion of Lincoln's two bodies derives in part from Ernst Kantorwicz's examination of the legal fictions employed in the construction of the king's two bodies in England and France. In medieval funeral processions the effigy of the king and his actual body represented two distinct images, the immortality of the crown and the transient remains of the mortal who inhabited the crown. See Kantorwicz, *The King's Two Bodies.*

17. See, for example, the comments by Henry Ward Beecher in his sermon delivered the Sunday following the death: Shea, *Lincoln Memorial,* 103.

18. See, for example, the speech by Henry W. Bellows, Unitarian minister and president of the U.S. Sanitary Commission, in ibid., 98. Also see Rogin's analysis of the symbolism of Lincoln's death in "The King's Two Bodies," in *Ronald Reagan, the Movie.*

19. For a brief discussion of the rituals in Washington see Mary P. Ryan, "The American Parade: Representations of the Nineteenth-Century Social Order," in Hunt, *New Cultural History,* 143.

20. Hamilton and Ostendorf, *Lincoln in Photographs,* 234. This observation is also quoted in Huntington and Metcalf, *Celebrations of Death,* 206.

21. Huntington and Metcalf write that as a result of the visibility of Lincoln's body, "public attitudes were made ready to accept the new techniques of embalming then being perfected": *Celebrations of Death,* 206–208; Pine writes that Lincoln's journey "brought about new public awareness of embalming" and that "people along its path became aware that it was possible to keep and view the dead for long periods of time": *Caretaker of the Dead,* 16.

13. The Business of Death in the Late Nineteenth Century

1. Larger towns and cities were significantly more receptive to these assumptions than were rural areas; they also provided the context in which the industry would experience its initial successes. This dichotomy is consistent with the changes related to burial in the antebellum period discussed in the first six chapters.

2. Kelley, *Shaping of the American Past,* vol. 2; Wiebe, *Search for Order;* Trachtenberg, *Incorporation of America;* and Sutherland, *Expansion of Everyday Life.*

3. Judith Walzer Leavitt, "Public Health and Preventive Medicine," in Numbers, *Education of American Physicians,* 251. For an excellent collection of essays on the history of public health see Part 2 in Leavitt and Numbers, *Sickness and Health in America.*

4. For a discussion on the efforts to address social problems in the nineteenth century,

see Boyer, *Urban Masses and Moral Order.* On how the notion of public health changed over the course of the nineteenth century see, for example, Rosenberg, *Cholera Years.*

5. Billings, "Registration of Vital Statistics," 33–59. Willcox, a historian of statistics, wrote in 1940 that "American citizens interested in the public-health movement and in the statistics of deaths as an important part of the foundation of that movement were much more numerous than those who cared about any other branch of vital statistics. For that reason the statistics of deaths became the starting point": *Studies in American Demography,* 201. Also see Habenstein and Lamers, *History of American Funeral Directing,* 450.

6. Waite, "Development of Anatomical Laws," 722; John B. Blake, "Anatomy," in Numbers, *Education of American Physicians,* 29–47; and Russell C. Maulitz, "Pathology," in the same volume, 122–142.

7. Humphrey, "Dissection and Discrimination," 821–823.

8. Ibid., 824; also see Waite, "Development of Anatomical Laws," 722–723.

9. Waite, "Development of Anatomical Laws," 722. Also see Starr's discussion of the changes in medical education encouraged by Charles Eliot, appointed president of Harvard University in 1869, in *Social Transformation of American Medicine,* 112–116. Finally, according to the historian Charles Bardeen, after 1870 the number of specialists in the field of anatomy increased significantly, and the prestige that the specialty assumed in medical training grew as well: "Anatomy in America," 98.

10. Waite, "Development of Anatomical Laws," 723.

11. The establishment of a national marketplace, the creation of a new class of professionals, and the emergence of an inventive discourse in marketing and advertisements promising "therapeutic release" from the anxieties and uncertainties that plagued everyday life contributed to the new culture. See the Introduction in Fox and Lears, *Culture of Consumption.* For other discussions of consumer culture at the end of the nineteenth century see Cotkin, *Reluctant Modernism;* and Trachtenberg, *Incorporation of America,* 130–139.

12. Although the term *casket* was current in this sense before the war, its usage became more widespread in the postbellum period. On the history of burial receptacles, see Habenstein and Lamers, *History of American Funeral Directing,* 251–310; Farrell, *Inventing the American Way of Death,* 169–172; and Harmer, *High Cost of Dying,* 89–97. Also see Habenstein and Lamers' discussion of the proliferation in styles of hearses after the war, 353–387.

13. Cotkin, *Reluctant Modernism,* 102–103.

14. Bledstein, *Culture of Professionalism,* 104. This work provides an excellent analysis of some of the trends associated with professionalism in the nineteenth century.

15. Quoted in "Modern Mummies," which describes a visit to Devore's offices: *Casket* 20, no. 10 (October 1895): 2.

16. According to the biographical sketch that serves as a preface to his reminiscences, Clarke's medical service in the Fifth Iowa Infantry "was of great value to him in later years when he became a teacher of embalming": Clarke, *Reminiscences of Early Embalming,* xxiv. Also see Habenstein and Lamers, *History of American Funeral Directing,* 344; Harmer, *High Cost of Dying,* 82; and Farrell, *Inventing the American Way of Death,* 163.

17. Farrell, *Inventing the American Way of Death,* 148.

18. On the creation of professional societies see Bledstein, *Culture of Professionalism,* 90.

19. For a fairly comprehensive discussion of "The Associational Impulse," see Habenstein and Lamers, *History of American Funeral Directing,* 445–503; also see Farrell's examination of the "Modernization of Funeral Service" in *Inventing the American Way of Death,* 146–183.

20. Funeral Directors' National Association, *Proceedings of the National Convention,* 19–20.

21. See the published record in Funeral Directors' National Association, *Second Annual Convention;* also see Farrell, *Inventing the American Way of Death,* 151.

22. *Second Annual Convention,* 33–35.

23. There are a number of religious histories of Protestantism that cover or focus on the period after the Civil War, including Ahlstrom, *Religious History,* 731–872; Marty, *Protestantism in the United States;* Carter, *Spiritual Crisis of the Gilded Age;* Saum, *Popular Mood of America;* and May, *Protestant Churches and Industrial America.*

24. Baker, *Mary Todd Lincoln,* 310–311.

25. Douglas, *Feminization of American Culture,* 240–272. Also see the discussion by Ariès in *Hour of Our Death,* 450–455.

26. Ahlstrom, *Religious History,* 490.

27. For an examination of the spiritualist movement during the nineteenth century see Braude, *Radical Spirits.*

28. Moorhead, "'As Though Nothing at All Had Happened,'" 461. An important primary source for Moorhead's study, as well as my own, is *That Unknown Country.* This work not only documents a range of postbellum Protestant beliefs but also includes writings from members of the Jewish and Catholic communities, presidents of universities, and representatives of "Asiatic clubs."

29. Ahlstrom, *Religious History,* 733–804; Marty, *Protestantism in the United States,* 197–206; and Curtis, *Consuming Faith.*

30. Ahlstrom, *Theology in America,* 75–76.

31. Gladden, "Thought of Heaven," 309, 313.

32. Gladden, *Christian Pastor,* 193–194.

33. Albanese, *America: Religions and Religion,* 102–103.

34. Henry Ward Beecher, "The Ages to Come," quoted in Goodwin, *Mode of Man's Immortality,* 236–237; also see Beecher, "Foretokens of Resurrection," in *Plymouth Pulpit.* Other examples of this tendency can be found in Goodwin's book. In the Methodist tradition, see, for example Stevenson, *Elements of Methodism.* Moorhead also examines these themes in "'As Though Nothing at All Had Happened.'"

35. Smith, "On the Day of Judgment," in *That Unknown Country,* 806.

36. For discussions of dispensational premillennialism see Ahlstrom, *Religious History,* 808–812; Albanese, *America: Religions and Religion,* 276–277; and Weber, *Living in the Shadow.*

37. Moorhead, "'As Though Nothing at All Had Happened'," 464.

38. Farrell, *Inventing the American Way of Death,* 44. Also see Saum, *Popular Mood of America,* 104–133.

39. Nugent, *Structures of American Social History,* 106–107.

40. See Wells, *Revolutions in Americans' Lives,* 126.

41. For an interesting discussion on the repercussions of declining mortality rates in the modern world, see Goldscheider, *Population, Modernization, and Social Structure,* 102–134.

42. Funeral Directors' National Association, *Proceedings of the National Convention,* 4–5.

Bibliography

Primary Sources

Alcott, Louisa M. *Hospital Sketches and Camp and Fireside Stories.* Boston: Robert Brothers, 1873.

Allegheny Cemetery: Historical Account of Incidents and Events Connected with its Establishment. Pittsburgh: Bakewell and Marthens, 1873.

Allen, Francis D. *Documents and Facts, Showing the Fatal Effects of Interments in Populous Cities.* New York: F. D. Allen, 1822.

Anderson, Jonathan. *The Recollections of Jonathan Anderson.* Boston: Christian Register Office, 1828.

Army and Navy Journal. Various issues, 1861–1865.

Articles of Agreement . . . between Captain Edward L. Hartz, Assistant Quarter Master, United States Army, of the one part, and Frank L. Sands of the City of Washington, D. C., of the other part. 5 May 1862. Manuscript Division, Library of Congress.

Atticus. *Hints on the Subject of Interments Within the City of Philadelphia: Addressed to the Serious Consideration of the Members of Councils, Commissioners of the Districts, and Citizens Generally.* Philadelphia: William Brown, 1838.

Barnes, Joseph K. *The Medical and Surgical History of the War of the Rebellion, 1861–1865.* Reprint. Wilmington, N.C.: Broadfoot, 1990.

Beecher, Henry Ward. *Plymouth Pulpit: Sermons Preached in Plymouth Church, Brooklyn.* New York: Fords, Howard and Hulbert, 1875.

Beecher, Lyman. *The Autobiography of Lyman Beecher.* Edited by Barbara M. Cross. 2 vols. Cambridge: Belknap, 1961.

Bentley, William. *The Diary of William Bentley, D.D., Pastor of the East Church, Salem, Massachusetts.* 4 vols. Gloucester, Mass.: Peter Smith, 1962.

Billings, John Shaw. "The Registration of Vital Statistics." *American Journal of Medical Science* 85 (1883): 33–59. Reprinted in *Medical America in the Nineteenth Century: Readings from the Literature.* Edited by Gert H. Brieger. Baltimore: Johns Hopkins University Press, 1972.

Billingsley, A. S. *From the Flag to the Cross: Or, Scenes and Incidents of Christianity in the War . . .* Philadelphia: New World, 1872.

Bond, Alvan. Journals, 1815–1873. Reverend Alvan Bond Collection. Old Sturbridge Village Research Library, Sturbridge, Mass.

Bradford, James H. "Military Order of the Loyal Legion of the United States. War Papers 11, 'The Chaplains in the Volunteer Army.'" Wyles Collection, University of California, Santa Barbara.

Brinton, John H. *Personal Memoirs of John H. Brinton, Major and Surgeon, U.S.V., 1861–1865.* New York: Neale, 1914.

Bucklin, Sophronia E. *In Hospital and Camp: A Woman's Record of Thrilling Incidents Among the Wounded in the Late War.* Philadelphia: John E. Potter, 1869.

Bullard Family Papers. Old Sturbridge Village Research Library, Sturbridge, Mass.

Bushnell, Horace. *Reverses Needed: A Discourse Delivered on the Sunday After the Disaster of Bull Run.* Hartford, Conn.: L. E. Hunt, 1861.

Cargill, John Milton. Family Papers, 1725–1923. American Antiquarian Society, Worcester, Mass.

The Casket. Various issues, 1876–1890.

Channing, William Ellery. *Memoir of William Ellery Channing with Extracts from His Correspondence and Manuscripts.* 6th ed. 2 vols. Boston: Crosby, Nichols, 1854.

Clark, Joel. Journal, 1797–1798. Old Sturbridge Village Research Library, Sturbridge, Mass.

Clarke, Joseph Henry. *Reminiscences of Early Embalming.* New York: Sunnyside, 1917.

[Coffin, John Gorman.] *Remarks on the Dangers and Duties of Sepulture: Or, Security for the Living with Respect and Repose for the Dead.* Boston: Phelps and Farnham, 1823.

Colyer, Edward. Letters. Colyer Collection. Manuscript Collection, Huntington Library, San Marino, Calif.

The Constitution of the Presbyterian Church in the United States of America, Containing the Confession of Faith, the Catechisms, and the Directory for the Worship of God . . . Elizabethtown, N.J.: Mervin Hale, 1822.

Cooper, James Fenimore. *The Last of the Mohicans.* New York: Airmont, 1962.

Daily Evening Bulletin (Philadelphia). Various issues, 1865.

Daily Post (Pittsburgh). Various issues, 1865.

Davis, Andrew Jackson. *The Great Harmonia: Being a Philosophical Revelation of the Natural, Spiritual, and Celestial Universe.* 5 vols. Boston: Banner of Light, 1850.

Davis, Mercy Lavinda. Diary. Davis Family Papers, 1794–1839. Old Sturbridge Village Research Library, Sturbridge, Mass.

Dearborn, Nathaniel. *A Concise History of, and Guide through Mount Auburn . . .* Boston: Nathaniel Dearborn, 1843.

Drew, Thomas. *The John Brown Invasion: An Authentic History of the Harper's Ferry Tragedy, with Full Details of the Capture, Trial, and Execution of the Invaders, and of All the Incidents Connected Therewith.* Boston: James Campbell, 1860.

Duncan, John M. *Travels Through Part of the United States and Canada in 1818 and 1819.* 2 vols. New York: W. B. Gilley, 1823.

Dwight, Timothy. *My Native Land: Life in America, 1790–1870.* Chicago: Phoenix, 1961.

———. *A Sermon on the Death of Mr. Ebenezer Grant Marsh . . .* Hartford, Conn.: Hudson and Goodwin, 1804.

———. *Theology Explained and Defended in a Series of Sermons.* 12th ed. 4 vols. New York: Harper and Brothers, 1858.

Eaton, Benjamin. *West Bridgewater Hearse Books and Notes, 1812–1813.* Baker Library, Rare Books Collection, Harvard University.

"An Elegy on the Death of Mr. Harfield Lyndsey, Aged 26 years." Broadside. Old Sturbridge Village Research Library, Sturbridge, Mass.

Emerson, Ralph Waldo. *The Complete Sermons of Ralph Waldo Emerson.* 4 vols. Edited by Albert J. von Frank. Columbia: University of Missouri Press, 1989.

———. *The Journals and Miscellaneous Notebooks of Ralph Waldo Emerson.* Edited by Alfred R. Ferguson. Cambridge: Belknap, 1964.

———. *Young Emerson Speaks: Unpublished Discourses on Many Subjects by Ralph Waldo Emerson.* Edited by Arthur Cushman McGiffert Jr. Boston: Houghton, Mifflin, 1938.

Finney, Charles G. "Eternal Life." In *The Promise of the Spirit.* Edited and compiled by Timothy L. Smith. Minneapolis: Bethany House, 1980.

———. "How to Change Your Heart." In *Sermons on Important Subjects.* New York: John S. Taylor, 1836.

Fisher, Sidney George. *A Philadelphia Perspective: The Diary of Sidney George Fisher Covering the Years 1834–1871.* Edited by Nicholas B. Wainwright. Philadelphia: Historical Society of Pennsylvania, 1967.

Frank Leslie's Illustrated. Various issues, 1861–1865.

Frothingham, Octavius B. *Seeds and Shells: A Sermon Preached in New York, November 17, 1861.* New York: Wynkoop, Hallenbeck, and Thomas, 1862.

Funeral Directors' National Association. *Proceedings of the National Convention at Rochester, New York.* Rochester: A. H. Nirdlinger, 1882.

———. *Second Annual Convention of the Funeral Directors of the United States.* Richmond, Ind.: T. E. De Yarmon, 1883.

"A Funeral Scene." *American Monthly* 1 (March 1824): 18.

"Funeral Thoughts, Excited by the Death of John Adams and Thos. Jefferson, on the Fourth of July, 1826, the Jubilee of Independence." Broadside. Rare Books Collection, Library of Congress.

Furness, W. H. *A Voice of the Hour: A Discourse Delivered by W. H. Furness, Minister of the First Congregational Unitarian Church.* Philadelphia: Crissy and Markley, 1864.

William Marton Gable Collection. Manuscripts Collection, Huntington Library, San Marino, Calif.

Gannett, Ezra S. *A Sermon Delivered in the Federal Street Meeting House for William Ellery Channing . . .* Boston: William Crosby, 1842.

General Orders of the War Department, 1861–1862. 2 vols. New York: Derby and Miller, 1864.

James Herbert George Collection. Manuscripts Collection, Huntington Library, San Marino, Calif.

Gladden, Washington. *The Christian Pastor and the Working Church.* New York: Charles Scribner's Sons, 1923.

———. *How Much is Left of the Old Doctrines? A Book for the People.* Boston: Houghton, Mifflin, 1899.

Glazier, James Edward. Letters, Glazier Collection. Manuscripts Collection, Huntington Library, San Marino, Calif.

Goodwin, T. A. *The Mode of Man's Immortality: Or, The When, Where, and How of the Future Life.* 2d ed. New York: J. B. Ford, 1874.

Hallock, Armstrong B. *Letters from a Pennsylvania Chaplain at the Siege of Petersburg, 1865.* Edited by Hallock F. Raup. London: Eden, 1961.

Harper's New Monthly Magazine. Various issues, 1861–1865.

Harper's Weekly. Various issues, 1861–1865.

Hawthorne, Nathaniel. "Roger Malvin's Burial." *The Portable Hawthorne.* Edited by Malcolm Cowley. New York: Viking, 1969.

Hobart, John Henry. *The Christian's Manual of Faith and Devotion* . . . New York: T. and J. Swords, 1814.

———. *A Funeral Address Delivered at the Interment of the Rev. Benjamin Moore* . . . New York: George Lund, 1816.

Holmes, Oliver Wendell. "Doings of the Sunbeam." In *Soundings, from the "Atlantic."* Boston: Ticknor and Fields, 1866.

———. "My Hunt After 'The Captain.'" In *Pages from an Old Volume of Life: A Collection of Essays, 1857–1881.* Vol. 8 of *The Works of Oliver Wendell Holmes.* 15 vols. Boston: Houghton, Mufflin, 1892.

Holmes, Oliver Wendell, Jr. *Touched with Fire: Civil War Letters and Diary.* Edited by Mark de Wolfe Howe. Cambridge: Harvard University Press, 1946.

Hone, Philip. *The Diary of Philip Hone.* Edited by Allan Nevins. New York: Arno, 1970.

Hough, Franklin B. *Washingtoniana: Or, Memorials of the Death of George Washington, Giving an Account of the Funeral Honors Paid to his Memory* . . . 2 vols. Roxbury, Mass.: Elliot Woodward, 1865.

Howe, Julia Ward. *Reminiscences, 1819–1899.* Boston: Houghton, Mifflin, 1900.

Humphreys, Charles A. *Field, Camp, Hospital, and Prison in the Civil War, 1863–1865.* Boston: George H. Ellis, 1918.

Hyde, Solon. *A Captive of War.* New York: McClure, Phillips, 1900.

"In the Board of Health, May 7, 1810 . . . " Broadside. Rare Books Collection, Countway Medical Library, Harvard University.

Johnson, Charles Benevyln. *Muskets and Medicine: Or Army Life in the Sixties.* Philadelphia: F. A. Davis, 1917.

Kean, Ellen. *Death and Funeral of Abraham Lincoln: A Contemporary Description by Mrs. Ellen Kean.* London: n.p., 1921. Illinois State Historical Library, Springfield.

Lake, Ann [Getz]. Correspondence, 1820–1872. Manuscripts Collection, Huntington Library, San Marino, Calif.

The Lincoln Memorial: A Record of the Life, Assassination, and Obsequies of the Mar-tyred President. Edited by John Gilmary Shea. New York: Bunce and Huntington, 1865.

Lippard, George. *The Quaker City: Or the Monks of Monk Hall.* New York: Odyssey, 1972.

Masur, Louis P., ed. *" . . . the Real War Will Never Get in the Books": Selections from Writers During the Civil War.* New York: Oxford University Press, 1993.

McAllister, Robert. *The Civil War Letters of General Robert McAllister.* Edited by James I. Robertson Jr. New Brunswick, N.J.: Rutgers University Press, 1965.

McLoughlin, William G., ed. *The American Evangelicals, 1800–1900: An Anthology.* New York: Harper Torchbooks, 1968.

Mesick, Jane Louise. *The English Traveller in America, 1785–1835.* New York: Columbia University Press, 1922.

Miller, William. *Memoirs of William Miller, Generally Known as a Lecturer on the Prophecies, and the Second Coming of Christ.* Boston: Joshua V. Himes, 1853.

Moody, Dwight L. *Glad Tidings: Comprising Sermons and Prayer-Meeting Talks.* New York: E. B. Treat, 1876.

Moore, Frank, ed. *Anecdotes, Poetry, and Incidents of the War: North and South, 1860–1865.* New York: printed for the subscribers, 1866.

Moss, Lemuel. *Annals of the United States Christian Commission.* Philadelphia: J. B. Lippencott, 1868.

Nevin, John W. *The Mystical Presence and Other Writings on the Eucharist.* Edited by Bard Thompson and George H. Bricker. Philadelphia: United Church Press, 1966.

New Hampshire Civil War Collection. Manuscript Collection, Huntington Library, San Marino, Calif.

New York Times. Various issues, 1861–1865.

Niemcewicz, Julian Ursyn. *Under Their Vine and Fig Tree: Travels Through America in 1797–1799, 1805, with Some Further Account of Life in New Jersey.* Edited and translated by Metchie J. E. Budka. Elizabeth, N.J.: Grassmann, 1965.

Page, Charles A. *Letters of a War Correspondent.* Edited by James R. Gilmore. Boston: L. C. Page, 1899.

Park, Louisa Adams. Journal. Park Family Papers, 1800–1890. American Antiquarian Society, Worcester, Mass.

Peck and Perez Family Papers, 1813–1899. Old Sturbridge Village Research Library, Sturbridge, Mass.

Phelps, Elizabeth Stuart. *The Gates Ajar.* Boston: Fields, Osgood, 1869.

Radcliffe, Napolean. "Journal of the War of the Rebellion, from August 21st, 1861, to July 22nd, 1865." Manuscript Collection, Huntington Library, San Marino, Calif.

Report of the Case: John Dorrance Against Arthur Fenner, Tried at the December Term . . . Providence, R.I.: Bennett Wheeler, 1802. Countway Medical Library, Rare Books Collection, Harvard University.

Report of the Committee on Laws, to the Corporation of the City of New-York, on the Subject of Interment, Within the Populous Parts of the City. New York: Mahlon Day, 1825.

Report of the Select Committee of the House of Representatives, on So Much of the

Governor's Speech, at the June Session, 1830, as Relates to Legalizing the Study of Anatomy. Boston: Dutton and Wentworth, 1831.

Rhodes, Elisha Hunt. *All for the Union: The Civil War Diary and Letters of Elisha Hunt Rhodes.* Edited by Robert Hunt Rhodes. New York: Orion Books, 1985.

Sanborn, F. B., ed. *The Life and Letters of John Brown, Liberator of Kansas and Martyr of Virginia.* 1885. Reprint. New York: Negro University Press, 1969.

Sargent, L. M. *Dealings with the Dead, by a Sexton of the Old School.* 2 vols. Boston: Dutton and Wentworth, 1856.

Smith, Adelaine W. *Reminiscences of an Army Nurse During the Civil War.* New York: Graves, 1911.

Smith, Ida. "My Absent Brother." *Zion's Herald and Wesleyan Journal* 34 (January 1863): 72–73.

Smith, Samuel Francis. Smith Collection. Manuscripts Collection, Huntington Library, San Marino, Calif.

Smith, Stephen. *Reports and Papers of the American Public Health Association, 1879.* Boston: Houghton, Mifflin, 1880.

Stevenson, D. *Elements of Methodism in a Series of Short Lectures Addressed to One Beginning a Life of Goodness.* Claremont, N.H.: Daniel Stevenson, 1879.

Stone, Josiah. Diaries, 1847–1849. Old Sturbridge Village Research Library, Sturbridge, Mass.

Story, Joseph. *An Address Delivered on the Dedication of the Cemetery at Mount Auburn, September 24, 1831.* Boston: Joseph T. and Edwin Buckingham, 1831.

Stowe, Harriet Beecher. *Uncle Tom's Cabin: Or, Life Among the Lowly.* Edited by Kenneth S. Lynn. Cambridge: Belknap, 1962.

Sunderland, Byron. *The Crisis of the Times: A Sermon Preached in the First Presbyterian Church, Washington, D.C., on the Evening of the National Fast, Thursday, April 30, 1863.* Washington, D.C.: National Banner, 1863.

That Unknown Country, or What Living Men Believe Concerning Punishment After Death. . . Springfield, Mass.: C. A. Nichols, 1899.

Thorburn, Grant. *Forty Years' Residence in America: Or the Doctrine of a Particular Providence Exemplified in the Life of Grant Thorburn, Seedsman, New York.* Boston: Russell, Odiorne and Metcalf, 1834.

Thoreau, Henry David. *Walden and Other Writings of Henry David Thoreau.* Edited by Brooks Atkinson. New York: Modern Library, 1965.

"Thou Shalt Not Kill." Broadside, 1845. Old Sturbridge Village Research Library, Sturbridge, Mass.

Townsend, George Alfred. *Campaigns of a Non-Combatant, and His Romaunt Abroad During the War.* New York: Blecock, 1866.

Trumball, H. Clay. *War Memories of an Army Chaplain.* New York: Charles Scribner's Sons, 1898.

Trumball, Louisa Jane. Diaries. Trumball Family Papers, 1773–1896. American Antiquarian Society, Worcester, Mass.

United States Sanitary Commission. *The Soldier's Friend.* Philadelphia: Perkinpine and Higgins, 1865.

"A Visit to General Butler and the Army of the James." *Fraser's Magazine for Town and Country* 71 (April 1865): 434–448.

Walker, Sarah. Letters. Old Sturbridge Village Research Library, Sturbridge, Mass.

Walter, Cornelia W., ed. *Mount Auburn Illustrated.* New York: R. Martin, 1847.

Webber, Mrs. Frank, consultant. WPA Federal Writers Project. Folklore Collection, Manuscripts Division, Library of Congress.

Webster, Samuel Derrick. "My Diary in Field and Camp, 1861–1865." Webster Collection. Manuscripts Collection, Huntington Library, San Marino, Calif.

West Bridgewater Hearse Books and Notes. Bridgewater, Mass., 1812–1813. Baker Library, Rare Books Collection, Harvard University.

Whitman, Walt. *Walt Whitman's Civil War.* Compiled and edited from published and unpublished sources by Walter Lowenfels. New York: Da Capo, 1960.

Wightman, Edward King. *From Antietam to Fort Fisher: The Civil War Letters of Edward King Wightman, 1862–1865.* Edited by Edward G. Longacre. London: Associated University Press, 1985.

Wightman, S. K. "In Search of My Son" [1865]. In *American Heritage* 14 (February 1963): 61–78.

Wills, David. *Revised Report of the Select Committee Relative to the Soldiers' National Cemetery* . . . Harrisburg, Pa.: Singerly and Myers, 1865.

Woodhull, Alfred A. *Catalogue of the Surgical Section of the United States Army Medical Museum.* Washington, D.C.: Government Printing Office, 1866.

Woodward, George W. Letters. Woodward Collection. Manuscripts Collection, Huntington Library, San Marino, Calif.

Secondary Sources

Aaron, Daniel. *The Unwritten War: American Writers and the Civil War.* New York: Random House, 1973.

Abels, Jules. *Man on Fire: John Brown and the Cause of Liberty.* New York: Macmillan, 1971.

Adams, George Washington. *Doctors in Blue: The Medical History of the Union Army in the Civil War.* New York: Henry Schuman, 1952.

Ahlstrom, Sydney E. *A Religious History of the American People.* New Haven: Yale University Press, 1972.

——, ed. *Theology in America: The Major Protestant Voices from Puritanism to Neo-Orthodoxy.* Indianapolis: Bobbs-Merrill, 1976.

Albanese, Catherine L. *America: Religions and Religion.* Belmont, Calif.: Wadsworth, 1981.

——. *Corresponding Motion: Transcendental Religion and the New America.* Philadelphia: Temple University Press, 1977.

——. *Nature Religion in America: From the Algonkian Indians to the New Age.* Chicago: University of Chicago Press, 1990.

Albrecht, Robert C. "The Theological Response of the Transcendentalists to the Civil War." *New England Quarterly* 38 (March 1965): 21–34.

Alexander, Jeffrey C., ed. *Durkheimian Sociology: Cultural Studies.* Cambridge: Cambridge University Press, 1988.

Alexander, John K. *Render Them Submissive: Response to Poverty in Philadelphia, 1760–1800.* Amherst: University of Massachusetts Press, 1980.

Appel, Theodore. *The Life and Work of John Williamson Nevin.* New York: Arno, 1969.

Ariès, Philippe. *Essais sur l'histoire de la mort en Occident du Moyen Age à nos jours.* Paris: Editions du Seuil, 1975.

——. *The Hour of Our Death.* Translated by Helen Weaver. New York: Vintage, 1982.

——. *Images of Man and Death.* Translated by Janet Lloyd. Cambridge: Harvard University Press, 1985.

——. *Western Attitudes Toward Death: From the Middle Ages to the Present.* Translated by Patricia M. Ranum. Baltimore: Johns Hopkins University Press, 1974.

Backer, Barbara, Natalie Hannon, and Noreen A. Russell. *Death and Dying: Individuals and Institutions.* New York: John Wiley and Sons, 1982.

Baker, Jean H. *Mary Todd Lincoln: A Biography.* New York: W. W. Norton, 1987.

Bardeen, Charles Russel. "Anatomy in America." *Bulletin of the University of Wisconsin* 3 (September 1905): 1–121.

Barron, Hal S. *Those Who Stayed Behind: Rural Society in Nineteenth-Century New England.* Cambridge: Cambridge University Press, 1984.

Becker, Ernest. *The Denial of Death.* New York: Free Press, 1973.

Bednarowski, Mary Farrell. *New Religions and the Theological Imagination in America.* Bloomington: Indiana University Press, 1989.

Bellah, Robert. "Civil Religion in America." In *Beyond Belief: Essays on Religion in a Post-Traditional World.* New York: Harper and Row, 1970.

Berger, Peter. *The Sacred Canopy: Elements of a Sociological Theory of Religion.* Garden City, N.Y.: Anchor, 1969.

Bledstein, Burton J. *The Culture of Professionalism: The Middle Class and the Development of Higher Education.* New York: W. W. Norton, 1976.

Bloch, Marc. *The Historian's Craft.* Translated by Peter Putnam. New York: Alfred A. Knopf, 1963.

Bloom, Harold, ed. *Nathaniel Hawthorne.* New York: Chelsea House, 1986.

Bode, Carl. *The Anatomy of Popular Culture, 1840–1861.* Berkeley: University of California Press, 1959.

Boller, Paul F. *American Transcendentalism, 1830–1860: An Intellectual Inquiry.* New York: Putnam, 1974.

Bowman, Leroy. *The American Funeral: A Study in Guilt, Extravagance, and Sublimity.* New York: Paperback Library, 1964.

Boyer, Paul. *Urban Masses and Moral Order in America, 1820–1920.* Cambridge: Harvard University Press, 1978.

Braude, Ann. *Radical Spirits: Spiritualism and Women's Rights in Nineteenth-Century America.* Boston: Beacon, 1989.

Braudel, Fernand. *Ecrits sur l'histoire.* Paris: Flammarion, 1969.

Brieger, Gert H., ed. *Medical America in the Nineteenth Century: Readings from the Literature.* Baltimore: Johns Hopkins University Press, 1972.

Brown, Peter. *The Body and Society: Men, Women, and Sexual Renunciation in Early Christianity.* New York: Columbia University Press, 1988.

Burns, Stanley B. *Sleeping Beauty: Memorial Photography in America.* Altadena, Calif.: Twelvetree, 1991.

Bushman, Richard L. *From Puritan to Yankee: Character and the Social Order, 1690–1765.* Cambridge: Harvard University Press, 1967.

Butler, Jon. *Awash in a Sea of Faith: Christianizing the American People.* Cambridge: Harvard University Press, 1990.

Butler, Jonathan M. *Softly and Tenderly Jesus Is Calling: Heaven and Hell in American Revivalism, 1870–1920.* Brooklyn, N.Y.: Carlson, 1991.

Bynum, Caroline Walker. *The Resurrection of the Body.* New York: Columbia University Press, 1995.

Camporesi, Piero. *The Incorruptible Flesh: Bodily Mutilation and Mortification in Religion and Folklore.* Cambridge: Cambridge University Press, 1988.

Carter, Paul A. *The Spiritual Crisis of the Gilded Age.* De Kalb: Northern Illinois University Press, 1971.

Cassedy, James H. *Medicine and American Growth, 1800–1860.* Madison: University of Wisconsin Press, 1986.

Charmaz, Kathy. *The Social Reality of Death: Death in Contemporary America.* New York: Random House, 1980.

Chesebrough, David B. *"No Sorrow Like Our Sorrow": Northern Protestant Ministers and the Assassination of Lincoln.* Kent, Ohio: Kent State University Press, 1994.

Chidester, David. *Salvation and Suicide: An Interpretation of Jim Jones, the Peoples Temple, and Jonestown.* Bloomington: Indiana University Press, 1988.

Clover, Carol. *Men, Women, and Chain Saws: Gender in the Modern Horror Film.* Princeton: Princeton University Press, 1992.

Coffin, Margaret M. *Death in Early America: The History and Folklore of Customs and Superstitions of Early Medicine, Funerals, Burials, and Mourning.* Nashville: Thomas Nelson, 1976.

Cole, James M., and Roy E. Frampton. *The Gettysburg National Cemetery: A History and Guide.* Hanover, Penn.: Sheridan, 1988.

Cole, Pamela Martha. "New England Funerals." *Journal of American Folk-Lore,* 8 (July–September 1894): 313–325.

Cole, Thomas. *The Journey of Life: A Cultural History of Aging in America.* Cambridge: Cambridge University Press, 1992.

"The Corpse and the Beaver Hat: One of the Causes Célèbres of Rhode Island; How Justice Was Administered in the Beginning of This Century." *Rhode Island Medical Journal* 50 (December 1967): 836–846, 855.

Corr, Charles A., Clyde M. Nabe, and Donna M. Corr. *Death and Dying, Life and Living.* Pacific Grove, Calif.: Brooks/Cole, 1994.

Cotkin, George. *Reluctant Modernism: American Thought and Culture, 1880–1900.* New York: Twayne, 1992.

Covey, Cyclone. *The American Pilgrimage: The Roots of American History, Religion and Culture.* New York: Collier, 1961.

Cox, Meg. "Death Conquers Bestseller Lists as Boomers Age." *Wall Street Journal,* 23 February 1994.

Cray, Robert E., Jr. "Memorialization and Enshrinement: George Whitefield and Popular Religious Culture, 1770–1850." *Journal of the Early Republic* 10 (Fall 1990): 339–361.

Cross, Whitney R. *The Burned-Over District: The Social and Intellectual History of Enthusiastic Religion in Western New York, 1800–1850.* Ithaca, N.Y.: Cornell University Press, 1950.

Curl, James Stevens. *The Victorian Celebration of Death*. Detroit: Partridge, 1972.

Curtis, Susan. *A Consuming Faith: The Social Gospel and Modern American Culture*. Baltimore: Johns Hopkins University Press, 1991

Darnton, Robert. *The Great Cat Massacre and Other Episodes in French Cultural History*. New York: Vintage, 1985.

———. *The Kiss of Lamourette: Reflections in Cultural History*. New York: W. W. Norton, 1990.

Davidson, Abraham A. *The Eccentrics and Other American Visionary Painters*. New York: E. P. Dutton, 1978.

Davis, William C., ed. *Touched by Fire: A Photographic Portrait of the Civil War*. 2 vols. Boston: Little, Brown, 1986.

Dawson, Grace D., John F. Santos, and David C. Burdick. "Differences in Final Arrangements Between Burial and Cremation as the Method of Body Disposition." *Omega: Journal of Death and Dying* 21 (1990): 129–146.

Deetz, James F., and Edwin S. Dethlefsen. "Death's Head, Cherub, Urn, and Willow." *Natural History* 76 (March 1967): 29–37.

Delumeau, Jean. *Sin and Fear: The Emergence of a Western Guilt Culture, 13th–18th Centuries*. Translated by Eric Nicholoson. New York: St. Martin's, 1990.

DeSpelder, Lynne Ann, and Albert Lee Strickland. *The Last Dance: Encountering Death and Dying*. Palo Alto, Calif.: Mayfield, 1983.

Doan, Ruth Alden. *The Miller Heresy, Millennialism, and American Culture*. Philadelphia: Temple University Press, 1987.

Dosse, François. *L'histoire en miettes: Des "Annales" à la "nouvelle histoire."* Paris: Editions la Découverte, 1987.

Douglas, Ann. *The Feminization of American Culture*. New York: Alfred A. Knopf, 1977.

Douglas, Drake. *Horrors!* Woodstock, N.Y.: Overlook, 1989.

Douglas, Mary. *Natural Symbols: Explorations in Cosmology*. New York: Pantheon, 1973.

———. *Purity and Danger: An Analysis of Concepts of Pollution and Taboo*. New York: Praeger, 1966.

Duncan, Louis C. *The Medical Department of the United States Army in the Civil War*. 19-?.

Eadie, Betty J. *Embraced by the Light*. Placerville, Calif.: Gold Leaf, 1992.

Eliade, Mircea. *Occultism, Witchcraft, and Cultural Fashions: Essays in Comparative Religions*. Chicago: University of Chicago Press, 1976.

Farrar, Samuel Clarke. *The Twenty-Second Pennsylvania Cavalry and the Ringgold Battalion, 1861–1865*. Pittsburgh: Twenty-Second Pennsylvania Ringgold Cavalry Association, 1911.

Farrell, James J. *Inventing the American Way of Death, 1830–1920*. Philadelphia: Temple University Press, 1980.

Febvre, Lucien. *Combats pour l'histoire*. Paris: Armand Colin, 1953.

Feifel, Herman, ed. *New Meanings of Death*. New York: McGraw-Hill, 1977.

Fiedler, Leslie A. *Love and Death in the American Novel*. Rev. ed. New York: Delta, 1966.

——. "The Male Novel." *Partisan Review* 37 (1970): 74–89.

Fischer, David Hackett. *Albion's Seed: Four British Folkways in America.* New York: Oxford University Press, 1989.

——. *Growing Old in America.* Oxford: Oxford University Press, 1978.

Florin, John W. *Death in New England: Regional Variations in Mortality.* Chapel Hill: University of North Carolina Press, 1971.

Foucault, Michel. *The Birth of the Clinic: An Archaeology of Medical Perception.* Translated by A. M. Sheridan Smith. New York: Pantheon, 1973.

Fox, Richard Wightman, and T. J. Jackson Lears, eds. *The Culture of Consumption: Critical Essays in American History, 1880–1980.* New York: Pantheon, 1983.

Fox, William F. *Regimental Losses in the American Civil War, 1861–1865.* Albany, N.Y.: Albany Publishing, 1889.

Frank, Neal. *Hawthorne's Early Tales: A Critical Study.* Durham, N.C.: Duke University Press, 1972.

Frankenstein, Alfred. *William Sidney Mount.* New York: Harry N. Abrams, 1975.

Frassanito, William A. *Antietam: The Photographic Legacy of America's Bloodiest Day.* New York: Charles Scribner's Sons, 1978.

——. *Gettysburg: A Journey In Time.* New York: Charles Scribner's Sons, 1975.

Fredrickson, George M. *The Inner Civil War: Northern Intellectuals and the Crisis of the Union.* New York: Harper and Row, 1965.

Gallup, George, Jr., with William Proctor. *Adventures in Immortality.* New York: McGraw-Hill, 1982.

Garrett, Elisabeth Donaghy. *At Home: The American Family, 1750–1870.* New York: Harry N. Abrams, 1990.

Gausted, Edwin S. *Faith of Our Fathers: Religion and the New Nation.* San Francisco: Harper and Row, 1987.

——, ed. *The Rise of Adventism: Religion and Society in Mid-Nineteenth-Century America.* New York: Harper and Row, 1974.

Geddes, Gordon E. *Welcome Joy: Death in Puritan New England.* Ann Arbor: UMI, 1981.

Geertz, Clifford. *The Interpretation of Cultures: Selected Essays.* New York: Basic, 1973.

Gillis, John. "From the Good Death to the Good Birth." Manuscript.

Goldscheider, Calvin. *Population, Modernization, and Social Structure.* Boston: Little, Brown, 1971.

Gorer, Geoffrey. *Death, Grief, and Mourning.* Garden City, N.J.: Doubleday, 1965.

Grollman, Earl A., ed. *Concerning Death: A Practical Guide for the Living.* Boston: Beacon, 1974.

Habenstein, Robert W., and William M. Lamers. *The History of American Funeral Directing.* Rev. ed. Milwaukee: Bulfin, 1962.

Hall, David. *Worlds of Wonder, Days of Judgment: Popular Religious Belief in Early New England.* New York: Alfred A. Knopf, 1989.

Halliwell, Leslie. *The Dead That Walk: Dracula, Frankenstein, the Mummy and Other Favorite Movie Monsters.* New York: Continuum, 1988.

Halttunen, Karen. *Confidence Men and Painted Women: A Study of Middle-Class Culture in America, 1830–1870.* New Haven: Yale University Press, 1982.

Hamilton, C., and L. Ostendorf. *Lincoln in Photographs: An Album of Every Known Pose*. Norman: University of Oklahoma Press, 1963.

Harman, Keith, J. *Charles Grandison Finney, 1802–1875: Revivalist and Reformer*. Syracuse, N.Y.: Syracuse University Press, 1897.

Harmer, Ruth M. *The High Cost of Dying*. New York: Crowell-Collier, 1963.

Harrington, Thomas Francis. *The Harvard Medical School: A History, Narrative and Documentary*. 3 vols. New York: Lewis, 1905.

Harris, Neil. *The Artist in American Society: The Formative Years, 1790–1860*. New York: George Braziller, 1966.

Hatch, Nathan O. *The Democratization of American Christianity*. New Haven: Yale University Press, 1989.

Hecht, Richard D., and Roger Friedland. "Reading the Body of Christ: The Politics of a Social Symbol." Manuscript.

Hertz, Robert. "Contributions to the Study of the Collective Representations of Death." In *Death and the Right Hand*. Translated by Rodney and Claudia Needham. Glencoe, Ill.: Free Press, 1960.

Hick, John. *Death and Eternal Life*. San Francisco: Harper and Row, 1976.

Houghton, Walter E. *The Victorian Frame of Mind, 1830–1870*. New Haven: Yale University Press, 1957.

Howe, David Walker. *The Unitarian Conscience: Harvard Moral Philosophy, 1805–1861*. Cambridge: Harvard University Press, 1970.

Hudson, Winthrop S. *Religion in America: An Historical Account of the Development of American Religious Life*. 4th ed. New York: Macmillan, 1987.

Huizinga, Johan. *The Waning of the Middle Ages: A Study of the Forms of Life, Thought, and Art in France and the Netherlands in the Fourteenth and Fifteenth Centuries*. New York: Anchor, 1954.

Humphrey, David C. "Dissection and Discrimination: The Social Origins of Cadavers in America, 1760–1915." *Bulletin of the New York Academy of Medicine* 49 (September 1973): 819–827.

Hunt, Lynn. *The Family Romance of the French Revolution*. Berkeley: University of California Press, 1992.

———, ed. *The New Cultural History*. Berkeley: University of California Press, 1989.

Hunter, James Davison. *Culture Wars: The Struggle to Define America*. New York: Basic, 1991.

Huntington, Richard, and Peter Metcalf. *Celebrations of Death: The Anthropology of Mortuary Ritual*. Cambridge: Cambridge University Press, 1979.

Jackson, Charles O., ed. *Passing: The Vision of Death in America*. Westport, Conn.: Greenwood, 1977.

Jaffe, A. J., and W. I. Laurie Jr. "An Abridged Life Table for the White Population of the United States in 1830." *Human Biology* 14 (September 1942): 352–371.

Johnson, Christopher Jay, and Marsha G. McGee, eds. *Encounters with Eternity: Religious Views of Death and Life After Death*. New York: Philosophical Library, 1986.

Johnson, Edward C. "A Brief History of United States Military Embalming." *The Director* (September 1971).

———. "Civil War Embalming." Reprint. *Funeral Director's Review*, Summer 1965.

Johnson, Paul E. *A Shopkeeper's Millennium: Society and Revivals in Rochester, New York, 1815–1837.* New York: Hill and Wang, 1978.

Jones, Donald G. *The Sectional Crisis and Northern Methodism: A Study in Piety, Political Ethics, and Civil Religion.* Metuchen, N.J.: Scarecrow, 1979.

Kantorowicz, Ernst. *The King's Two Bodies: A Study in Medieval Political Theology.* Princeton: Princeton University Press, 1957.

Kearl, Michael C. *Endings: A Sociology of Death and Dying.* New York: Oxford University Press, 1989.

Kelley, Robert. *The Shaping of the American Past.* 2 vols. Englewood Cliffs, N.J.: Prentice-Hall, 1982.

Kennedy, J. Gerald. *Poe, Death, and the Life of Writing.* New Haven: Yale University Press, 1987.

Kertzer, David I. *Ritual, Politics, and Power.* New Haven: Yale University Press, 1988.

King, Moses. *King's Handbook of New York City: An Outline, History, and Description of the American Metropolis.* 2d ed. Boston: Moses King, 1893.

Kselman, Thomas A. *Death and the Afterlife in Modern France.* Princeton: Princeton University Press, 1992.

Kubler-Ross, Elisabeth. *On Death and Dying.* New York: Macmillan, 1969.

Kunhardt, Dorothy Meserve, and Philip B. Kunhardt Jr. *Twenty Days: A Narrative in Text and Pictures of the Assassination of Abraham Lincoln and the Twenty Days and Nights that followed: The Nation in Mourning, the Long Trip Home to Springfield.* North Hollywood, Calif.: Newcastle, 1985.

Kushner, Howard I. *Self-Destruction in the Promised Land: A Psychocultural Biology of American Suicide.* New Brunswick, N.J.: Rutgers University Press, 1989.

Laderman, Gary. "Locating the Dead: A Cultural History of Death in the Antebellum, Anglo-Protestant Communities of the Northeast." *Journal of the American Academy of Religion* 63 (Spring 1995): 27–52.

Laqueur, Thomas. *Making Sex: Body and Gender from the Greeks to Freud.* Cambridge: Harvard University Press, 1990.

Larkin, Jack. *The Reshaping of Everyday Life, 1790–1840.* New York: Harper and Row, 1988.

Leavitt, Judith Walzer, and Ronald Numbers, eds. *Sickness and Health in America: Readings in the History of Medicine and Public Health.* Madison: University of Wisconsin Press, 1978.

Le Goff, Jacques. *The Birth of Purgatory.* Translated by Arthur Goldhammer. Chicago: University of Chicago Press, 1981.

——, ed. *La nouvelle histoire.* Paris: Editions Complexe, 1988.

Le Goff, Jacques, and Pierre Nora, eds. *Constructing the Past: Essays in Historical Methodology.* Cambridge: Cambridge University Press, 1985.

Linden-Ward, Blanche. *Silent City on a Hill: Landscapes of Memory and Boston's Mount Auburn Cemetery.* Columbus: Ohio State University Press, 1989.

Linderman, Gerald F. *Embattled Courage: The Experience of Combat in the American Civil War.* New York: Free Press, 1987.

Linenthal, Edward Tabor. *Changing Images of the Warrior Hero in America: A History of Popular Symbolism.* New York: E. Mellon, 1982.

——. *Sacred Ground: Americans and Their Battlefields.* Urbana: University of Illinois Press, 1991.

Livermore, Thomas L. *Numbers and Losses in the Civil War in America, 1861–1865.* 1900. Reprint. Bloomington: Indiana University Press, 1957.

MacCloskey, Monro. *Hallowed Ground: Our National Cemeteries.* New York: Richards Rosen, 1969.

Marks, Geoffrey, and William K. Beatty. *The Story of Medicine in America.* New York: Charles Scribner's Sons, 1973.

Marsden, George M. *The Evangelical Mind and the New School Presbyterian Experience: A Case Study of Thought and Theology in Nineteenth-Century America.* New Haven: Yale University Press, 1970.

Marty, Martin E. *Protestantism in the United States: Righteous Empire.* 2d ed. New York: Charles Scribner's Sons, 1986.

Masur, Louis P. *Rites of Execution: Capital Punishment and the Transformation of American Culture, 1776–1865.* New York: Oxford University Press, 1989.

Maxwell, William Quentin. *Lincoln's Fifth Wheel: The Political History of the United States Sanitary Commission.* New York: Longmans, Green, 1956.

May, Henry. *Protestant Churches and Industrial America.* New York: Harper and Brothers, 1949.

Mayer, Robert G. *Embalming: History, Theory, and Practice.* Norwalk, Conn.: Appleton and Lange, 1990.

Mayfield, John. *The New Nation, 1800–1845.* Rev. ed. New York: Hill and Wang, 1982.

McDannell, Colleen. *The Christian Home in Victorian America, 1840–1900.* Bloomington: Indiana University Press, 1986.

McDannell, Colleen, and Bernhard Lang. *Heaven: A History.* New York: Vintage, 1988.

McIntosh, James. "Nature and the Frontier in 'Roger Malvin's Burial.'" *American Literature* 60 (May 1988): 188–204.

McLoughlin, William G. *Revivals, Awakenings, and Reform: An Essay on Religion and Social Change in America, 1607–1977.* Chicago: University of Chicago Press, 1978.

McManners, John. *Death and the Enlightenment: Changing Attitudes to Death Among Christians and Unbelievers in Eighteenth-Century France.* New York: Oxford University Press, 1981.

——. "Death and the French Historians." In *Mirrors of Mortality: Studies in the Social History of Death.* Edited by Joachim Whaley. London: Europa, 1981.

McPherson, James M. *Battle Cry of Freedom: The Civil War Era.* New York: Ballantine, 1989.

Meinwald, Dan. "Memento Mori: Death in Nineteenth-Century Photography." *California Museum of Photography Bulletin* 9 (1990).

Michaels, Walter Benn, and Donald Pease. *The American Renaissance Reconsidered.* Baltimore: Johns Hopkins University Press, 1985.

Miller, Perry. *Errand into the Wilderness.* Cambridge: Belknap, 1956.

——. *The Life of the Mind in America from the Revolution to the Civil War.* San Diego: Harcourt Brace Jovanovich, 1965.

Mitchell, Allan. "Philippe Ariès and the French Way of Death." *French Historical Studies* 10 (Fall 1978): 684–695.

Mitchell, Reid. *Civil War Soldiers*. New York: Viking, 1988.

———. *The Vacant Chair: The Northern Soldier Leaves Home*. New York: Oxford University Press, 1993.

Mitford, Jessica. *The American Way of Death*. New York: Simon and Schuster, 1963.

Moody, Raymond A. *Life After Life*. Covington, Ga.: Mockingbird, 1975.

Moore, R. Laurence. *In Search of White Crows: Spiritualism, Parapsychology, and American Culture*. New York: Oxford University Press, 1977.

———. *Religious Outsiders and the Making of Americans*. New York: Oxford University Press, 1986.

Moorhead, James H. *American Apocalypse: Yankee Protestants and the Civil War, 1860–1869*. New Haven: Yale University Press, 1978.

———. " 'As Though Nothing at All Had Happened': Death and the Afterlife in Protestant Thought, 1840–1925." *Soundings* 67 (Winter 1984): 453–471.

Morin, Edgar. *L'homme et la mort*. Paris: Editions du Seuil, 1970.

Mosse, George. *Fallen Soldiers: Reshaping the Memory of the World Wars*. Oxford: Oxford University Press, 1990.

Nevins, Allan, ed. *Lincoln and the Gettysburg Address: Commemorative Papers*. Urbana: University of Illinois Press, 1964.

Nichols, James Hastings. *Romanticism in American Theology: Nevin and Schaff at Mercersburg*. Chicago: University of Chicago Press, 1961.

Novack, Barbara. *American Painting of the Nineteenth Century: Realism, Idealism, and the American Experience*. 2d ed. New York: Harper and Row, 1979.

Nugent, Walter T. K. *Structures of American Social History*. Bloomington: Indiana University Press, 1981.

Numbers, Ronald L., ed. *The Education of American Physicians: Historical Essays*. Berkeley: University of California Press, 1980.

Numbers, Ronald L., and Jonathan M. Butler, eds. *The Disappointed: Millerism and Millenarianism in the Nineteenth Century*. Bloomington: Indiana University Press, 1987.

Oates, Stephen B. *To Purge This Land with Blood: A Biography of John Brown*. New York: Harper and Row, 1970.

Paluden, Phillip Shaw. *"A People's Contest": The Union and the Civil War, 1861–1865*. New York: Harper and Row, 1988.

Penley, Constance. "Spaced Out: Remembering Christa McAuliffe." *Camera Obscura* 29 (May 1992): 179–214.

Pike, Martha V., and Janice Gray Armstrong, eds. *A Time to Mourn: Expressions of Grief in Nineteenth-Century America*. Stony Brook, N.Y.: The Museums of Stony Brook, 1980.

Pine, Vanderlyn R. *Caretaker of the Dead: The American Funeral Director*. New York: Irvington, 1975.

Powell, Earl A. *Thomas Cole*. New York: Harry N. Abrams, 1990.

Praz, Mario. *The Romantic Agony*. Translated by Angus Davidson. 2d ed. London: Oxford University Press, 1970.

Prior, Lindsay. *The Social Organization of Death: Medical Discourse and Social Practices in Belfast*. London: Macmillan, 1989.

Pryor, Elizabeth Brown. *Clara Barton: Professional Angel.* Philadelphia: University of Pennsylvania Press, 1987.

Quimby, Rollin W. "Recurrent Themes and Purposes in the Sermons of the Union Army Chaplains." *Speech Monographs* 31 (November 1964): 425–436.

Randall, Ruth Painter. *Mary Todd Lincoln: Biography of a Marriage.* New York: Little, Brown, 1953.

Reynolds, David. *Beneath the American Renaissance: The Subversive Imagination in the Age of Emerson and Melville.* New York: Alfred A. Knopf, 1988.

———. *George Lippard.* Boston: Twayne, 1982.

Richardson, E. P. *Painting in America: The Story of 450 Years.* New York: Thomas Y. Crowell, 1956.

Richardson, Ruth. *Death, Dissection, and the Destitute.* London: Penguin, 1988.

Richey, Russell E., and Donald G. Jones, eds. *American Civil Religion.* New York: Harper and Row, 1974.

Ring, Kenneth. *Heading Toward Omega.* New York: William Morrow, 1984.

Rinhart, Floyd, and Marion Rinhart. "Rediscovery: An American Way of Death." *Art in America* 55 (September 1967): 30–31.

Risch, Erna. *Quartermaster Support of the Army: A History of the Corps, 1775–1939.* Washington, D.C.: Office of the Quartermaster General, 1962.

Robertson, James I., Jr. *Soldiers Blue and Gray.* Columbia: University of South Carolina Press, 1988.

Rogin, Michael. "The King's Two Bodies: Lincoln, Wilson, Nixon, and Presidential Self-Sacrifice." In *Ronald Reagan, the Movie, and Other Episodes in Political Demonology.* Berkeley: University of California Press, 1987.

Rosenberg, Charles E. *The Care of Strangers: The Rise of America's Hospital System.* New York: Basic, 1987.

———. *The Cholera Years: The United States in 1832, 1849, and 1866.* Chicago: University of Chicago Press, 1987.

Rowe, David L. *Thunder and Trumpets: Millerites and Dissenting Religion in Upstate New York.* Chico, Calif.: Scholars, 1985.

Ruby, Jay. "Post-Mortem Portraiture in America." *History of Photography* 8 (1984): 201–222.

Rumford, Beatrix T. "The Role of Death as Reflected in the Art and Folkways of the Northeast in the Eighteenth and Nineteenth Centuries." Master's thesis, State University of New York at Oneonta, 1965.

Runblad, Georgeanne. "From 'Shrouding Woman' to Lady Assistant: An Analysis of Occupational Sex-Typing in the Funeral Industry, 1870–1920." Ph.D. diss., University of Illinois, Urbana-Champaign, 1992.

Ryan, Mary P. *Cradle of the Middle Class: The Family in Oneida County, New York, 1790–1865.* New York: Cambridge University Press, 1981.

Sandburg, Carl. *Abraham Lincoln: The Prairie Years and the War Years.* New York: Harcourt, Brace, 1954.

Saum, Lewis O. *The Popular Mood of America, 1860–1890.* Lincoln: University of Nebraska Press, 1990.

———. *The Popular Mood of Pre–Civil War America*. Westport, Conn.: Greenwood, 1980.

Scharf, J. Thomas, and Thompson Westcott. *History of Philadelphia, 1609–1884*. 3 vols. Philadelphia: L. H. Everts, 1884.

Schlereth, Thomas J. *Victorian America: Transformations in Everyday Life, 1876–1915*. New York: HarperCollins, 1991.

Schneider, A. Gregory. *The Way of the Cross Leads Home: The Domestication of American Methodism*. Bloomington: Indiana University Press, 1993.

Schorsch, Anita. *Mourning Becomes America: Mourning Art in the New Nation*. Harrisburg, Penn.: William Penn Memorial Museum, 1976.

Schwartz, Barry. *George Washington: The Making of An American Symbol*. New York: Free Press, 1987.

A Service of Death and Resurrection. Nashville: Abingdon, 1979.

Shattuck, Gardiner H., Jr. *A Shield and A Hiding Place: The Religious Life of the Civil War Armies*. Macon, Ga.: Mercer University Press, 1987.

Shryock, Richard Harrison. *Medicine and Society in America: 1660–1860*. Ithaca, N.Y.: Cornell University Press, 1960.

———. *Medicine in America: Historical Essays*. Baltimore: Johns Hopkins University Press, 1966.

Sloane, David Charles. *The Last Great Necessity: Cemeteries in American History*. Baltimore: Johns Hopkins University Press, 1991.

Slotkin, Richard. *Regeneration Through Violence: The Mythology of the American Frontier, 1600–1860*. Middletown, Conn.: Wesleyan University Press, 1973.

Smillie, Wilson G. *Public Health, Its Promise for the Future: A Chronicle of the Development of Public Health in the United States, 1607–1914*. New York: Macmillan, 1955.

Smith, Albert. *History of the Town of Peterborough, Hillsborough County, New Hampshire*. Boston: George H. Ellis, 1876.

Smith, Daniel Scott. "Differential Mortality in the United States Before 1900." *Journal of Interdisciplinary History* 8 (Spring 1983): 735–759.

Somkin, Fred. *Unquiet Eagle: Memory and Desire in the Idea of American Freedom, 1815–1860*. Ithaca, N.Y.: Cornell University Press, 1967.

Stannard, David E. *The Puritan Way of Death: A Study in Religion, Culture, and Social Change*. Oxford: Oxford University Press, 1977.

———, ed. *Death in America*. Philadelphia: University of Pennsylvania Press, 1974.

Starr, Paul. *The Social Transformation of American Medicine*. New York: Basic, 1982.

Steere, Edward. *The Graves Registration Service in World War II*. Washington, D.C.: Office of the Quartermaster General, 1951.

Steiner, Paul E. *Disease in the Civil War: Natural Biological Warfare in 1861–1865*. Springfield, Ill.: C. C. Thomas, 1968.

Stephenson, John S. *Death, Grief, and Mourning: Individual and Social Realities*. New York: Free Press, 1985.

Stevenson, Louise L. *The Victorian Homefront: American Thought and Culture, 1860–1880*. New York: Twayne, 1991.

Stokes, Mack B. *Major Methodist Beliefs*. Nashville: Abingdon, 1961.

Stone, Lawrence. "Death and Its History." *New York Review of Books,* 12 October 1978, 22–32.

Sullivan, Lawrence E., ed. *Death, Afterlife, and the Soul.* New York: Macmillan, 1989.

Sutherland, Daniel E. *The Expansion of Everyday Life, 1860–1876.* New York: Harper and Row, 1990.

Sweet, Leonard I., ed. *The Evangelical Tradition in America.* Macon, Ga.: Mercer University Press, 1984.

Sweet, Timothy. *Traces of War: Poetry, Photography, and the Crisis of the Union.* Baltimore: Johns Hopkins University Press, 1990.

Tenenti, Alberto. *La vie et la mort à travers l'art du XVe siècle.* Paris: Colin, 1952.

Thomas, Louis-Vincent. *Rites de mort: Pour la paix des vivants.* Paris: Fayard, 1985.

Thompson, W. Fletcher, Jr. *The Image of War: The Pictorial Reporting of the American Civil War.* New York: Thomas Yoseloff, 1959.

Thurow, Glen E. *Abraham Lincoln and American Political Religion.* Albany: State University of New York Press, 1976.

Trachtenberg, Alan. "Albums of War: On Reading Civil War Photographs." *Representations* 9 (1985): 1–32.

———. *The Incorporation of America: Culture and Society in the Gilded Age.* New York: Hill and Wang, 1982.

Turner, Bryan S. *The Body and Society: Explorations in Social Theory.* New York: Basil Blackwell, 1984.

Turner, Justin G., and Linda Leavitt Turner. *Mary Todd Lincoln: Her Life and Letters.* New York: Alfred A. Knopf, 1972.

Tuveson, Ernest Lee. *Redeemer Nation: The Idea of America's Millennial Role.* Chicago: University of Chicago Press, 1968.

Ulrich, Laurel Thatcher. *A Midwife's Tale: The Life of Martha Ballard, Based on Her Diary, 1785–1812.* New York: Vintage, 1990.

Van Gennep, Arnold. *The Rites of Passage.* Translated by Monika B. Vizedom and Gabrielle L. Caffee. Chicago: University of Chicago Press, 1960.

Veatch, Robert M. *Death, Dying, and the Biological Revolution: Our Last Quest for Responsibility.* New Haven: Yale University Press, 1976.

Vinovskis, Maris A. *Fertility in Massachusetts from the Revolution to the Civil War.* New York: Academic, 1981.

———. "The Jacobson Life Table of 1850: A Critical Reexamination from a Massachusetts Perspective." *Journal of Interdisciplinary History* 8 (Spring 1978): 703–724.

———. "Mortality Rates and Trends in Massachusetts Before 1860." *Journal of Economic History* 32 (March 1972): 184–213.

———, ed. *Toward a Social History of the American Civil War: Exploratory Essays.* Cambridge: Cambridge University Press, 1990.

Vovelle, Michel. "A Century and One-Half of American Epitaphs (1600–1813): Toward the Study of Collective Attitudes about Death." *Comparative Studies in Society and History: An International Quarterly* 22 (October 1980): 534–547.

———. *Histoires figurales: Des monstres médiévaux à Wonderwoman.* Paris: Usher, 1989.

———. *Ideologies and Mentalities.* Translated by Eamon O'Flaherty. Chicago: University of Chicago Press, 1991.

———. *La mort et l'Occident de 1300 à nos jours.* Paris: Gallimard, 1983.

———. *Mourir Autrefois: Attitudes collectives devant la mort aux XVIIe et XVIIIe siècles.* Paris: Gallimard, 1974.

———. *Piété baroque et déchristianisation en Provence au XVIIe siècle.* Paris: Editions du Seuil, 1978.

Vovelle, Michel, and Gaby Vovelle. *Visions de la mort et de l'au-dela en Provence.* Paris: Armand Colin, 1970.

Wach, Joachim. *Types of Religious Experience, Christian and Non-Christian.* Chicago: University of Chicago Press, 1951.

Waite, Fredrick C. "The Development of Anatomical Laws in the States of New England." *New England Journal of Medicine* 233 (December 1945): 716–726.

———. "Grave Robbing in New England." *Bulletin of the Medical Library* 33 (1945).

Waller, Gregory A., ed. *American Horrors: Essays on the Modern American Horror Film.* Urbana: University of Illinois Press, 1987.

Warner, W. Lloyd. *The Living and the Dead: A Study of the Symbolic Life of Americans.* New Haven: Yale University Press, 1959.

Warren, Louis A. *Lincoln's Gettysburg Declaration: "A New Birth of Freedom."* Fort Wayne, Ind.: Lincoln National Life Foundation, 1964.

Was, Hannelore, and Robert A. Neimeyer, eds. *Dying: Facing the Facts.* 3d ed. Washington, D.C.: Taylor and Francis, 1995.

Weber, Timothy P. *Living in the Shadow of the Second Coming: American Premillennialism, 1875–1925.* New York: Oxford University Press, 1979.

Weisberger, Bernard A. *They Gathered at the River: The Story of the Great Revivalists and Their Impact upon Religion in America.* Boston: Little, Brown, 1958.

Wells, Robert V. *Revolutions in Americans' Lives: A Demographic Perspective on the History of Americans, Their Families, and Their Society.* Westport, Conn.: Greenwood, 1982.

White, Trentwell Mason, and Ivan Sandrof. "That Was New York: The First Embalmer." *New Yorker* 18 (November 1942): 43–46.

Wiebe, Robert H. *The Search for Order, 1877–1920.* New York: Hill and Wang, 1967.

Wiley, Bell I. *The Life of Billy Yank: The Common Soldier of the Union.* 1952. Reprint. Baton Rouge: Louisiana State University Press, 1978.

Wilkinson, Warren. *Mother, May You Never See the Sights I Have Seen: The Fifty-Seventh Massachusetts Veteran Volunteers in the Army of the Potomac, 1864–1865.* New York: Quill, 1990.

Willcox, Walter F. *Studies in American Demography.* New York: Russell and Russell, 1971.

Wills, Garry. *Lincoln at Gettysburg: The Words That Remade America.* New York: Simon and Schuster, 1992.

Wilson, Charles Reagan. *Baptized in Blood: The Religion of the Lost Cause, 1865–1920.* Athens: University of Georgia Press, 1980.

Wilson, Edmund. *Patriotic Gore: Studies in the Literature of the American Civil War.* New York: Oxford University Press, 1966.

Wolf, Brian Jay. *Romantic Re-Vision: Culture and Consciousness in Nineteenth-Century American Painting and Literature*. Chicago: University of Chicago Press, 1982.

Wright, Conrad. *The Beginnings of Unitarianism in America*. Boston: Starr King 1955.

Yasuba, Yasukichi. *Birth Rates of the White Population in the United States, 1800–1860: An Economic Study*. Baltimore: Johns Hopkins University Press, 1962.

Zaleski, Carol. *Otherworld Journeys: Accounts of Near-Death Experience in Medieval and Modern Times*. Oxford: Oxford University Press, 1987.

Ziegler, Jean. *Les vivants et la mort*. Paris: Editions du Seuil, 1975.

Index